The Giant Book Of Children's Sermons

Matthew To Revelation

260 Children's Object Lessons

Wesley T. Runk

CSS Publishing Company, Inc., Lima, Ohio

THE GIANT BOOK OF CHILDREN'S SERMONS:
MATTHEW TO REVELATION

I dedicate this book of children's object lessons to eight wonderful grandchildren (Joey, Jeremy, Shane, Dan, Aaron, Elijah, Marley, and Raina) and their parents (David and Beth, Jeff and Ellen, and Tim and Megan) who teach them daily the desire to be dependent on God while independent in their thinking of the world that surrounds them. May they grow in richness of God's grace and be of the humble understanding that they have been called to his service.

For more information about CSS Publishing Company resources, visit our website at www.csspub.com or e-mail us at custserv@csspub.com or call (800) 241-4056.

ISBN 0-7880-1956-2 binder
ISBN 0-7880-1913-9 paperback

PRINTED IN U.S.A.

Introduction

Being part of a ministry to children is one of the more exciting opportunities in the Christian ministry. Each child is a reflection of the teaching he/she receives at home, in school, and in our own congregation. In later years the children will learn to disguise their learning, but at the ages we see them when giving a children's sermon, they are a delight and open to all the love we can share with them.

When you share your love in using one of these object lessons, you also encourage the entire family to be a part of worship on a regular basis. It is the intention of each lesson to bring children into the worship experience and make them a part of the whole worship service.

Each of these children's sermons is a field-tested experience. It is my hope that you will enjoy using them as much as I did the first time I had the opportunity to introduce one of God's revelations to one or more of his chosen people.

Wesley T. Runk

Table Of Contents

Your Name Is Important

Matthew 1:18-25

"She will bear a son, and you are to name him Jesus, for he will save his people from their sins." (v. 21)

Object: a baby book with a list of names

Good morning, boys and girls. Today we are going to talk about something that is very important to you. We are going to talk about your names and the names of others. All of you have names, don't you? (*let them answer*) Let's tell everyone your name. (*encourage each of them to stand and speak his or her name*) We not only call each other by a name, but we write our names on important papers. And when we get married we usually give our last names, if we are a boy, to the girl that we marry or, if we are a girl, we often take the name of our husband, but not always. You have a choice. There are a lot of things that we use our names for and that is what makes a name so important.

I have a list of names in this book that parents sometimes use when they are waiting for their baby to be born. Every name that you can think of is listed in this book and it also says what the name means. I picked some names out of the Bible to see what they mean and I will share them with you. Did you know that the name David means "beloved" or that Ruth means "companion"? Here is a good one: Philip means a "lover of horses." And, of course, Peter means "rock." Martha is another way of saying "lady" and the prophet Malachi was named to mean "my messenger." Those are just a few of the names in the Bible that have a special meaning to us.

But here is the most special one of all. Do you know what the name Jesus means? Do you remember that an angel of God came and spoke to Joseph, and told him that Mary, the woman he loved, was going to have a baby boy? (*let them answer*) The angel also told Joseph what God wanted Joseph and Mary to name the baby. Did you remember that also? (*let them answer*) The angel told Joseph that God wanted this baby to be called Jesus. Do you know why God wanted them to call him Jesus? (*let them answer*) Because, the name Jesus means "to save God's people from their sins." That is what the name Jesus means. Your name means something: the name Philip means "lover of horses" and Jesus means "saving God's people from their sins." That's what Jesus did. That is why the name of Jesus is so important and why God did not name him Pat or Henry or Bill or any other name. God wanted people to know Jesus and also to know what Jesus was going to do. Now you know why names are so very important and why Jesus' name is the most important of all.

Saved In The Nick Of Time

Matthew 2:13-18

Now after they had left, an angel of the Lord appeared to Joseph in a dream and said, "Get up, take the child and his mother and flee to Egypt, and remain there until I tell you; for Herod is about to search for the child, to destroy him." (v. 13)

Object: some stones, clubs, swords, and knives

Good morning, boys and girls. Today I must tell you an awful story and one that we should never forget. It is the story of how a lot of babies were killed by a very jealous king. It is also a story about Jesus and God's plan to save him from death as a baby.

King Herod, the King of Israel at the time of Jesus' birth, was a very jealous king who heard that a baby had been born in Bethlehem who was going to be a king. Now, kings were always afraid that someone else was going to take their place, so they kept large armies around them to protect them from any danger. But, when Herod heard that this king was only a baby, he decided he would kill the child now, and never have to worry about him later. He sent soldiers to Bethlehem and told them to kill every boy child who was two years old and younger. The soldiers did not like the king's order, but they were soldiers, so they went to Bethlehem to do what they were told. God knew of Herod's evil plan and so he sent an angel in a dream to Joseph and told Joseph to take Jesus and Mary and travel to Egypt as fast as they could go. Joseph woke Mary, bundled the baby Jesus and went into Egypt.

Meanwhile, the soldiers came to Bethlehem and carried out the king's orders. With swords, knives, rocks, and clubs they killed every boy baby they could find. It was awful. No one will ever forget it. God will never forget it, and he reminds us with a day every year. December 28 is the day that the church remembers all of the children who were killed by Herod. Of course, he did not kill the one whom he wanted to kill. Joseph, Mary, and Jesus escaped to Egypt and lived there until Herod died. After Herod died, the holy family of God came back to Nazareth to live.

Murder is a terrible sin. The murder of children, like the little boys in Bethlehem, is horrible. But God remembers these children, and he asks us to remember them. Jesus lived and finally died for all of our sins, even the sins of Herod.

Maybe, when you think about Jesus today, you will remember the children who gave their lives so that Jesus could live to teach us and help us to know God.

12

Grow Like A Fruit Tree

Matthew 3:1-12

"Even now the ax is lying at the root of the trees; every tree therefore that does not bear good fruit is cut down and thrown into the fire." (v. 10)

Object: an ax

Good morning, boys and girls. I have with me this morning a tool that not many of you have used. It is a dangerous tool and you must be very careful when you use it. I am sure that you have seen your father or someone else use it when he had a certain kind of job to do that needed chopping. We call it an ax. How many of you know what you might chop with an ax? (*let them answer*) That's right; you can chop up firewood. You can also chop down a tree, make stakes for your tent, or, if you wanted to, you could build a log cabin as people used to do. There are a lot of ways to use an ax, but the most important use for an ax is to chop down and get rid of things that you want to get rid of around your home or work.

Jesus once talked about using an ax when he was telling a parable. A parable is a story that teaches us something. Jesus said that when fruit trees stop making fruit we should get rid of them. Chop them down and use them for firewood or whatever you need the wood for. There is no sense letting a fruit tree that is not making good fruit stand and take up space where another fruit tree could grow. That sounds right, and I am sure that all of us agree with Jesus.

But Jesus told that story with a teaching because he wanted us to learn something about ourselves and about the way that we belong to God. We are like fruit trees, Jesus said, and that means that we are supposed to grow fruit like trees do. Of course, we can't actually grow fruit. Do you know anyone who grows apples or pears or oranges at the ends of their fingers or elbows? (*let them answer*) I don't either. But we are expected to grow in our love and our forgiving others who may have hurt us. We should grow in believing that Jesus is the Son of God and our Savior. We should believe those things more today than we did yesterday, and that is growing. We should grow in sharing our money and our time with people who need them. Now if we are not growing, then Jesus says that we could be like the fruit tree that does not grow any fruit. That tree is taken away or cut down so that another tree can grow in its place.

You don't want anyone to take your place with Jesus, do you? (*let them answer*) Good, I don't want you to lose your place either, so we must grow up in our belief in Jesus and that we are going to share him with the whole world.

Look What Water Does!

Matthew 3:13-17

Then Jesus came from Galilee to John at the Jordan, to be baptized by him. (v. 13)

Object: water at the baptismal font

Good morning, boys and girls. Today we are going to talk about something very special. It is called water. How many of you thought that water is very special? (*let them answer*) It is very special because it is necessary for us to live. We could not live without water. That sounds strange because you have never had to try to live without water, but if you ever had to live one day without water, you would know how important it is. Just think of all the things that you use water for in one day's time. (*let them name some of the uses of water*) You see how important it is. That is why we call it special. Very special.

Water is also used in something very special that we call baptism. How many of you are baptized? (*let them answer*) Do you know why you were baptized? (*let them answer*) Baptism does a lot for you, such as making you part of God's world and helping you understand that you will live with God forever. But another reason that you were baptized with water was because Jesus told you and your parents that you should be baptized. Jesus was baptized. He asked John the Baptizer to baptize him, and John finally did it. John thought that Jesus was too good to be baptized by anyone, including himself, and he said so. But Jesus wanted John and everyone else to know that he was one of us, and therefore he had to be baptized also.

It makes you feel good to know that Jesus wants to be one of us. He went to the same river where John was baptizing others and Jesus was baptized with the same water that others had been baptized with. Jesus was trying to tell us that, with him, sin died. If we are baptized in water, then our sin is drowned and it cannot live. That is one of the reasons that you were baptized. Your sins were drowned and they died, and you became one with Jesus.

Water can be used for lots of things, but the most important thing that it is ever used for is to become one with Jesus in our baptism.

I don't know if you will think about your baptism every time you use water, but if you think about it once in a while, it will be good. Jesus came to John the Baptizer to be baptized so that he could be with us and we could be with him, John baptized him with the water from the river and we have chosen to be like him ever since.

Those Tempting Crayons

Matthew 4:1-11

Then Jesus was led up by the Spirit into the wilderness to be tempted by the devil. (v. 1)

Object: some crayons and scissors

Good morning, boys and girls. Today we are going to talk about a word that I am sure all of you have heard many times but you may not be sure what it means. The word is *tempted* or *temptation*. How many of you have heard that word used before? (*let them answer*) How many of you know what it means? (*let them answer*) Those are very close answers. Let me see if I can help explain it a little better.

I brought with me some crayons and some scissors. How many of you have crayons at home? Almost all of you. What do you do with crayons? (*let them answer*) That's right, you color pictures. Sometimes we use them in coloring books and sometimes we use them just on a piece of paper. That is the right place to use them. No problem and no temptation.

But have you ever used them anywhere else, or thought about using them somewhere else? Have you ever colored a wall in your house, or thought about coloring the wall or maybe a table or your bed? If you thought about it, and you wanted to do it, then you were tempted. You could almost hear a little voice that said, "Go ahead and color the table, or go ahead and color the wall. It's all right, no one will ever know." That is temptation. Of course, if you color it, then the temptation is over. You have done something wrong. But if you just think about it and you want to do it and you think it might be all right, then you are being tempted.

Jesus was tempted. Did you know that Jesus was tempted? He was. The Bible tells us how the devil tried to get him to follow him rather than the Father in heaven. Jesus knew it was wrong but he listened to the devil tell him how he would make him wonderful, and how he would give him land and all the food he could eat. Jesus listened to the devil and he was tempted. How many of you knew that Jesus listened to the devil, or as the Bible calls him, Satan? (*let them answer*)

That's a true story. Jesus was high on a mountain and that devil came and tried to get Jesus to follow him just like that little voice tries to get you to color the table.

But Jesus did not give up. He was tempted, but he told the devil to get away for he was not going to do anything that was a sin against God. After three times of the devil offering Jesus everything he had, the devil left Jesus and went away.

We must often do the same thing. There are things that we know are wrong, but they sound wonderful. That is temptation and we must be strong and put it away. Temptation is strong, but God is even stronger. If you listen to both voices and ask God for his help, you will do it God's way.

Turn Around!

Matthew 4:12-23

From that time Jesus began to proclaim, "Repent, for the kingdom of heaven has come near." (v. 17)

Object: a framed picture with the back showing

Good morning, boys and girls. Today we have one of the simplest lessons to learn, but one of the hardest things to do that we have ever talked about. I brought along a picture with me and I am going to put it right in front of you so that you can see it very clearly. (*put up the picture with the back facing them*) It's a beautiful picture and one that I enjoy having in my house. Sometimes I just stand in front of it and look at all of the wonderful things that it describes. It must have taken someone a long time to paint such a beautiful picture, and I hope that you enjoy it as much as I do. (*by this time the children are telling you that they can't see it and you must turn it around*) You can't see it? You mean that it is going in the wrong direction? If you are to see this beautiful picture, I must first turn it around. I will if you will listen to me for just one more minute.

Jesus used to preach, "Repent," and he would say it over and over again. "Repent, repent, repent." Do you know what repent means? (*let them answer*) It means to turn around. Jesus was telling people that they were going in the wrong direction with their sin, and they should stop and turn around and come back to God. In other words, when Jesus was saying, "Repent," he could have said, "Turn around, turn around, turn around." The right way to go is toward God and not away from him. When we commit sin we are going away from God and Jesus tells us to turn around.

Now I am going to turn the picture around because this is the way it was meant to be. No one ever painted a picture to be hung on the wall facing the wall. When people paint pictures, they want them to be seen.

When God made us, he meant for us to go in the right direction and he didn't make us to sin. But we do sin and we do head in the wrong direction. That's why Jesus preaches for us to repent, to turn around and head in the right direction.

The next time you see a picture and it is hanging so that you can see it, I want you to remember the day that someone asked you to look at the back of the picture. We know it was the wrong way and we had to turn it around. That is the same thing that we must do with our lives after we sin. We must repent and turn them around.

The Constitution Of Our Faith

Matthew 5:1-12

Then he began to speak, and taught them, saying: (v. 2)

Object: a constitution (United States, state, or local government) and slips of paper for each child with Matthew 5:1-12 written on them

Good morning, boys and girls. Today we are going to talk about something that you may have heard about a lot of times but perhaps you have never seen. How many of you have heard the word *constitution*? (*let them answer*) That's good. How many of you know what a constitution is? (*let them answer*) You have some good ideas. A constitution is something that people write for their organization to tell how it should be run and what they believe in. I have a copy of the United States Constitution that tells how our government should be set up and what we believe in as Americans. This is a great constitution, and it is something that we pay a lot of attention to every day of our lives. There are other constitutions such as the one for our state, and we have one for our church. I can show you the one that we have for our church. Constitutions are important and a lot of thinking and planning goes into every one. If you follow the constitution of your county, your church, or your club, then you will be a better citizen, church person, or club member.

Jesus gave the Christian church a kind of constitution one day when he was teaching his disciples and a lot of other people what it meant to be a follower of God. The words that he taught are thought to be some of the most important words that have ever been spoken by anyone to someone else. I cannot think of any words that are more important because these tell me exactly what a Christian is supposed to be like, according to Jesus. I am not going to read the words to you today, but I am going to tell you where you can find them in the Bible, and I hope your mother and father will sit down with you today and go over them.

Each of the words that Jesus used was carefully chosen, and it teaches us the importance of love and how we are to use the love that God gives to us. It tells us how to care for each other and how God cares for us. These verses are called the Beatitudes, but they could be called the Constitution of our Faith. I hope that you will spend some time today reading the Bible with your parents and listening to the words that Jesus taught us about how to live. How many of you will do that? (*let them answer*) That's good.

Telltale Fingernails

Matthew 6:24-34

"And can any of you by worrying add a single hour to your span of life?" (v. 27)

Object: some fingernail clippings or any sign of some nervous habit

Good morning, boys and girls. I brought something with me this morning that I know you have never seen anyone carry with him or her before. I have these things in a small box, and I am going to show you what they are in a minute. They have to do with worry, or being nervous. Can you imagine what they might be? What do some people do when they are nervous? (*let them answer*) I am going to open the box now, and I want you to take a good look and then let me know what you think they are. (*show them*)

Fingernails! That's right, they are fingernail clippings. How many of you have ever chewed your fingernails when you were nervous? Some of you do. Do you keep them in a box? You don't, do you? Why do you bite your fingernails? (*let them answer*) Does it help you solve a problem? When you chew off a nail, do you have more clothes to wear? Does each fingernail mean that you will get over a cold or will it help you pass a test in school or buy you more food when you are hungry? Of course not. Why should we worry and do things like bite our fingernails?

Jesus talked about this one day, and he asked the people if they ever saw a bird go without food or a flower without clothes? Doesn't God give the birds everything they need to fly and to live, and doesn't God take care of all the flowers so that they look beautiful? Of course he does. If God will do that for birds and flowers, then just think what God will do for you whom he loves so much. Jesus said there is no need for people to worry, but that instead they should trust God and love him and everything will be all right.

The next time that you want to bite your fingernails, say a prayer instead. No one should worry when he has God who cares for everything. Let your fingernails grow and cut them off with clippers. Use your mouth for prayer and everything will be all right.

Gordon Glove And Henry Hand

Matthew 7:21-29

"Not everyone who says to me, 'Lord, Lord,' will enter the kingdom of heaven, but only the one who does the will of my Father in heaven." (v. 21)

Object: a glove on a stick

Good morning, boys and girls. I brought a little friend with me to help us learn something this morning, My friend's name is Gordon. His full name is Gordon Glove, and he belongs to another friend of mine by the name of Henry Hand. Henry is not here this morning, but I think you will know why when I tell you a little bit about Gordon. I asked Gordon to come because he is pretty close to Henry. Gordon is the kind of a friend who thinks he knows everything. Whenever I want to know something and I begin to ask a question, Gordon pops up on the hand of Henry and waves around in the air. Gordon does not even wait for me to ask the whole question. He just hears me ask, "Where do you think?" and there is Gordon Glove waving around in the air like a big flag.

If you say the word "what" then Gordon is waving. If you ask, "Why," Gordon is waving. Gordon likes to think that he knows all of the answers, and he just raises Henry Hand every time you ask a question. Do you know anyone like that? (*let them answer*) Of course you do. We all know the Gordons. Some of us are like Gordon. We are waving our hands before we hear the question.

Jesus knew about people like that, too. There were people running around calling him "Lord, Lord," but they did not really mean it. They must thought that this was a good thing to say since they had seen or heard about the wonderful things that he did. Of course, the people did nothing. They just said, "Lord, Lord, Lord."

But Jesus is looking for disciples who are doing more than talking or raising their hands. Jesus is looking for Christians who are willing to share their lives with other people. Jesus wants people to love and help the people who are not loved.

There is a lot more to being a Christian than shouting his name a lot of times. You must be ready to forgive people who hurt you or say bad things about you. You must be willing to share your money with people who need food and clothing. Just calling Jesus a pretty name like "Lord," does not mean a whole lot. But Jesus says it really counts when you are willing to visit a sick friend or write a letter or draw a picture for someone who is lonely. I know a lot of people like Gordon Glove who just like to wave their hands around but never have an answer. We are looking for people who have answers and are willing to share the answers with others.

The next time you see someone just waving a hand who does not have the answer, perhaps you will remember the time that Jesus said, "Don't call me a pretty name like 'Lord,' but do the things that God wants you to do, and then share your life with others." That is the real test of being a Christian.

19

A Paper Bag Is Worth A Lot

Matthew 8:1-13

The centurion answered, "Lord, I am not worthy to have you come under my roof; but only speak the word, and my servant will be healed." (v. 8)

Object: a paper bag and a bunch of fruit — a dozen apples or oranges or anything that a child would have trouble holding in his or her hands

Good morning, boys and girls. How much are you worth? Has anyone every asked you how much you are worth? (*let them answer*) It isn't the kind of question that very many people ask one another, but people like to know how much they are worth to other people. Sometimes we think we are worth a lot to some people and not very much to others.

There was a man who came to Jesus one day and asked him to heal his servant. The servant must have been very good to him because the man who was asking was very important to most people. Yet when he asked Jesus to heal his servant the man did not think that he himself was worth very much to Jesus.

I suppose that a lot of us who know Jesus would feel as the important man did. Parents feel as though they are worth a lot to their children, and children feel that they are worth a lot to their parents. The members of a congregation are worth a lot to the pastor, and the pastor is important or worth a lot to his or her members. The same is true of doctors and their patients, teachers and their classes, and so on.

But how important are any of us to Jesus? Can we be worth much to Jesus?

Suppose that a person was a paper bag. Can you imagine that? (*hold up the paper bag*) A paper bag does not look very important and there are a lot of paper bags. I don't think that many of you would agree with me if I told you that this paper bag is worth a lot. But let me show you something. I need a volunteer for this little experiment. (*choose someone to help you*) Now I want you to hold some oranges for me. (*begin to hand the child one at a time*) It is important to me that you hold all of the oranges, so try hard. (*keep handing them until the child can hold no more*) That's too bad. I wanted you to be able to hold all of the oranges but I can see that you are not able to. If you had something to hold them in, you would be able to carry all of them. Maybe you understand now how important a paper bag can be. It is worth a lot to someone who needs one.

Every person is worth something to God. As a matter of fact, God tried to show how much all of us were worth when he sent Jesus into the world to work with us, and for us. We are really important to God, and we all have worth to him. The important man in our story did not think that he could be worth much to Jesus, but Jesus showed him that he cared a lot by healing his servant.

Jesus feels the same way about us. We are all worth a lot to him, and he uses us to do good for him and for others.

20

The Doctor For Sin

Matthew 9:9-13

But when he heard this, he said, "Those who are well have no need of a physician, but those who are sick." (v. 12)

Object: a thermometer, a heating pad, and a bad cough

Good morning, boys and girls. I brought to share with you a few things that I have been using this week. (*bring out the heating pad and thermometer*) I have had all of the aches and pains that a person have and still be living. In addition to this I have been coughing. (*give them an example of your very best cough*) When I cough it hurts right down to my toes. I don't know which are worse, the days or the nights. Have any of you been sick this week? (*let them answer*) I just feel awful and I feel doubly bad because it is so nice outside with the beautiful sunshine. You don't feel so badly when the weather is bad outside and you are sick, but when the weather is good and you feel ill, then you feel twice as bad.

I don't seem to be getting any better. Can you think of anything else that I can do besides take my temperature and use the heating pad? (*wait until someone suggests that you see a doctor*) Why should I see a doctor? I have seen lots of doctors and they look just like other people. (*let them tell you what a doctor does for the sick*) Oh, I see! The doctor will help me to get well. He knows how to cure me from my sickness.

That must be what Jesus was talking about when he said that the sick people need a doctor but that people who are healthy do not need a doctor. Only he meant something a little different. He was not talking just about people with coughs and colds. He was talking about people with sins. How many of you like people who sin a lot? (*let them answer*) Do you know anyone who cheats, steals, lies, and tries to hurt people? Are those people your friends? (*let them answer*) Do you wish that they were in church with you this morning? (*let them answer*) Probably not. But where should they be? (*let them answer*) Isn't this the place that people learn not to cheat, lie, steal, and hurt others? Isn't this where boys and girls come to learn about Jesus and how to love and forgive, and help one another? (*let them answer*) Jesus spent a lot of time with people whom you and I don't like, and he changed them into good people. I wish that all of the bad people in the world, or the ones who we think are bad, would come and learn about Jesus, and I wish that boys and girls like you would teach them.

If you are sick, you want to go to a doctor. If you are filled with sin and it causes you to hate instead of love, then you need Jesus. He can make the sin-sick people better just as a doctor can help you get rid of a cough. That's something to remember and something for all of us to think about.

Better Than A Million-Dollar Policy

Matthew 9:35—10:7

"And as you go, proclaim the good news, 'The kingdom of heaven has come near.' " (v. 7)

Object: a life insurance policy

Good morning, boys and girls. Today I have brought something that I know almost all of you have heard about, but something you probably have not seen. (*hold up an insurance policy*) This is a valuable piece of paper. We call it an insurance policy, a life insurance policy. It is worth a lot of money. Some insurance policies are worth millions of dollars. Some are only worth a thousand dollars or so. It depends on how much you think your life is worth to someone else and how much money you have to pay for it. If you think that your life is worth a million dollars to your wife, husband, or to one of your children, and you have the money to pay for it, then you can buy a million dollars' worth of life insurance.

How would you like for someone to give you a million dollars? (*let them answer*) There is only one catch. The only way you get the million dollars is when the person who bought it for you dies. That's right, the person must die before you get the million dollars. That means that your million dollars can only come later.

But I have something that is even more valuable than a million-dollar insurance policy and you can have it right now. It is a free gift given by God. Jesus tells us about it, and he will give it to you immediately. Some of you may already have it. It lasts forever and it is worth more than all of the money in the world. It is worth more than money because it gives you all of the things that you hope money will give you. The kingdom of God brings you happiness. It means that you will never have another worry. It gives you forgiveness, friends, love, joy, and peace. The kingdom of God is filled with all of these things and more.

You have to wait for money from an insurance policy because you must wait for the person who bought it to die. You must wait for a lot of things that are good, but you don't have to wait for the kingdom of God. It is here now and you can belong to it by asking Jesus to bless you and share his love with you. When you have Jesus in your heart, then you have all of the other things that I told you about. Peace, joy, love, happiness, and not have worry, hate, sadness, and other things like that.

Join God's kingdom today and if you already know that you belong, then share it with your friends. It is better than life insurance, money, or anything else that everyone works so hard for and must wait so long to have. You can have the kingdom today. God bless you.

Counting Fish, Birds, And Hair

Matthew 10:26-33

"So do not be afraid; you are of more value than many sparrows." (v. 31)

Object: an aquarium with many fish (minnows or guppies can be purchased at bait shops, pet stores, or pet departments)

Good morning, boys and girls. How many of you have ever gone fishing? (*let them answer*) When you were fishing did you wish that you could be under the water to see the fish? (*let them answer*) It would be a lot easier if you knew where they were and how many were in one spot.

I brought some fish with me today so that you could watch them swim around and also listen to a story that I have to tell you. Look at all of the fish in this one aquarium. There must be hundreds of them. Have you ever tried to count fish swimming or birds when they are flying? (*let them answer*) That's a hard job and sometimes it is almost impossible. They keep moving and you can't remember which ones you have counted. There are thousands of birds and thousands of fish in very small areas. I guess when there are so many of them, one of them does not seem to be so important. If you lose a fish or miss a bird, it really doesn't matter does it? (*let them answer*) What's another fish?

But Jesus says that each one of them is important to God. God knows where each fish is swimming and where each bird is flying. He knows if they are in any kind of trouble, or if they are sick, or if they die. God cares about all of the things he made, and he made everything. It must be wonderful to be a bird or a fish and know that God cares about you. It is hard for us to believe that every bird and every fish is important, but that is what the Bible says about all of God's creatures.

If birds and fish are important, then what about us? Do you think that God is concerned about us? Does he care as much for us as he does the birds and fish? (*let them answer*)

He sure does! Jesus tells us that we are so important that God counts the hairs on our head. That's right. He knows how many hairs you have on your head. How many do you think that is? (*let them answer*) I don't know. If you were bald, it would be easier to count, but since none of you is bald, I couldn't begin to count all of your hairs. There must be thousands. You must really be important to God if he knows that much about you — and he does!

The next time you see some fish or birds, or comb your hair, you might think about how important we all are to God and how glad we are that he cares.

Cold Water And Kindness

Matthew 10:34-42

"And whoever gives even a cup of cold water to one of these little ones in the name of a disciple — truly I tell you, none of these will lose their reward." (v. 42)

Object: cups of cold water to be shared with all of the children

Good morning, boys and girls. How many of you think that you are a kind person? (*let them answer*) Being kind is a wonderful thing because everyone likes kind people. Kind people are good to people they know and also to people they do not know. Some people think they are kind but they are good only to their friends or to people who can help them. Kind people really do not live like this. They are the same to everyone. The Bible teaches us that Christians are kind people. Jesus taught all of his disciples to be kind people. It did not make any difference to Jesus if you lived next door or in another country, he taught us to be kind to everyone. Jesus did not care if you were black or white, red or yellow; you should be kind to all people. Jesus said that God knew and rewarded people for their love that they shared with each other.

Let me show you the example that Jesus used. Water is very precious to people in the country where he lived. There is not a lot of water and most of what water they have is warm because the rocks that the water passes over are also warm from the hot sun. Those people just did not give water away or waste it. You must know how important water is to people who live there. Jesus said that when a person gives cold water to a child then God remembers that giving, and rewards the person who gives it. I am going to share some cold water with you this morning so that you know that God thinks you are important and that my kindness should be shared with you.

But I am also sharing the water, the cold water, so that you will also remember to share things that you have with others. Being a Christian means that we should share our lives and our kindnesses with everyone. We must even be ready to share the most important things that we have with other Christians and people who are not Christian.

God told about the person who shared the cold water. You may have something that is more important than water to share with others and God says that your kindness will be rewarded.

The next time you see someone sharing something important, or you share something important, I hope you will remember that God blesses you for your kindness.

24

Jesus' Job Description

Matthew 11:2-11

Jesus answered them, "Go and tell John what you hear and see: the blind receive their sight, the lame walk, the lepers are cleansed, the deaf hear; the dead are raised, and the poor have good news brought to them." (vv. 4-5)

Object: a blackboard, some chalk, and some ideas on the job description of a mother

Good morning, boys and girls. Have you all been busy since I saw you last week? I know I have been busy. Sometimes it seems like adults are always busy, doesn't it? I think some of the busiest people are mothers. I thought that we might make a list of some of the things that your mother does, and then we can all see how busy she is. You tell me what your mother does for you and I will make a list on the blackboard. (*invite some responses and prod where necessary with some things that they may not think about*)

That is quite a list. And we have forgotten a lot of the things that a mother does every day. I know this: if I showed this list of things to someone who was not here this morning they would guess right away that we were talking about a mother's job.

Now I am going to give you another list and I want you to tell me who you think this job belongs to. This person makes the blind see, the crippled walk; he heals the very sick and can make deaf people hear. This person can even make the dead come back to life and, finally, he takes care of the poor and gives them hope with which to live. Do you now who can do all of this and even more? (*let them answer*)

That's right; this was the job that Jesus was sent to do. That is the work of the Savior, and no one else in the whole world can do that job but he. No doctor or preacher or father or mother, or anyone else can do it. Just the Savior.

A long time ago John the Baptizer sent his disciples to ask Jesus if he was the one that everyone was waiting for or if they should look for another. Jesus told them just what I told you. He told John's disciples to look around and see what was happening and to realize that this was the work of the Savior. Then he told them to go back to John and tell him what they saw.

Each of us has something that we are supposed to do, just as our mothers do all of the things that mothers can do. But the job of Jesus is a very special one, and we call his work the work of the Savior.

The next time someone asks you about Jesus' work, you can tell them the things that he does that no one else can do.

Ouch! Those Thistles!

Matthew 13:1-9

"Other seeds fell among thorns, and the thorns grew up and choked them." (v. 7)

Object: weeds, some with thorns and thistles

Good morning, boys and girls. Guess what I had to do this week that almost no one likes to do? (*let them guess*) I don't like to do many of those things either, but this week I did one of my most unfavorite things. I pulled weeds. How many of you like to pull weeds? (*let them answer*) It is an awful job because if you do not get the roots of the weed, you have to do it again in a very short time. But these weeds were really awful because they had thorns. Let me show you one of the weeds that I pulled. (*show them the weed with the thistles*)

This is a mean weed. First, you pull the weed out of the ground and then you pull the thorns out of your hand. Does that hurt! These kind of weeds are particularly bad because if you let them grow, they will choke out the vegetables you are growing for food and the grass that you want to cover your yard. They are mean things, these kind of weeds. They grow so fast and are so tough that you have to dig many of them out instead of just pulling them.

Jesus tells us a story that helps us look out for sin that is just like this kind of weed. Some people learn about God and know how he loves them, but they never get rid of the things that cause them trouble. Let's suppose that your sins are like weeds with thorns. You go to church, learn about Jesus and how he lives you, but you never get rid of your sin. Your sin keeps growing. Maybe you don't want to sin, but you keep doing it anyway. Today you are learning about God, but tomorrow you are telling lies, hating your brother or sister, and taking pennies and nickels out of your mother's purse. Those sins are like thorns on weeds and they just choke out all of the good things that you have learned about God. Pretty soon you will quit coming to Sunday school and church, and you will continue to do the things that you don't like to do, but which seem so easy. You wish that you were closer to God, but God is choked out of your life like the vegetable plants are in the garden. The only way that you can help yourself is similar to the way that I helped my garden. It isn't easy to do, but you must do it if you want a good life. You must pull the weeds and get rid of them if you want a good garden. You must pull out your sins and stay away from the places that cause you to sin. That way, your life will look as good as my garden does this week.

It is not an easy thing to do the first time, but if you stay at it every day of your life, there will be fewer weeds and more vegetables. If you stay close to God and get rid of your sins, you will have a beautiful life that will be loved by all.

Bad Mixed With Good

Matthew 13:24-30

"But while everyone was asleep, an enemy came and sowed weeds among the wheat, and then went away." (v. 25)

Object: some wheat seeds and some weed seeds

Good morning, boys and girls. Today we are going to look at something that troubles all of us. Have you ever wondered why there are mean people in the world and why God lets them live with the good people? That is a hard question. We read in the paper or watch on television about some of the worst things that happen to people, and we are always surprised that it was one person who did something mean to another person. Why does God let mean people live?

That is a question people have always asked. Let me share with you the answer that Jesus gave to his disciples. He told the story about a farmer who planted wheat in his field. It was good wheat and it should have grown up to be a fine crop. But one night after he had planted his wheat, an enemy came with some weed seeds and planted them with the wheat. (*show the children both kinds of seeds; mix them together*) The people came and told the farmer what had happened, but it was too late. What could the farmer do? If he dug up the seeds, there would be no wheat. If he tried to cut only the weeds after they started to grow, he could cut up the wheat also. There was only one thing to do. Let the wheat and the weeds grow together until the wheat was ready to cut, and then cut the weeds with it. Only after the wheat was cut would you separate out the bad weeds and throw them away.

That is the way God is working with us. God knows that there are a lot of bad people mixed in with the good people. There are a lot of people who want to share their love with one another and with God, and there are some who hate and are selfish. But if God sent a bad storm, he would kill the good with the bad. If he took away the sun and the rain, he would do the same. So God has decided to wait until the right time to do something about the bad. At the right time, when Jesus comes again, God will get rid of the bad and cause them to be sorry. Until then, you must know that the bad are going to live with the good, and the good are going to live with the bad. It is the way that God chose to do it. That's why Jesus told his story about the farmer and the seeds of wheat and weeds. The weeds stayed until the wheat was ready to be taken in, and then it was gotten rid of for good. The same will be true of people. When the time comes, God will take care of the people who love and share, and he will take good care of them. But he will also get rid of the bad so that they will not hurt the good anymore.

The Great Picnic

Matthew 14:13-21

And all ate and were filled; and they took up what was left over of the broken pieces, twelve baskets full. (v. 20)

Object: a basketful of pieces of broken bread

Good morning, boys and girls. How many of you have heard of the time that Jesus fed 5,000 people with just a couple of loves of bread and some fish that a little boy had in his basket? (*let them answer*) We call that happening a miracle. No one else could have done this, except for Jesus, and he did it several times. We can't explain it and we don't even try to. All we know is that a lot of people were with him one day at supper time and no one had anything to eat. The disciples wanted to send the people away, but Jesus told them that they should invite the people to stay and be fed. It seemed impossible to feed that many, but they knew that Jesus could do some amazing things, so they invited the people to sit down and wait for something to happen.

Jesus sent the disciples out to find whatever little bit of food they could and bring it back to him. They found one little boy whose mother had packed him a lunch of bread and fish. When the disciples came back with it, Jesus took the bread and fish and thanked God for it and then broke it up into little pieces. Each disciple was given some of the pieces to give to all of the people who were there. Each person thanked the disciples and then ate all that he wanted. Some of the people took more than they could eat at first because they were afraid that there might not be enough. But as the disciples kept going to each group of people and giving them the bread and fish, there was more than when they started. Pretty soon everyone had enough to eat and still there was some left.

Jesus told the disciples to take and basket and collect the leftovers. They went out and people started putting back what they could not eat. Do you remember that they started with only five loaves of bread and two fish? When the disciples came back, there were twelve baskets full of bread and fish left over. What a picnic! No one had ever been to one like it before. Can you imagine what it must have been like to have been there that day with Jesus? You would never forget it, would you? (*let them answer*)

The next time you sit down to your table and you see bread in a basket, perhaps you will think about the day that Jesus showed the power of God with a great picnic lunch.

The Clean Plate Club

Matthew 15:21-28

She said, "Yes, Lord, yet even the dogs eat the crumbs that fall from their master's table." (v. 27)

Object: bread crumbs

Good morning, boys and girls. How many of you are good eaters? (*let them answer*) Do a lot of you belong to the clean plate club? (*let them answer*) If I came to your house and ate dinner with you, would I find anything left on your plate? (*direct your question to a clean plate club member*) You mean that I would not find even a crumb of food left somewhere around where you eat? (*let them answer*) Not many of us eat all of the crumbs. When one of your parents cleans up the table after each meal, he or her usually must take a cloth and wipe off all the crumbs that are left behind. Crumbs, bread crumbs, are something that we hardly even see.

A long time ago, people would clean up the dining table by sweeping all of the bread crumbs onto the floor. Then the dogs would eat everything that fell on the floor. Things were different then than they are now, but I am sure that you have seen a dog look all over the floor for anything that might have fallen by accident. They eat almost everything that falls to the floor.

Jesus had a kind of funny thing happen to him one day with a woman from another country who had been following him. This woman had a daughter who was very sick. She heard about Jesus and the things that he could do for sick people. She was not of the same nationality as Jesus, and foreigners were not well liked by most people. But she wanted her sick daughter to be healed. She began to ask Jesus for help, and he listened to her, but he also tested her. She asked for help and Jesus told her that he did not give his bread to foreigners. But she didn't give up. She wanted help for her daughter and she knew that a doctor from her country was not the answer. Jesus looked right at her while she thought about what she was going to say and then she said it. She told Jesus to pretend that she was just a dog because even a dog was allowed to eat the crumbs that fell on the floor. She was positive that Jesus could help, and even a little bit of help would be enough to cure her daughter. Jesus admired her faith in him and helped her immediately.

That is the story of Jesus and the bread crumbs. It doesn't take much of Jesus' power to solve our problems if we only bring our problems to him to solve.

So the next time you see some bread crumbs, I want you to think about the day that a woman was willing to compare herself to a dog so that she could get some help from Jesus to cure her daughter.

Jesus' Public Opinion Poll

Matthew 16:13-20

Now when Jesus came into the district of Caesarea Philippi, he asked his disciples, "Who do people say that the Son of Man is?" (v. 13)

Object: a public opinion poll

Good morning, boys and girls. Today we are going to pretend that we are very grown up people and that I am a news reporter who is trying to get some very important information. I will ask you some questions, and I will then write down your answers for the newspaper. It is very important that you tell me exactly how you feel.

Here is my first question. "Do you think that the President of the United States is doing a great job?" (*let them answer*) Second question: "Do you like cartoons on Saturday morning television or would you rather have them on school nights?" (*let them answer*) Third question: "Which are the best teachers, men or women?" The last question is: "Do my parents love me more than anyone else in the whole world?" That is our public opinion poll and I will turn your answers into our newspaper for their study and information. Thank you.

Newspapers and magazines run a lot of polls. Americans think that polls are very important and a lot of important decisions are made on the information that is received from people like you.

Jesus once had a public opinion poll of his disciples. He asked all of the disciples what they had heard about him. He wanted to know what people were thinking about him and who they thought that he was. He asked each disciple. Some of them said that he was the prophet Elijah and others thought that he was the prophet Jeremiah. Some were talking about him being John the Baptizer. There were a lot of different ideas of who Jesus really was and each of these people that they talked about were important people in Jewish history. Jesus listened very carefully to what the people thought, but then he asked one more question. He asked the disciples who *they* thought he was. This was really an important question. You would have thought that it would have taken a lot of thought and some real time. But Peter was listening to Jesus, and he just said in a hurry what was on the tip of his tongue. "You are the Christ, the Son of the Living God." That was a mouthful. He was right, and Jesus told him that he was right. But he also told Peter that he did not think up that answer on his own. That answer came from God the Father in heaven, and it was given for Peter to say. It was something that no one would ever forget. The answer that Peter gave was the thing that Christians have been saying for almost 2,000 years when people have asked who Jesus is.

The next time that you hear about a poll that was taken you think about the one that Jesus took one day while he was walking through a town called Caesarea Philippi. It was Peter's answer that we will always remember. Jesus is Christ, the son of the Living God.

Such A Good Time

Matthew 17:1-9

Then Peter said to Jesus, "Lord, it is good for us to be here; if you wish, I will make three dwellings here, one for you, one for Moses, and one for Elijah." (v. 4)

Object: a bag of popcorn or peanuts

Good morning, boys and girls. Tell me about some place you have been where you really had a good time. (*let them answer*) What place did you visit where you wished that you did not to leave and come home very soon? (*let them answer*) I just love to go to the movies and watch a very good picture show. Sometimes I hope that the show will not end and I can go on watching it forever.

Have you ever felt like I feel? (*let them answer*) I would like to have a bag of popcorn and a good seat and just sit there and watch the movie. Of course, I would like to have a big bag of popcorn and go to a baseball or basketball game. When I eat popcorn, it reminds me of something that I like to do so much that I don't care if I ever stop.

The reason I told you about the popcorn is because it reminds me of one day when Peter, James, and John were with Jesus on the top of a mountain. Something wonderful happened. While the disciples were looking around, Jesus turned the whitest white they had ever seen. His clothes were so white they seemed to shine. Also while they were watching him, two other people appeared whom they had never seen before. They had not climbed the mountain, but suddenly they were just there and it amazed the three disciples. Even though no one told them, they knew who the other two men were, and they said so. It was Moses and Elijah, and even though they had been dead for many, many years, the disciples knew who they were. It was a wonderful moment and one that they would never forget.

If you can imagine seeing something like this, you will also understand what Peter meant when he looked at Jesus and told him that he would be glad to build three tents so that they could stay a while. Peter did not want to leave. He wanted to build a place for Jesus, one for Elijah, and one for Moses so that they could be comfortable. Peter did not want to leave. Does that sound familiar? It should. That is the way that all of us feel when we are doing something that we like so much. Peter loved it. It was the most wonderful thing that had ever happened to him and he wanted to stay.

Of course, they didn't stay on the top of the mountain and Peter did not build the three tents. You don't stay in the movies or at the ballgame after it is finished. But the next time that you eat some popcorn or go to the show and you are having such a good time that you don't want to leave, then think about Peter and the time that he shared with Jesus, Moses, and Elijah, on the mountain and you will understand why he didn't want to leave either.

31

Sunday's Special Breakfast

Matthew 18:15-20

"For where two or three are gathered in my name, I am there among them." (v. 20)

Object: some orange juice, toast, and cereal

Good morning, boys and girls. I brought along a few friends that I used this morning that I thought I would share with you and help us all to learn something about one of the teachings of Jesus.

First of all, you must be ready to tell me what these things remind you of when you see them together. (*bring out the orange juice, toast, and cereal*) Here are three of my very favorite things to eat. I love orange juice to drink, toast and cereal to eat, and I like them especially at a certain time of the day. What do these three things remind you of when you see them together? (*let them answer*) That's right; breakfast. Whenever you have two or three of these things gathered together you have breakfast. What a wonderful time of the day it is when you sit down to a good breakfast. It helps the whole day get off to a good start.

The same thing is true in a way about people, certain people. The Bible tells us that whenever you have two or three Christians gathered together that Jesus will be there also. It is like our church service on Sunday morning. You put us all together and let us sing our hymns, read our Bibles, and talk about God, and you can be sure that Jesus is here with us. You can feel him here just as you know that it is breakfast when you see orange juice, toast, and cereal sitting on the table. It just has to happen.

Jesus loves to share himself with us on a Sunday morning in worship or in Sunday school. He listens to what we say and gives us ideas about a better way to live. But the Bible tells us that this is not the only time when he is sharing his life with us. The Bible tells us that whenever there are only two or three of us together and we are sharing the name of Jesus that he will be there also. That means that Jesus could be with you when you are playing in your yard with your friends or at school when you are learning about his world or when you are eating dinner with your family. Whenever you meet with people who love God and like to share their lives with others, then Jesus will be there with you.

The next time that you sit down to eat some breakfast and you have a few things that you always eat that make you think of breakfast, I hope you will remember how often Jesus is ready to share his life with you and your friends who love him.

Hermon, The Camel Who Was Humbled

Matthew 19:24

"Again I tell you, it is easier for a camel to go through the eye of a needle than for someone who is rich to enter the kingdom of God." (v. 24)

Object: none

Do you know what it means to be humble? (*let them answer*) Most people like to think that they are humble, but many of them are not. How many of you think that it is good to be proud? People are always telling us that we should be proud of doing this or doing that. If you get good grades in school or can play ball very well, people might tell you that you should be very proud. Maybe there are different ways to be proud but we know that Jesus approved of the humble and taught us not to think too much of ourselves or be proud.

There is one sentence in the Bible I would like to tell you about this morning. I think it has something to say about being proud or being humble. At the time this sentence was spoken, Jesus was talking to people about entering into the kingdom of God and what they should be like for God to give them passage. Jesus said that it would be harder for a rich man to enter heaven than it would be for a camel to pass through the eye of a needle. You know how large a camel is and you know how big the eye of a needle is, don't you? Well, if you do, then maybe you will understand a little better the story I am going to tell you.

Once upon a time there was a camel by the name of Hermon. Now Hermon was no ordinary camel; he was the best-looking camel anyone had ever seen. He had a magnificent hump and this made him even prouder. Because Hermon was so fine, he didn't associate with just any camel. When Hermon went someplace he looked beautiful. Long red cords with gold emblems surrounded his head and neck. High upon his hump there was a seat that looked like a carriage and it was covered in velvet with jewels of ruby and sapphire dotting the length and height of it. When Hermon walked with his very practiced sway, he was something to behold. The other camels looked like poor relatives when compared to Hermon.

One day the very rich owner of Hermon emerged from his tent in a hurry and mounted the handsome camel in haste. "Now, Hermon," the owner said in a loud voice, "we must hurry to Jerusalem, for the enemy is on his way toward us, and if we are not safely within the gate before nightfall we shall be taken captive." Hermon knew of what enemy his owner spoke, and he knew that they were cruel people who would treat him roughly and make him carry heavy pieces of freight and other things that a fine camel was not used to carrying. Off Hermon went at a very fast gait. Still it did not seem fast enough for the owner as he kept urging Hermon on to greater and greater speeds. "Hermon," he said, "if we don't go faster the gate to the city will be closed and we will have to enter the great city through the eye of the needle."

"The eye of the needle," Hermon thought, "how will we do that?" Hermon knew what an eye of the needle was, for many times the tailor had been to his owner's tent to measure

33

him for a new blanket or to do some work on the beautiful carriage, and the tailor worked with needles. The needle was small enough that Hermon could use it as a toothpick and the eye of the needle was so small that he couldn't even see it. Faster and faster Hermon went, cutting across the desert sands under the hot sun. The sand burned his hoofs as he raced over it. Never before had his owner asked him to use himself in such a way and it upset him that he should make him work so hard on such a hot day.

"At last, there is the city of Jerusalem ahead, and it's about time," gasped Hermon. Hermon liked Jerusalem because he knew the other camels and some of the other animals would look at him and say to one another what a handsome camel he was. Hermon thought how he would stretch his long and gracefully curved neck in such a way that no one could help but notice him.

"Oh, no," said the owner from high upon his back, "the gates are closed, and we will have to enter through the needle's eye." The owner knew what a proud camel Hermon was, and he knew his feelings would be hurt when his handsome camel saw what he must do to enter the city. There really was no other way, for the enemy was fast closing in on them. It was about then that Hermon saw that the gates to the city were closed. He realized he would be taken captive and the next thing would be hard work for the enemy.

"What is the needle's eye?" Hermon asked, almost in such a way that the owner could understand him.

"That is the little gate and we must enter the city on our knees through the little opening in the great door," said his owner.

Sure enough, there was a very small door in the big door where a camel could get through only if he crawled on his knees, pulled in his long neck, and scraped his hump. Only one could enter at a time, and it prevented the city from being attacked by an army. "Oh, my," said Hermon, "my beautiful garments are going to get dirty and the other camels will laugh when I come crawling into the great city so awkwardly."

Hermon had almost made up his mind to be taken captive when his owner commanded him to fall to his knees. Hermon began to inch through the small gate. What a squeeze for such a mighty animal! But at last he was through. There was the great city, the needle's eye was closed and locked behind him, and there were the other camels watching him. Hermon lowered his head with shame as he just knew what the other camels were saying. They never did like him but this was too much!

But wait a minute, the other camels were not laughing; they were cheering. "Proud Hermon," they said, "has humbled himself and was saved from the enemy." Hermon felt good because he had not only done what had been asked of him and brought his owner to safety, but also the other camels liked him for the first time. It felt good to be humble.

I suppose you know, boys and girls, the same thing is true of us. We too feel good when we are humble and not proud. God teaches us to use ourselves for other people's happiness and that in so doing we will be blessed with happiness ourselves. I can tell you Hermon was a lot happier camel after he passed through the eye of the needle than he was before, and so will we be when we lose our pride and accept humility.

The Last Is First

Matthew 20:1-16

"So the last will be first, and the first will be last." (v. 16)

Object: a circle of children holding hands

Good morning, boys and girls. Today we are going to be objects of the sermon. Usually we bring something from home or something that we use around the church, but today we are going to use you to teach us what Jesus taught his disciples.

I need a volunteer, someone who would like to be first. (*select the first person that raises his/her hand*) You are my first choice. Do you like being first? (*let him or her answer*) That is very good. We need leaders and people who will take the risk and be first. I want you to stand here and hold out both of your arms from your sides. The reason for you standing in that position is because I am going to select another volunteer to join and stand on your right side. (*select another child*) Do you like being second if you cannot be first? (*let the child answer*) It is good to have someone who is willing to follow the person who goes first. It means that you know how to cooperate very well. I want you, the second person, to hold out both of your arms and take hold of the first person's right hand with your left hand. Now we have someone who was first and someone who was second. (*continue to select people and have each one take the right hand of the previous person until you have only one child left*)

Now we have used everyone except the last person. Do you feel lonely? (*let him/her answer*) How does it feel to see everyone up there holding hands? It is a very straight line that we have at this point, and I think that they look nice together, don't you? (*let them answer*) You are the last one to be used, but in a moment you are going to be the very first one to make something happen. What do you think I am going to use you for? (*let him or her answer*) You don't know?

See what you think of this. All of the other people were told to stand beside someone and hold one of the hands of each person. You are the last one and I am going to ask you to hold the hands of two people. You are the last one chosen but you are the first to complete a circle. (*take the child up and have him or her form the circle*) This means that the last person used becomes the first person in the circle. You are the last and the first, and the first person that we asked becomes the last person to make the circle.

Actually we are all the same. Jesus taught us a long time ago that it doesn't make any difference when we come to be a part of his group. We will all be treated the same. Some people are afraid that if they are not first with Jesus they will be shortchanged. But Jesus said that this is not the way with God. No matter when we are chosen, if we are first or last, we will all be the same in God's world. Living with God is like being in a circle, the first is last and the last is first.

"Hosanna!"
(Appropriate for use on Palm Sunday)

Matthew 21:1-11

The crowds that went ahead of him and that followed were shouting, "Hosanna to the Son of David! Blessed is he who comes in the name of the Lord! Hosanna in the highest heaven!" (v. 9)

Object: spoons and water glasses

Good morning, boys and girls. I brought along with me some things that I thought you might help me make noise with today. Don't you just love to make noise in church and not have anyone tell you to be quiet? (*let them answer*) Usually your mom or dad is telling you to be quiet in church, but not today. I need your help because we are going to pretend that we are watching a special parade that only ever happened once.

How many of you have ever heard someone tap a glass with a spoon? (*let them answer*) It is a good way to get other people's attention.

Now we are going to pretend that we are lining up on a street leading into Jerusalem and we have heard that Jesus is going to pass by us. There has been a lot of talk about Jesus where we live. Some have said that they saw him heal people who were deaf and blind and very sick with terrible diseases. Other people say that he talks like a man who has talked out loud with God. He teaches wonderful news about God and how he loves people. Some people, like the priests and the rich, don't like Jesus, but I guess there is no one whom everyone likes. A lot of people have been following him from town to town and now he is coming into the great city of Jerusalem.

We are going to be part of the crowd that welcomes Jesus. When I see him coming, I will tell you, and I want you to shout, "Hosanna! Hosanna!" and I also want you to tap your glass with the spoon. It will make Jesus feel welcome and let him know that we are his followers also. (*pass out the glasses and spoons*)

It sounds like a crowd is coming over the hill. I can hear voices. As soon as I see Jesus, I will tell you and you can begin to shout. Let's practice it just once. Say, "Hosanna!" and tap your glass.

Now we must watch. Isn't this exciting? Just think; we are standing on the street where Jesus is going to pass us by. We will be able to see him, listen to him, and maybe even touch him if we can get close enough. I think I see the crowd coming. Yes, there is someone running toward us to tell us that Jesus is not far behind. There he is. I see him. Don't forget. Shout, "Hosanna!" (*let the children shout and tap their glasses*)

Wasn't that wonderful? Did you ever think that it would happen to you? You were there the day that Jesus came riding on a donkey into Jerusalem. I know that it is a day that you will never forget. Thank you for being a part of the great Palm Sunday Parade and welcoming Jesus into our town.

Who'll Do The Dishes?

Matthew 21:28-32

"What do you think? A man had two sons; he went to the first and said, 'Son, go and work in the vineyard today.' He answered, 'I will not'; but later he changed his mind and went. The father went to the second and said the same; and he answered, 'I go, sir,' but he did not go." (vv. 28-29)

Object: a broom and dustpan

Good morning, boys and girls. Did all of you know that Jesus was a super storyteller? (*let them answer*) Of course you did, and I have one of those stories to tell this morning, only I am going to change the objects so that you will understand it better. How many of you have ever cleaned the floor with a broom and dustpan? (*let them answer*)

This is the story about a brother and sister who lived at home with their mother and father. The mother had worked very hard one day and was so tired when she was eating supper that she could hardly keep her eyes open. Just before finishing her cup of coffee, she asked her son and daughter if they would mind helping sweep the floor that night so she could get a little rest. The son had played very hard that day and also felt pretty tired, and so when his mother asked, he said that he would not help since he was so tired. The daughter always liked to make her mother feel happy and she said that she would be glad to help if she could. The mother was very disappointed in her boy and said so, but then she went in and sat down in her favorite chair.

As soon as mother was out of the kitchen, the daughter, who had told her mother how glad she would be to help sweep the floor, slipped out the back door and forgot all about the dirty floor. The son, who had said he would not help, thought about how hard his mother worked and was very sorry for what he said. He went into the kitchen and swept the floor and picked up all the dust in the dustpan and carried it out to the trash. Which child do you think the mother was happiest with? (*let them answer*)

That's right; the mother was happier with the son who knew that he had done wrong in refusing his mother but was sorry and came back to help, than she was with the daughter who said the words the mother wanted to hear but did not keep her word.

God is like that with boys and girls and moms and dads. He would rather have people come back to him after they have committed a sin and tell him that they are sorry than to have people make all kinds of promises that they never keep.

If you have done something wrong and you are sorry for it, then tell God. He loves you and he will forgive you. That is better than promising and not keeping your promise.

God has a special love for people who do wrong and are sorry about it. God loves forgiven sinners.

An Invitation

Matthew 22:1-10 (11-14)

"Those slaves went out into the streets and gathered all whom they found, both bad and good; so the wedding hall was filled with guests." (v. 10)

Object: an impressive invitation (try to plan at least part of your service, if not the whole thing, for the children that day to make the point)

Good morning, boys and girls. I have a great surprise for you today. How many of you think that church is just for big people? (*let them answer*) Don't you think that Sunday school is for children and that church is for mom and dad and all of the other big people? (*let them answer*) How many of you listen to the sermon when I preach in the pulpit? How many of you go to sleep or draw in the church bulletin when I am preaching? How about all of the other things that mean you must read and be quiet while the pastor prays or talks? Do you listen to what I say? Not many of you do.

This is my surprise. Today we are going to have church for you. I have an invitation, a special invitation that has been written just for you and it says, "Welcome to worship, bring your mom and dad a special service for children on Sunday morning at 10:30 a.m." This invitation is for all of the children who are here. I wish there were more so that we could fill the church with children to worship God. Let me tell you why I would like this.

Jesus told a parable or story one day about a king who had a big party for his son who was getting married. He invited all of his friends and the friends of his son. But on the day of the party, no one that he invited could come. They all had excuses and did not come to the party. Of course the king was unhappy. But what could he do? Should he call the party off and disappoint his son? Of course not. He sent some of his people out so that they could find other guests. He wanted his palace filled. He stopped people on the street, went to their houses, and to their jobs and invited them to the party. None of these people had ever been to the king's palace and they didn't know him at all, but they went to the party and they had a good time.

Jesus told us this story because sometimes people feel that God needs them and that God cannot live without them. God does some things that are surprises just like the king did in the story. God is going to have people who love him just as the king was going to have a party for his son. The people he invites first may not come, but there will still be people working with God.

This morning we are having a surprise service just for the children so that all of us will learn that God can make a surprise for us just like the king did to his people. We want to be a party of God's world and that means paying attention to what God expects of us.

I hope that you enjoy church this morning and your special surprise for the day.

Jars Of Bad Candy

Matthew 22:15-21

But Jesus, aware of their malice, said, "Why are you putting me to the test, you hypocrites?" (v. 18)

Object: a jar full of candy

Good morning, boys and girls. How many of you have heard the word *hypocrite* spoken by someone? (*let them answer*) It is one of the favorite words for big people. They use it a lot. It is usually someone else they are talking about, but sometimes they even use it when they are talking about themselves. It is a big word. Say it with me: hypocrite. One more time: hypocrite. Do you think that a hypocrite is someone good or bad? (*let them answer*)

I have an example of a hypocrite with me this morning, only it isn't a person. I hope you will understand a little better what a hypocrite is when we finish talking about it this morning. You will know if a hypocrite is good or bad.

I have a large jar of candy. It has every kind of candy that I could find and it makes my mouth water just to look at it. How many of you like candy? (*let them answer*) How would you like to sit down right now and just eat every piece of candy you wanted until your tummy was filled? (*let them answer*) I know how you feel. Just think of all the candy you can eat and it would not cost you a dime. It looks good, it tastes good, and a lot of people would eat it. But before you eat it, I want you to know that this candy would be like poison to you if you ate it all. No matter how good it looks, the sugar in this candy would make your teeth rotten. If you ate this candy and some more like it, you would soon find that you were not only very fat, but that your teeth would almost fall out of your mouth.

Do you remember that we said it looks good and tastes good, but now I want you to know that it would be bad for you. It is a bad trap to rot your teeth.

Hypocrites are like a big jar of candy. They look wonderful and talk wonderful, but they are mean inside and try to cause trouble. There were many hypocrites trying to trap Jesus into saying or doing something that would be against the law. They wanted Jesus to go away so that they would not have to see the good that he did and then could do the bad without being ashamed. Jesus made the hypocrites feel ashamed.

If you ate that jar of candy, the worst would happen to you. That is too much candy. If you talk and act one way and think another, you can be a hypocrite. The next time you see something that is tempting and looks so good but you know it is really bad for you, then you will want to think about the hypocrites and the way that they tried to trap Jesus.

Who Ends Up Happiest?

Matthew 23:1-12

"All who exalt themselves will be humbled, and all who humble themselves will be exalted." (v. 12)

Object: very pretty ribbon and some plain old string

Good morning, boys and girls. I brought along some friends with me this morning and I know that you will enjoy having them here with us. As you can see they are quite different looking, but they both hang around in the same drawer at my house.

First of all I would like to introduce you to Randy Ribbon. Randy is a little strange and actually has very few real friends in the drawer. Occasionally the pearl-handled pocketknife and Randy talk to one another, but most of the other folks in the drawer ignore him. They think he is a bore. Randy likes to talk a lot about himself and very seldom listens to what other people have to say. He really thinks that he is too good for the other drawer people. He says that he is handsome and when people complain about the fact that he never works, he only tells them that he is being saved for something special. That's Randy.

But I also want you to meet Sally String. Now Sally is a good old girl and everyone likes her. She also stays in the drawer when she is not being used. Sally is different from Randy. Sally is used for a lot of different projects. One time she is used to help hold a piece of furniture together that is being glued, while at another I tie her around my finger to help me remember something I don't want to forget. Why, one time Sally was even used as a toy for the brand new kitten. They rolled Sally up into a ball and then rolled her on the carpet. She talks to everyone in the drawer and everyone talks to Sally.

My reason for showing you my friends is because there is something to be learned from Randy and Sally. One day there was a birthday party at my house and it came time to wrap the presents. Sally would have loved to have been used on the bright shiny paper that the birthday present was wrapped in and said so, but she knew that she would never be chosen. She was too plain and common. But Randy was ready. He looked up and held out his cut end and waited to be picked. Sure enough, Randy was chosen. I will have to admit Randy looked just great on the present. He is so good looking he could hardly wait until someone said something. But instead of anyone talking about Randy, they simply tore him apart and looked inside the package. Randy was crushed and torn and thrown away. Now the best part is yet to come. Poor Sally who wanted so badly to be used on the bright birthday paper was also finally chosen. The present was a kite and today Sally flies high in the sky while Randy was rescued from the garbage can.

The Bible tells us why this happened. The Bible says that anyone who thinks too much of himself will be humbled and the humble will be well thought of. Something for you and me to remember and for Randy to learn. God bless you.

When Is Jesus Coming Back?

Matthew 24:37-44

"Therefore you also must be ready, for the Son of Man is coming at an unexpected hour." (v. 44)

Object: an egg timer, a clock, and a television schedule

Good morning, boys and girls. Did you know that Jesus Christ is coming back to earth? (*let them answer*) That's what the Bible says. It teaches us that Jesus is coming back at a certain time and that only the Father in heaven knows just when.

We know the time of almost everything we do or want to do in the future. If I wanted to cook some eggs and make sure that they were just right, I would use this egg timer, set it for just the right time, and then wait for the timer to go off. If I want a three-minute egg, I turn the egg timer just the right number of times, and it will alert me when the cooking time is up so that my eggs come out perfect.

I can do the same thing with a clock. Let's suppose that I want to get up in the morning at 7:15. I set the alarm on the clock and go to sleep knowing that the alarm will go off and wake me up at 7:15.

I can also know when my favorite television show is going to be on the air by looking at the television schedule and finding the hour of the day that it is going to be on. I will not miss it by a minute.

But, now, let's suppose that I want to know when Jesus is coming back to earth. People have waited for a long time to see Jesus again, but it has not happened. I could tell you that it is going to happen tomorrow, but I don't really know when he is coming back. You could read the Bible from cover to cover and you would not know the time that Jesus is coming back. You can ask your mom or dad or any of your friends, but as much as they want to know themselves, they do not know. God has a reason for not telling us when he is coming back. He wants us to always be expecting him and to live as if he were coming back today.

If you thought that Jesus were not coming to your house to live this afternoon, would you not get ready for Jesus in a special way? Would you live a little differently if you knew that Jesus was going to meet you in your living room today? I know that you would, and it is for this reason that God is not telling us when he is coming. He is asking us to live every day as if he was coming today.

You may know when you are getting up, how you like your eggs, and when your favorite television show is on the air, but you will never know when Jesus is coming until the day and the moment he arrives.

God's Bankers

Matthew 25:14-30

"Then you ought to have invested my money with the bankers, and on my return I should have received what was my own with interest." (v. 27)

Object: a bank savings book

Good morning, boys and girls. How many of you have ever been to a bank? (*let them answer*) Almost all of you. What do you do at a bank? (*let them answer*) You put money in the bank and you take money out of the bank. Banks are very important places because they not only protect our money and keep it safe but they also do a lot of other things to help people.

One of the things that banks do is pay us for keeping our money in their bank. If I give the bank one dollar and let them keep it for a year they will give me back the dollar and six cents extra (*adjust figure to current interest rate*) for letting them use it for one year. The six cents we call interest.

That is why people save their money in banks rather than saving it at home. If you keep your dollar at home for one year you will only have one dollar at the end of the year. So you make money by letting the bank save it for you. The bank pays interest. If you save your money at a bank they give you a print-out that will tell you how much they are paying you for letting them use your money.

You are also a kind of banker. You are God's banker. He gives you a part of his world and he wants you to do something with it. He wants you to pay him interest. He gave you a brain and he wants you to learn. If you did not learn you would not use your brain. That is like keeping your money at home. You are not paying God interest on your brain. God gave you love. If you do not use the love that he gave you, then you are losing God's love. It is not being used. There is no interest on God's love. God gave you forgiveness. If you do not forgive other people then you are not paying interest on God's forgiveness. God gave you a yard to play in. If you do not play in the yard and take care of the yard, then you have wasted the yard that God gave you. God gives us everything that we have and he expects us to use it and to share it with others so that they can use it also. It is part of God's plan for the whole world and it is a good plan.

Use the things that God gives you so that there is more of it. If he gives you love, then you love, and he gets interest on his love just like the bank gives interest on the money. If he gives you forgiveness, then forgive others, and God will have interest on his forgiveness. You are God's bankers and whatever God gives you, then you must also give to others so that God makes interest on whatever he gives to you.

Sharing With Others

Matthew 25:31-46

And the king will answer them, "Truly, I tell you, just as you did it to one of the least of these who are members of my family, you did it to me." (v. 40)

Object: an item of canned food that might be given to a food pantry

Good morning, boys and girls. How many of you have ever given food, toys, or clothes to share with another family at Thanksgiving, Christmas, or some other time? (*let them answer*) Do you want to tell me what you gave? (*let them answer*) Those are really good gifts to share with someone who would not have that if it were not for you. When you give like that, you are going to make someone very happy, and not only are they going to thank you for your sharing, but they are also going to thank God for having people remember them.

God teaches us a lot of things, but one of the things that he teaches us most often is to share the things that we have with others. Sometimes he wants us to share our time so that we can go and visit people who are sick or in prison, or who are new in town and have no friends, and things like that. Other times God wants us to share our talent so that people with good voices sing in choirs, and people who can paint, make beautiful pictures, and people who can take care of a house make their homes beautiful. That is sharing talent.

But then sometimes God asks us to share things like our food with people who are poor or can't work because they are old or injured and have run out of money. That is when we do things like collecting food to give to a food pantry. Jesus says that when you do this for the poor people, then it is just like giving it to him. That is really something because we all want to share our things and our lives with Jesus. When we give to the poor, we are giving to Jesus. When we share any of our lives with people who need it, we are sharing our life with Jesus.

All of us want to share Jesus and this is one way that we can do it well. So the thing to remember today is that when you give to some person who needs it, you have given it to Jesus and he thanks you for it.

Reuben, The Rooster With A Reminder

Matthew 26:34

Jesus said to him, "Truly I tell you, this very night, before the cock crows, you will deny me three times." (v. 34)

Object: none

Good morning, boys and girls. How many of you know what I mean when I talk about reminders? Can anyone think of something which we might call a reminder? (*let them answer*) That's pretty good.

When I think of a reminder I can't help but think of a string that my mother used to tie around my finger so that I would not forget about the time that I was supposed to be home or do the job that she wanted me to do. That was one kind of reminder, but there are a lot of others.

For instance whenever I leave the dentist's office there is a nice lady at the desk who gives me a little card with the time written on it for my next appointment. It says, "Don't forget to come back and see us next Tuesday at 10:15 a.m." How about the reminder the firefighter gets when there is a fire? BONG! BONG! BONG! The big bell in the firehouse goes off whenever there is a fire.

Today, though, I would like to tell you the story about a friend who was a reminder, a real reminder. It is the story about one of our animal friends named Reuben. Now Reuben was a rooster, a beautiful rooster, and he had one of the best cock-a-doodle-dos that you have ever heard. I mean this was no ordinary rooster, but a rooster with one of the most powerful voices in the rooster kingdom. Well, Reuben used to wonder why God had given him such a powerful voice. Most roosters could wake up the people in their own yards or houses, but Reuben seemed to be able to let people know all the way across town that he was alive and kicking.

One day Reuben was lounging around the chicken house without too much to do and not having anywhere to go. Little did Reuben know how important he was going to be later on. The night before, on the other side of town, Jesus had been arrested and had gone through a whole series of awful experiences. One of his most loyal followers was a man named Peter who had told Jesus that he would stick by him no matter what happened. Jesus told Peter that it was a nice thought, but that Peter would pretend not to know Jesus three times before the rooster crowed.

Well, as you know the soldiers came and arrested Jesus and took him away. At first Peter put up quite a fight, so good as a matter of fact, that he actually cut off one of the soldier's ears. Jesus told him that this was not the way that Christians did things, and he healed the man who had lost his ear. Then Peter followed the soldiers and Jesus, but he stayed a long way back so that no one could see him.

44

While Peter was standing by a fire trying to keep warm, a woman came up to Peter and asked if he was a friend of Jesus. "No," Peter said, "I have never known him." Two more times people asked Peter if he did not know Jesus and if he was not a follower. Each time Peter told them that he did not know Jesus. When he said it the third time there was a pretty quiet moment and, just as Jesus said it would happen, from far across town came the strong voice of the rooster, Reuben. "COCK-A-DOODLE-DOO" said Reuben, and Peter put his hands to his face and covered his eyes in shame. "I have denied the Lord Jesus three times just as he said I would." Reuben had been a reminder of what Jesus had said.

I don't know if Reuben ever knew what he did with his voice and his loud cock-a-doodle-doo, but it was good. Reuben was such a good reminder that Peter not only bowed his head in shame and sorrow, but he also asked God's forgiveness. That's right, Peter heard the reminder and he went and prayed and asked God to give him another chance. Peter went on to be one of the very great Christian leaders. Many times he told how God gave him another chance with the reminder from Reuben.

That's the way it can be with you, boys and girls. You will do wrong things and all of a sudden you will see or hear something that will be a reminder of the wrong thing which you have done. For Peter it was a rooster, but for you it might be a Bible verse or one of the commandments or even a string tied around your finger.

Reuben was a reminder, and the next time you see a rooster, perhaps you will remember what happened the day that Peter tried to forget all about Jesus and think only of himself. Reuben woke Peter up and made him feel sorry, and then Peter asked for God's forgiveness.

The Ladder And The Sponge

Matthew 27:45-49

At once one of them ran and got a sponge, filled it with sour wine, put it on a stick, and gave it to him to drink. But the others said, "Wait, let us see whether Elijah will come to save him." (vv. 48-49)

Object: a picture of a ladder and a sponge

Good morning, boys and girls. This morning I want you to imagine Jesus hanging on the cross and the Roman soldiers dice games for his clothes. Imagine a horrible afternoon in Jerusalem. The Bible tells us that at noon, when the sun is usually at its brightest, there was nothing but darkness. It looked like it was night time, and there was a big storm coming. The people who stood around the cross were cold and crying since the people they loved were dying on crosses. The soldiers watched the people to make sure that none of them tried to rescue Jesus or the other two criminals who were being crucified that day.

The pain of standing on a nail driven through his feet was terrible for Jesus, and his arms were tired from being held outstretched on the nails. But there was nothing he could do except look to his Father in heaven and pray for new strength. One of the criminals was yelling at Jesus to save them if he was the Son of God. "If you have that kind of power, why don't you use it?" he screamed at Jesus. The other thief felt something different about Jesus and told the screaming thief to be quiet.

The pain was unbelievable, and Jesus began to sweat drops of blood where the crown of thorns bit into his head. His throat was dry and he had to make a major effort even to breathe. Still, he looked out with love in his eyes for all of the people, including the ones who tormented him, with words like, "If you are the Son of God save yourself, come down from the cross." When he did nothing, they laughed at him. None of the followers of Jesus laughed but instead they prayed for death to come quickly so that Jesus would not have to suffer long.

Once when everything seemed quiet and the soldiers were watching some black clouds move toward the hill on which they were standing, Jesus let out a yell in Hebrew that sounded like this, *Eli, Eli, lema sabachthani.* It scared the soldiers to see someone so near to death be able to shout in such a loud voice. Some of the people who were not paying attention very closely thought that Jesus was calling for Elijah. What Jesus had said was, "My God, my God, why have you forsaken me?" Those who heard him felt awful. If Jesus felt that God had given up on him, then what was left: It was for his heavenly Father that he did what he did. Did Jesus feel that God had really left him to die all alone? Later, when men had a chance to think, they remembered that these words from a Psalm. Jesus knew how we feel when we have sinned and God seems so far away.

One of the soldiers ran over to Jesus with a stick with a sponge on the end, and climbed a ladder. He took the sponge and put it to Jesus' dry lips. The sponge was filled with sour wine or vinegar and it tasted terrible. But now it was for something else. It made his dry lips and throat feel better, and it was supposed to help kill the pain. At least one of the soldiers was beginning to feel something different for Jesus.

But the other people who were not followers of Jesus and the other soldiers began yelling at this one who tried to help. "Let him alone," they shouted. "Let's see if Elijah comes and saves him." Then all of these people let out a big laugh since they know that Elijah had been dead for hundreds of years. The soldier came down from the ladder, but he could not take his eyes off Jesus. The soldier could see that even with all Jesus' pain and sorrow, Jesus was filled with love and forgiveness for those who hated him.

I have a small picture of that ladder and sponge of you. I hope that you will keep it somewhere so you can remember the day that Jesus felt all of our sin and the sins of the whole world crush him. You will also remember how one soldier began to think a little differently about Jesus and tried to tell him that he was sorry. Maybe when you think of the soldier you will remember to tell Jesus that you are sorry for your sins.

Joining The Team

Matthew 28:16-20

"Go therefore and make disciples of all nations, baptizing them in the name of the Father and of the Son and of the Holy Spirit." (v. 19)

Object: some baseball team caps — all of them with the same letter team logo

Good morning, boys and girls. I brought something with me that all of you will know something about. (*take out the baseball caps*) Do you know who these belong to? (*let them answer*) That's right, these caps belong to our high school team. How do you know that they all belong to the same team? (*let them answer*) Very good, you know that they all belong to our team because they all have the same letter on the front of them and they are all the same color. That is important because when you are all on the same team, you want to look alike. It makes you feel like you are part of something that is very important. You are very important when you are a member of the team.

Jesus taught his disciples to go out and make a new team. Jesus wanted the disciples to go everywhere in the whole world and teach them about the good things that God had done and still wanted to do for the people in the world. Jesus told the disciples to go everywhere and make everyone a member of his team. He didn't give them ball caps or uniforms, but he told them to do something else that would make them members of his team. Do you know what he told the disciples to do to everyone that wanted to be a part of his team? (*let them answer*) He told them to baptize people who loved and trusted in God.

That is the way you became a member of the Jesus team. That is how you became a Christian. You were baptized and when you were baptized, you started calling yourself a member of the Christian team.

Baseball teams have caps and uniforms, and when you see a team of baseball players, they are all dressed in the same kind of a uniform. They look just great.

The same thing is true of Christians. All Christians are members of Jesus' team. They love God and they share God's love with other Christians and all of the people in the world.

The next time you see a baseball team or you see a baseball cap with a sign on the front, you can be sure that the person who owns that cap is a member of the team. The next time that you see a baby or an adult baptized, you can also be sure that they have just become part of God's team and that they are followers of Jesus. God bless you very much.

Give Someone A Jesus-Hug

Mark 1:4-11

And a voice came from heaven, "You are my Son, the Beloved; with you I am well pleased." (v. 11)

Object: a hug

Good morning, boys and girls. Today we are going to talk about something really wonderful that I am sure all of you will enjoy. We are going to talk about the way God the Father felt about Jesus. We don't think much about that kind of thing because we all know that the Father loved Jesus. But even though we know that, it is still good to think about it sometimes and talk about it when we are together.

Before we talk about Jesus and the Father, I want to show you something. I want to give each of you a hug and tell you how much I care about you. I don't think that I have ever done that with you before, but I want to do it today so that you will know that you are really important to me. (*begin to hug the children*) I look forward to seeing you every Sunday morning here at the time for the children's sermon. This is a very important time to me and I plan it each week so that we can be together. Do you like to be hugged? (*let them answer*) Of course you do. All of us really like to be hugged because it shows us that someone else really cares about us.

God the Father cared about Jesus. The day that Jesus was baptized by John the Baptizer in the River Jordan, the Father did something that Jesus would never forget for as long as he lived on earth. When Jesus was coming up out of the water, the clouds in the sky separated and there was a voice which came from heaven that said, "You are the Son that I love in a special way and I am really happy with the way that you are doing things." God the Father is the one that said this to Jesus and it made him feel great.

All of us feel great when our mom or dad gives us a special hug and tells us how much we mean to them. I like it a lot when you tell me I am special to you. I feel like I can do things that I would not be able to do if you did not love me in a special way.

That's why I wanted to give you a hug today so that you would know that you are really special to me, and I appreciate you very much. Maybe you will want to give someone else a hug today and tell them that they are special and make them feel as good as you feel.

The next time someone gives you a hug — or you give one to someone else — I want you to remember the day Jesus was baptized. For on that day the Father showed Jesus how pleased he was with him and it made Jesus feel good! Will you do that? Will you give someone a hug today to show them how much you care about them? That's wonderful. God bless you.

Follow Me

Mark 1:14-20

And Jesus said to them, "Follow me and I will make you fish for people." (v. 17)

Object: fishing equipment

Good morning, boys and girls. When Jesus was looking for disciples, he chose some men who not only became good followers of his but who could also be leaders of other people. All of us need to follow a leader, but when the leader tells us what to do and how to do it, then we must be ready. Jesus needed good people who would help other people to find Jesus and follow him.

Some of the people Jesus asked to follow him were fishermen. These men worked every day at catching fish. That was their job. What kind of a job does your father or mother have? (*let them answer*) If one of your parents is a doctor, then he or she goes to work every day to help people feel better. If one of them works in a store, then he or she goes to work every day to sell the things that are in the store. If one of them works in an office, he or she goes every day to work to do office work. The disciples had jobs like your father and mother have jobs, only their job was to catch fish so that people could have them to eat. It was a hard job, but the kind of a job that they liked doing.

Jesus told the disciples that he wanted them to be a different kind of fisherman. When they fished for fish, they had to catch the little things or big things that swam around in the water.

How many of you have ever gone fishing? (*let them answer*) If you went fishing, you took a pole, some worms, a stringer, a box like this with all sorts of little things, a net, and maybe some other parts that I don't even have.

Jesus told his new friends, the disciples, that he did not want them to only catch fish out of the lake. Jesus wanted his fishermen to start catching people. He wanted the disciples to find people and tell them what he had taught them and make them followers just like they were followers. That is why Jesus told them to fish for people.

You can be a fisher of people just like Peter, John, James, and Andrew were. You can be a disciple of Jesus. You can look for boys and girls like yourselves and bring them to Jesus. Jesus will love them as he loves you and teach them all of the good things there are to know about God.

The next time you go fishing, or you see someone fishing, I want you to think about the time that Jesus invited some fishermen to come to work for him and help him teach others about God.

A Treasure Hunt

Mark 1:29-39

When they found him, they said to him, "Everyone is searching for you." (v. 37)

Object: a jewelry box hidden somewhere in the chancel

Good morning, boys and girls. Today I need your help to find something which seems to be missing and is a really great treasure. I know that you will be a great help to me since it is somewhere in the front of the church. It isn't lost, but it is hidden and I can tell you that it is very valuable.

How many of you like to look for things which are hidden? (*let them answer*) Good. Now let me tell you what it looks like. (*describe your jewelry box and make it sound as valuable as you possibly can*) Remember, we are looking not only for the box, but the most gorgeous jewels that you can imagine. Take good care and hunt quietly until you have found it. (*when someone has found it, have him bring it back and look through the box to make sure that nothing is missing*)

That was good work and you did it so quickly. I am proud of you for both finding and box and also for making all the people who use it happy again. Finding that jewelry box reminds me of the time when needed some rest after a very hard day of teaching people and healing them of their many diseases.

Jesus was just exhausted and needed to be by himself for a little while, so he got up very early one morning and went out to a very lonely place where he could pray. But while he was gone, other people came to where he was staying and they brought other people who were sick and crippled and asked for Jesus.

The disciples were also tired but they thought that Jesus was close by. However they could not find him. Peter, John, James, and all the others, looked here and looked there, but they could not find Jesus anywhere. The people were going crazy because they wanted to see Jesus very much and no one seemed to know where he was. Finally, the disciples started a search, just as you did this morning. They began to hunt everywhere until they found him.

Jesus was more valuable to the people than a jewelry box. He was as important to them as life itself. They wanted Jesus, and they were willing to hunt for him as long as it took to find him. They searched and searched until they saw Jesus in his lonely spot praying. Quickly they ran up to him and told him how much the people were looking for him and how glad they were to discover him when they thought that he was lost. Jesus was glad to see his disciples but he told them that he must move on now to other places where there were other people who needed him as much as the people did in this village.

The next time you see a jewelry box or something very valuable, I hope you remember the day you searched for one in the front of the church and how you found it. Then you will also remember the day the disciples searched for Jesus and found him praying to his heavenly Father. How many of you will remember? That's wonderful.

Standing Room Only

Mark 2:1-12

So many gathered around that there was no longer room for them, not even in front of the door; and he was speaking the word to them. (v. 2)

Object: some signs ("Standing Room Only," "Full," or "Sold Out")

Good morning, boys and girls. How many of you have ever gone to a really good movie and could not get in because all of the seats were taken? (*let them answer*) Maybe you went to a game or you tried to get into a parking lot and there were so many cars that they could not take one more in the lot. If you did any of these things then you will have seen the kind of signs that I brought with me this morning. Look at these signs because I am going to tell you a story that you will always remember about Jesus. (*hold up your signs and let them read them very slowly*) "Sold Out," "Standing Room Only," and "Full." Those are the kind of signs that you see when you have gotten to the place that you wanted to go and there was no room for you to get in.

A long time ago Jesus was having a wonderful time traveling through small villages and the countryside. Wherever he went he healed the sick people and he preached about God and his wonderful world. The people came from everywhere. As soon as they heard that Jesus was coming, the town would begin looking for him and making plans of how to get the sick people in their family to Jesus so he could heal them. People would run ahead for miles to announce to their friends that Jesus was coming.

One day on such a trip, the people put away their work, cleaned up their houses, and looked for ways to carry their friends who were sick to a place where they could meet Jesus. You must remember that they didn't have cars, busses, or trains. They had to carry people on stretchers or put them in carts. Jesus came to town and went to the biggest house he could find and began to teach. Pretty soon the crowd was so large that there was no room in the house. It was full, sold out, there was not any standing room. All of the space was gone. Most of the people stood outside and hoped that they would get to see him when he left.

But not everyone felt that he could wait. Some people had a friend who was paralyzed. He could not walk. So these friends thought of another plan. They heard that there was not one space left in the house, around the doors, or even in the windows, so they climbed to the roof. After they reached the top of the roof, they took part of it off and then, holding ropes on both ends of the stretcher, they let their friend down through the hole in the roof until he was right in front of Jesus. How Jesus must have laughed at the sight of seeing this man coming to him out of the sky! Of course he healed him and he told the men "Thanks" for thinking so much of him and of their friend. Isn't that a good story?

If you see a "Sold Out," "Standing Room Only," or "Full" sign someday I hope that you will remember the time when Jesus was preaching to a full house and how he healed the man who came to him out of the sky.

Why Is Sunday Special?

Mark 2:23-28

Then he said to them, "The sabbath was made for humankind, and not humankind for the sabbath." (v. 27)

Object: some aspirin or some other kind of pill or capsule

Good morning, boys and girls. How many of you remember some special story about Jesus? (*let them answer*) What is your favorite story? (*let a few of them tell you something they remember about Jesus*) I am going to tell you a favorite story of mine about Jesus, and it is about a special day like Sunday. Sunday is very special to all of us. What do you do on Sunday? (*let them answer*) You go to church. What else do you do? (*let them answer*) You go to Sunday school, you have a big dinner after church, and you visit with your relatives. It is a special day. Some people think of Sunday as a special day because it is a time when they do not work like they work on other days of the week. There used to be laws that said that you could not work on Sunday and if you did work, you would be in big trouble. Did you ever think that you could get in trouble for working? Most of the time we get in trouble for not working.

One day Jesus was walking through a field where there was some food growing and since his disciples had not had anything to eat, they picked it and ate it. On any other day it would have been all right. But they did this on their Sunday and it was against the law. Some people saw them do it and they were very angry with them for breaking the law and they said so. Jesus told them to relax. God made the day of rest for us to use but he did not make it as a law so that we would be punished, or hurt by it.

Let me show you what I mean. We take medicine to help us when we are sick. If we use the medicine right, then we will get well. Medicine can be very good for us. But some people take the medicine when they are not sick. We call people who do this drug users. They make themselves sick because they are letting the medicine use them rather than them using it. Pills are meant to help us and not hurt us.

Jesus told the men who wanted to make Sunday a law, that they should remember why God made the day.

Sunday is God's day and it was made for us to use so that we would know God better. It is a time to love God and share our lives with him. It is not a time of law, but of love and we should use Sunday as a time when we can enjoy God in our life. Sunday makes our life better and never worse. The next time you see some pills remember how they are supposed to be used and not misused. The same thing is true about God's special day, Sunday. God made it for us as a special day to share with him and not as a law that should punish us.

53

A Man Who Changed His Mind

Mark 3:13-19

And he appointed twelve, whom he also named apostles, to be with him, and to be sent out to proclaim the message, and to have authority to cast out demons. (vv. 14-15)

Object: none

Good morning, boys and girls. Have you ever changed your mind? Did you ever think that you were absolutely right and find out that you were not and admitted it? (*let them answer*) Today we are going to talk about such a man. Admitting that you are wrong is one thing, but doing something about it is something else.

There was a man named Simon, and he was the kind of person who believed that he was always right. He did not like to give in to anyone, and he worked very hard to prove that he was right.

Simon knew how to hate. He hated people who were against his ideas. He would do anything to stop them from winning their way. Simon especially hated the Romans who lived in Israel for a short time, and then when their time was served, they would return home and some more Romans soldiers would come to take their place. These men did not care about the people, or the land of Israel, but cared only about keeping the order for the Roman governor who lived in Jerusalem. Simon used to spend whole days just thinking about the Romans and how he could help to get rid of them, making fun of them and scaring them. He thought of every mean thing he knew to make the Romans miserable. Simon was that kind of a man. When Simon prayed, he prayed for a leader to come to Israel whom he could follow and who would drive the Romans away from his land. He prayed that God would send Israel a great soldier with a mighty sword.

When Simon first heard about Jesus, he heard that people were calling Jesus the Messiah. This meant to Simon that Jesus was a great soldier, a leader who was going to free the people of Israel from the Romans. He could hardly wait to meet him, and when the opportunity came he was overjoyed. Simon wanted to belong to a group that traveled with Jesus.

One day when Simon was least expecting it, Jesus came and asked Simon to follow him. This was the time he was waiting for, and he knew it. He told Jesus that he would be glad to follow him and that he would go wherever he went.

Can you imagine how shocked Simon was when he listened to Jesus teach and preach about love and not hate? Jesus told Simon that he must love his enemies, and that if he were hit on one side of his face, he must turn his cheek instead of hitting back. Hating a person is like committing murder, Simon was told, and God would never agree to that.

Simon listened to Jesus, and at first he almost laughed out loud. This was the silliest thing he had ever heard. How could the Israelites ever win and throw the Romans out of the country with that kind of talk and action? He thought that people only did something out of fear and never because of love.

But Simon stayed and watched Jesus work. He was there the day that a Roman captain came to Jesus and begged for his help, and when he got it, the captain fell on his knees and thanked Jesus. Simon saw other people changed by the love that Jesus showed them, and he liked what he heard.

It wasn't easy. Every once in a while Simon wanted to punch someone in the nose or threaten to kill a Roman, but he didn't. Simon was never the same after he met Jesus. He learned that love was stronger than hate. He learned that people are changed by loving them and that they are not changed by hating them.

A lot of us are like Simon. We forget what Jesus taught, and we try to make others like us with our strength and hate, but the people never change. They may do something because they are afraid of us for a while, but they never do anything because they want to. Then we remember what Jesus taught, and we try it his way.

What a difference! People do change when we love them. We change when we are filled with love. It isn't easy, but it works. That's what Simon learned and that is what we all must learn if we are going to follow the teachings of Jesus.

Simon was a man who changed his mind, and he was glad that he did.

Just The Right Time

Mark 4:26-34

"But when the grain is ripe, at once he goes with his sickle, because the harvest has come." (v. 29)

Object: some ears of corn

Good morning, boys and girls. How many of you have a garden? (*let them answer*) Do any of you grow corn in your garden? (*let them answer*) The farmers tell me that corn should be as high as a farmer's knee by the Fourth of July. I like to watch corn grow. You start by planting just one little seed. Then pretty soon you will see something that looks like lots of grass growing in a field, but before too long the grass grows tall and soon you have big leaves. Finally we will see the ears growing on the stalk.

Have you ever looked closely at an ear of corn? (*let them answer*) Can you believe that all of those kernels of corn grew from just one little seed? It's true. But we have to be careful to pick the corn at just the right time. If you pick it too soon, the corn is hard and you can't eat it. If you wait too long, the corn is chewy and doesn't taste good at all. You have to pick the corn at just the right time.

God chooses just the right time also. God has a plan for all of the people in this world, and he has chosen a time that none of us knows to start a brand-new world. God is like a good farmer. He knows just the right time to start his new world, just like a good farmer knows when to pick his corn. Some people think that God has waited too long. Some people wish that God would wait forever, but God knows the right time to begin his new world, and he wants you to be a part of it.

You and I should not worry about when God will start his brand-new world with us. We don't worry about the farmer picking his corn because we know that he will choose the time that is best. If we don't worry about the farmer, we should certainly not worry about God because God knows the exact time that he wants to begin his new world.

The next time you see an ear of corn or you eat it some night for dinner, thank the farmer for knowing just the right time to pick it. While you are thanking the farmer, give thanks to God for his knowing when the right time will be to start his new world.

The Day The Winds Came

Mark 4:35-41

And they were filled with great awe and said to one another, "Who then is this, that even wind and sea obey him?" (v. 41)

Object: a large electric fan

Good morning, boys and girls. How many of you have ever been caught in a big wind? (*let them answer*) It can be kind of scary, can't it? I'm going to turn on a big fan, an electric fan, and we are going to pretend that this wind that is caused by the fan is one of God's own winds.

Pretend that you are on a big lake and the wind is blowing you in the face and on your arms, but pretty soon the waves are filling up the boat with water. If you have a bucket, you can try to bail out some of the water before the boat sinks, but you will have to bail very fast because now the waves are getting bigger and bigger and the boat is being filled with more and more water. You wish the wind would stop, but have you ever tried to stop the wind?

Can you push the wind? (*let them answer*) Can you yell at the wind and make it stop? (*let them answer*) If you have a lot of friends and you all work hard together, can you make the wind stop blowing? (*let them answer*) Of course not. The wind just keeps blowing and moving and getting bigger and bigger. Once in a while it turns another way, but then it comes back and now seems stronger than ever. Just imagine being in a boat on a big lake and having a wind blow like that. It's kind of scary, isn't it? (*let them answer*) It scares me.

Maybe if you know how frightened you would be, you can appreciate how the disciples felt one night when they were on the sea of Galilee. Jesus was riding in the boat but he was asleep. Everyone knew how hard Jesus had worked that day and many days before that. They did not want to wake him, but they were so afraid. The water in the boat was getting higher and higher and the winds were getting stronger and stronger and soon they thought they would sink. Finally, Peter shook Jesus by the shoulder and told him how afraid he was.

When Jesus opened his eyes and looked around and saw how frightened all the disciples were, he raised his hand and told the wind to stop. Can you imagine that! Jesus made the wind stop blowing. No one else could ever make the wind stop blowing just by talking to it, but Jesus did. That's what makes Jesus such a special person. He has such great power. He can even make the wind stop blowing when he wants it to.

The next time you are standing on a hill or just playing outside in your backyard or maybe watching the waves on a lake, you can think about the day that Jesus made the wind stop blowing and the sea to become very calm. Jesus was really something special. He could do things that no one else could do. Jesus could even make the rain stop raining, the sun stop shining, and the wind to stop blowing as he did in today's Gospel story. Jesus is really someone special, and I hope that you never forget it as long as you live. God bless you very much.

Filled Up With God

Mark 5:21-24a, 35-43 or 5:24b-34

But overhearing what they said, Jesus said to the leader of the synagogue, "Do not fear, only believe." (v. 36)

Object: a large glass of water and a clear straw

Good morning, boys and girls. Today we are going to have an experiment. How many of you like to do experiments? (*let them answer*) Good. I like to do experiments also because it is a fun way to learn. I brought along a glass of water with me, a full glass of water, and a clean straw; and we are going to learn something about the way that God teaches us to believe. If I put my clear straw in this glass of water, the straw will fill up with water, but when I take the straw out of the glass, there is no water in the straw. If I put my clear straw in the water, let it fill up as high as there is water in the glass, and then put my finger over the end of the straw and lift it out of the glass, my straw will be filled with water. Let me show you how I did this again. (*demonstrate that several times*)

Let's pretend that the straw is you and the water is faith or belief in God. When we do not believe in God, we are afraid. We are afraid of living, dying. We are afraid that people don't like us; we are afraid of the dark and lots of other things. We are empty when we don't believe in God, and that is why we are so afraid. Some people come to church, but they don't believe, and they are afraid. Many people don't go to church and they, too, are empty and afraid. But the secret is to not only come to church but to believe what you have learned from God.

When I put my straw in to the water but don't have my finger on the end of it, it is like listening and learning about God but not believing what we hear and see. It is just doing and coming. But when I put my finger on the end of the straw, it is keeping and trusting in what I have learned, and we call that believing in God. When I fill my straw or when I believe in God, I am not empty and I am not afraid. We want to be believers, and that means not only filling up but keeping inside of us what we have filled up with.

The next time you see a straw in a glass of water, you can try the same experiment, and when you do, you will remember what Jesus taught us when he told us not to be afraid but to believe. That's what Jesus shared with many people, and all believers in Jesus know that it is true.

Make A Friend For Jesus

Mark 6:7-13

He ordered them to take nothing for their journey except a staff; no bread, no bag, no money in their belts, but to wear sandals and not put on two tunics. (vv. 8-9)

Object: a big walking stick

Good morning, boys and girls. How many of you like to walk? (*let them answer*) What's the farthest distance that you have ever walked? (*let them answer*) Have you ever walked a mile, two miles, five miles, ten miles? Do you think you could walk 100 miles all at one time? (*let them answer*)

A long time ago before there were any cars or buses or trains or airplanes, people did a lot of walking. Sometimes they rode a horse or maybe even in a chariot, but it's hard to take care of a horse and it takes a lot of time, so most people found it easier to walk. A good walker used to carry a walking stick. It helped the person to climb hills and to jump across brooks and streams. It also helped the person to fight off animals and thieves. If you were going to walk 100 miles, you would want to have a good walking stick.

When Jesus sent the disciples out to teach everyone about God the Father, he told them to walk. He also told them what to take when they took this long walk. He told them not to take any bread. He told them not to take a bag full of clothes. He told them not to even take any money. The only things that they were supposed to take were the clothes they had on their backs, a pair of sandals for their feet, and a walking stick. It was a good plan that Jesus gave them, because with no money and no food, they had to trust God and make friends with everyone. If you didn't have any money or any food but only a walking stick, you would learn to make a lot of friends and to depend upon God also. They had no place to stay except in the homes of the people they talked to. They had no food to eat except for the food that the people they stayed with and worked for shared with them. Jesus told them to go out and make friends with the world, and he taught them to believe that God would direct them to the right places where they could share their lives with others. The disciples made a lot of friends for Jesus and for themselves, hundreds of people at first, and soon there were thousands.

Today, because of what the disciples did for Jesus over 2,000 years ago, there are millions and millions of people who believe in God and who trust one another. We called these millions of people Christians.

The next time you take a long walk, maybe you will want to do it for Jesus. Find yourself a good walking stick. Wear a pair of shoes and the clothes you have on, and see how many friends you make for Jesus and how many you also make for yourself.

You Have To Change The Inside

Mark 7:1-8, 14-15, 21-24

"... there is nothing outside a person that by going in can defile, but the things that come out are what defile." (v. 15)

Object: a ballpoint pen out of ink, several empty pens that the cartridge can be put into, and a new replacement cartridge

Good morning, boys and girls. I have with me this morning a little favorite object that I do a lot of writing with in my work. It is just a dandy little ballpoint pen that seems to write everywhere, under water, on paper, wood, or cardboard. It is a good little pen. Well, it was a good little pen until yesterday, and then it quit. I brought it along with me this morning, and I thought, if all of us would say something nice to my little pen, it would get better and start to write again. (*ask each of the children to say something nice to the pen*)

That was really nice of you to talk to my little pen that way, and I am going to sit down and write my mother a letter. (*begin to write or try to write*) Uh-oh. All of the nice things you said did not make any difference. It won't write. I know what I will do. I am going to change the cover on the pen. Maybe if I give it a red cover instead of a green one that it is wearing, it will write. (*begin to change covers, try to write with it, and then change it to another cover*)

Well, we have tried the red and the blue and the yellow and none of them work. I think my pen has died. It is a dead pen. We have talked to it nicely, we have dressed it up in many different colors, and the pen will not write. I guess there must be something else wrong with it. Maybe the thing that is wrong with the pen is on the inside and not on the outside like we have been trying to fix. If I put a different inside into the pen, maybe it would work again. (*put in a good ballpoint cartridge*) "Dear Mom." It writes! I changed the inside of the pen, and the pen is fixed!

That is a little bit like the story that Jesus told us today about people. Jesus said that the only thing that is wrong with people is not what happens to them on the outside or what they eat or how they eat their food. The thing that is wrong with people is in their heart and in how they think.

If you are going to change and be a Christian, a better person, it doesn't make any difference what kind of clothes you wear or the fancy manners that you might have. You have to change your heart and be ready to forgive and share your love with other people. That is how a person is fixed. That is how people change.

People are like pens. They quit working like God's people when they go wrong inside. Changing their clothes or the way that they eat or the house that they live in, will not make the difference. If you want to change and be a Christian, you have to change on the inside and love God and God's people. That is the way Jesus taught us and that is the real way.

60

Lose Your Life In God

Mark 8:30-38

"For those who want to save their life will lose it, and those who lose their life for my sake, and for the sake of the gospel, will save it." (v. 35)

Object: instant cocoa powder and a spoon; also a container for the children to dump the powder into afterward

Good morning, boys and girls. Today we are going to talk about something that can be hard to understand unless you are thinking just right. I want to talk to you about giving your life to Jesus. How many of you want to give your life to Jesus? (*let them answer*) Good. Almost all of you want to give your life to Jesus. That would mean doing things Jesus wants you to do more than doing the things that you want to do. There is even more to it than that, but this is a good place to begin.

Let me show you what I mean. I brought some cocoa with me. How many of you like cocoa? (*let them answer*) Almost all of you. Would you like some right now? (*let them answer*) Good, you can have it. (*begin to spoon out the cocoa grains to each child*) How do you like your cocoa? Aren't you going to drink it? (*let them answer*) What's wrong? You need something else? Do you know what you need? (*let them answer*) I see; I must mix it with something else before you can drink it. The cocoa must lose itself in some hot water or milk. I put the cocoa in a cup and pour some hot water over it and then you can drink it. That sounds like a good idea. (*instruct the children to dump the cocoa powder into the container*)

The little grains of cocoa have to die to give up what they are like to something bigger if they are going to be any good. The little pieces of cocoa are nothing by themselves. They need to be drowned in some water before they are any good to you or me.

You are like a piece of cocoa. You are nothing as long as you belong only to yourself. You need to be used by God and by other people. God tells us that when we give our lives to him then we become something wonderful just like the little pieces of cocoa become something wonderful after they are dissolved in the water.

That is what Jesus means when he talks about giving our lives to him. He calls it losing our lives and saving them. If we keep Jesus out of our life, then we are like little pieces of cocoa. We look kind of pretty but we are not much good. When Jesus enters our life and we stop being just ourselves, then we become something very important to the whole world.

The next time you want a cup of cocoa, I hope you think about how the little pieces of cocoa have to give up being just themselves to be important. Then you will think about giving up your life to God and finding out how your life can become really important. Will you do that? Wonderful!

Beloved Of God

Mark 9:2-9

Then a cloud overshadowed them, and from the cloud there came a voice, "This is my Son, the Beloved; listen to him!" (v. 7)

Object: a hidden tape recording that can be played, telling the children how much they are loved

Good morning, boys and girls. Do you remember what time of year we celebrate Valentine's Day and the birthdays of presidents Washington and Lincoln? Valentine's Day is exciting and we have a lot of fun. (*tape recorder breaks in with a loud voice telling the children how much they are loved*)

What was that? Did you hear something? (*play tape again*) I don't know where the voice is coming from, but I do think I know who the voice was talking about. Do you know who the voice was talking about? (*let them answer*) That's wonderful, you think that the voice was talking about you. How does that make you feel to know that you are loved? (*let them answer*) It makes you feel good. Does it make you feel good because you know that someone else likes you almost as much as your mom and dad, your brothers and sisters, and your grandparents? It is wonderful to know that this person, whoever he is, thinks you are wonderful children who love God.

I will never forget the story in the Bible about the time that Jesus was on a mountain with some of his disciples, and while they were watching Jesus, a voice that came from heaven told the disciples that he was the beloved Son of God and that the people should listen to him. Did you ever hear that story? It is a wonderful story. Jesus took his disciples up a mountain to pray, and while they were there, Jesus was changed into the most brilliant bright light that the disciples ever saw. They also thought that they were visited by some men by the names of Moses and Elijah who had died many years before. Did you ever hear of them? (*let them answer*) Of course you have. While the disciples were watching and listening, they heard this voice come out of heaven and say that the one speaking was really proud of Jesus. The voice said that they should listen to Jesus. Of course the voice belonged to God and God called Jesus his Son. Peter and James and John knew immediately that the voice was God's. But think how good Jesus must have felt to have his heavenly Father talk to them.

Do you remember how good you felt when you heard the voice this morning talking about you? Then maybe you have a little idea of how good Jesus felt the day he was changed into the brightest light you and I can imagine and this heavenly Father spoke to his friends. It is quite a feeling and one that Jesus never forgot. I hope that you don't forget it either.

In The Power Of His Name

Mark 9:38-50

But Jesus said, "Do not stop him; for no one who does a deed of power in my name will be able soon afterward to speak evil of me." (v. 39)

Object: a bottle of shampoo

Good morning, boys and girls. I brought one of your best friends with me this morning. (*show them the bottle of shampoo*) How many of you like shampoo? (*let them answer*) Do you like to put the shampoo on your head when you are taking a bath? Isn't it fun to feel all of those wonderful suds just working away to make your hair cleaner than a whistle? (*let them answer*) Most of you like it, some of you think it is a waste of time, and others don't like to get the shampoo suds in their eyes. But have you ever noticed how often your mom and dad shampoo their hair? (*let them answer*) They like it a bunch. They can hardly wait to wash their hair. Some parents do it everyday.

Someday you will shower once a day, brush your teeth four times a day, shampoo your hair once a day, comb your hair four or five times a day, and wash your hands six or seven times a day. And guess what? You will love it. That's when you will start telling others to make the big change and to start to do those things as often as you are. Good things happen when you are clean. You have fewer colds and other kinds of sickness and you smell good, too.

Jesus knows about changing sides. One day his disciples were upset because some people who hardly knew Jesus were preaching and teaching and even trying to heal people in the name of Jesus. They were not his disciples, but they went from town to town doing these kinds of things. The disciples were upset because they knew that these people had never even met Jesus. They wanted Jesus to stop them. But Jesus knew something very important and he told the disciples to stop worrying about the other people. Jesus told them that when the other people found out the good things that were happening in the name of Jesus, they would also begin to believe. He said even though they did not know him, they would soon become followers of Jesus. When good things happen to you and to others, you change.

Sometimes we wonder about other Christians who worship differently than we do. We want everyone to be like us. But they talk about Jesus, pray like Jesus, sing songs about Jesus, and read about Jesus, and we realize they are followers of Jesus just like us. We don't all have to be the same; we just need to love Jesus.

So when you see a stranger using the name of Jesus and he/she doesn't sound like you do when you talk about Jesus, remember how Jesus told his disciples to relax and enjoy. Change happens to all of us who know the Lord. Even strangers find Jesus to be good. The next time you have to take a bath, ask your mom or dad if you can also have a shampoo. Tell them you have changed just like Jesus' disciples changed their feelings about strangers who used the name of Jesus.

63

Have A Good Marriage

Mark 10:2-16

"Therefore what God has joined together, let no one separate." (v. 9)

Object: a clock

Good morning, boys and girls. Today we want to share some ideas on marriage. Are any of you planning to get married pretty soon? (*let them answer*) How many of you hope to be married someday? (*let them answer*) What kind of a husband or wife would you like? What would be the most important thing to you in a husband or wife? (*let several of them answer*) This is a pretty important thing in our life. We want to make sure that we choose the right person, for whomever we choose should last us for the rest of our lives. The Bible teaches us that we should be married for as long as both people live, but that if one of the two people die, then we can marry again.

One day, Jesus taught some people that when someone marries someone else, the two people become one person. Let me show you what I mean. I have a clock with me, and it is a good clock. It tells me the right time all of the time. I like this clock. It has two hands, doesn't it? (*let them answer*) You can see that those two hands are very important. If you take away one of the hands, you can't tell what time it is. Take away the big hand, and you have no idea how many minutes there are after the hour. Take away the little hand, and you don't know what hour it is. It takes two hands to tell the right time.

A divorce is like taking away one of the two hands. The motor in the clock still runs. The one hand keeps turning, but the time is gone. Jesus talked about the problem of divorce, and he said it shouldn't happen. When two people get married, they are supposed to stay married until one of them dies. That is what Jesus said. Two people become one person, he said. Just like the two hands on a clock make one time. That is the way that it should be. Now everything is not the way it should be. People do get divorced. Both people are still living, but they don't live with one another. Their marriage is over. It happens, and when it does the people who are divorced are very sad. Divorced people would tell you that it is very important that you should be careful whom you choose for your wife or husband, so that your marriage works as well as my clock. God forgives people who are divorced or whose marriage is broken. I want you to know that, but I also want you to know how pleased God is with good marriages that do work.

The next time that you see a clock like mine, with two hands that work, maybe you will think about marriage, and how it should be when two people work together. Someday, I hope your marriage works just as well as my clock and even better. Jesus hopes so too.

64

The Eye Of The Needle

Mark 10:17-31

"It is easier for a camel to go through the eye of a needle than for someone who is rich to enter the kingdom of God." (v. 25)

Object: a needle and your pet dog or cat

Good morning, boys and girls. How many of you have ever been to a zoo? (*let them answer*) Did you like it? (*let them answer*) I love to go to zoos and see all of the wonderful animals that God made to live in this world. One of the animals in the zoo that I have visited is a very strange animal. It is called a camel. How many of you know what a camel looks like? (*let them answer*) Will you describe a camel to me? (*let someone tell you about the camels he or she has seen*) That sounds like the same camel I saw.

I wanted to bring a camel with me to church this morning because that is the animal that Jesus talked about in the lesson that I read to you today. But I couldn't find one anywhere so I thought that I would bring the next best thing. (*bring out your dog or cat*) This is my cat (dog), and I just love him (her).

I also brought along a needle with me because Jesus also talked about needles. Jesus said that it was easier for a camel to walk through the eye of a needle than it was for a person to get into the kingdom of heaven. Do you know what the eye of a needle is? (*let them answer*) It's not very big, is it? Do you think a camel is bigger than my cat? (*let them answer*) Do you think I can put my cat through the eye of the needle? (*let them answer*) I am going to try and put my cat through the eye of this needle. (*make an attempt to put your cat or dog through the needle*) I don't think this is going to work. If this is true, and we know that a camel is even bigger, then I think Jesus must have meant that it will be very difficult for a rich person to get into heaven. Don't you?

I think Jesus told this little story to make all of us think pretty hard about what is really important. Putting a camel through the eye of a needle is impossible. But Jesus wanted us to know that being rich is not the greatest thing in the world. Having money is not so great. It is far greater to be a part of God's people. If we have money, we should share it and help people with our money. Money is a gift from God like being a teacher or a doctor or like anything else that is meant to be shared. If we keep all of our money to ourselves, then we are not sharing our gift. If we do not share, then we are selfish, and that is the kind of a sin that could keep us out of heaven. Jesus knew some things about us that we don't like to know. The more money we have the more we want and very often the less we share.

If you are like that or you know someone like that, then tell them what Jesus said about the camel and the eye of a needle. If you want to be part of God's world, then share and give so that you don't have the same kind of trouble that my cat had with the needle this morning.

Keep Your Promise

Mark 11:1-10

"If anyone says to you, 'Why are you doing this?' just say this, 'The Lord needs it and will send it back here immediately.' " (v. 3)

Object: something that you could borrow, like a gallon of milk or a loaf of bread

Good morning, boys and girls. How many of you have ever borrowed something? (*let them answer*) We borrow lots of things, don't we? Does your mother ever send you next door or to someone's house to borrow a gallon of milk or some bread? (*let them answer*)

When I was a little boy I used to go to my neighbor's house and borrow bread or milk or coffee. They were always so nice about lending me whatever I needed. Do you know why? (*let them answer*)

When you borrow something, what do you have to do? (*let them answer*) That's right, you have to give it back. If you borrow a tool you must give the tool back. If you borrow food, then you must buy some new food at the store the next time you go to the store and replace what you borrowed. Borrowing and giving back makes good neighbors.

Jesus borrowed something once. Do you know what he borrowed? (*let them answer*) It is the lesson for today. Do you remember that he needed a donkey and didn't have one? So what did he do? (*let them answer*) That's right; Jesus had to borrow a donkey. We don't know the name of the man that he borrowed it from, but we do know that Jesus knew him. When he sent the disciples to borrow the donkey, he told them to tell the owner he would send the donkey back right after he was finished riding it. Jesus knew how to be a good borrower. He promised the man when he borrowed the donkey that he would return it.

I suppose you remember the story of now Jesus rode that donkey into the city of Jerusalem and how the crowds came out of their houses and lined the streets to cheer him. It was a wonderful kind of parade. Jesus rode among the people, and they broke off branches from the palm trees to wave at him and shout praises. Some of the people even took off their coats to make a kind of carpet and let the donkey walk on them so that Jesus would know how much they thought of him. It was a thrilling day for everyone, probably even the donkey. We call this day Palm Sunday and it is one of the great days in the church year.

But the thing that I remember is the way that Jesus kept his promises. When he was through with the donkey, I just know that he returned it to the man who owned it. That is the kind of a person Jesus is. When God and Jesus make a promise, they keep it.

Signs Of The Kingdom

Mark 12:28-34

And when Jesus saw that he answered wisely, he said to him, "You are not far from the kingdom of God." After that no one dared to ask him any question. (v. 34)

Object: some signs that note only one mile from your town like "Boston, 1 Mile" and a sign that reads "Kingdom Of God, Very Close"

Good morning, boys and girls. When you ride in car, do you read the signs along the side of the road that tell you how far it is to the next town? Sometimes the sign may say "Indianapolis, 50 Miles" or "St. Louis, 120 Miles." Those kinds of signs are nice because they tell you how far you have yet to go. But the signs I like to read are the ones that tell me something like this: "Boston, 1 Mile." To me that means that I am very close to home. It will only be a minute or so until I am in my hometown. It is good to get home. That is where I eat best, sleep best, and play best. I like home, and I like to be close to it when I am not there. We all like to get back home, for it makes us feel good.

I guess the only sign that could make me feel better than the one that I have just shown you is the next one that I am going to show you. Suppose that you saw a sign that said, "Kingdom of God, Very Close." How would that make you feel? (*let them answer*) That would mean that you were very close to heaven, wouldn't it? (*let them answer*) It sure would! If we see a sign that says the kingdom of God is only one mile away, it would mean that we have understood a lot of things that Jesus had taught, and that we had believed them. It would also mean that we were soon to see Jesus and his Father and all of the other believers. What a wonderful feeling that would be. It would be better than any homecoming that we ever knew because this is what we pray for every day of our lives.

A long time ago a very religious man asked Jesus a lot of questions and Jesus answered them. Jesus also asked him a question and the same man answered it in the way that Jesus wanted him to answer it. When he told Jesus the answer, Jesus said that he was very close to the kingdom of God. He now only had the answer, but he also believed in the answer that he gave. You and I are very close to the kingdom of God. It is only a little while until we see it, even though we are living in it right now.

You may see some road signs that tell you that you are close to home. "Boston, 1 Mile" means a lot to me and to you too, but the best sign of all will be the one that will tell us we are soon to be with God our Father and his Son Jesus Christ. That will be quite a day, one that all of us will enjoy more than any other.

Watch Out! He's Coming!

Mark 13:33-37

"Beware, keep alert; for you do not know when the time will come." (v. 33)

Object: the pose of someone on a sheep-keeping watch, with binoculars

Good morning, boys and girls. This morning we are looking forward to the time when Jesus will return and that means we should be keeping watch. How many of you have ever seen a movie or a picture of a person keeping watch on a ship? (*let them answer*) Good, a lot of you have seen that. What do people do who are keeping watch? (*let them answer*) That's right, they sort of stretch their necks, puts their hands over their eyes so that the sun doesn't affect them, and look in all directions. If they do see something, they lift their binoculars up to their eyes and take a closer look. (*pretend you are looking through binoculars, or use them if you have them*) That is called keeping watch.

Christians should always be keeping watch for the return of Jesus. We don't know when Jesus is coming back, but we should be ready for him when he does come back. There were only a few who were looking for him when he came the first time, but all of us have been told to be ready for him when he comes again.

How would you get ready for Jesus if you thought he might come here to our church today or to your home tonight? (*let them answer*) All of those ideas sound pretty good to me, but the important thing to do is to be sure that we know when he arrives. Put your hand over your eyes on your forehead and begin to look around to see if you can see Jesus anywhere. Do you see him? (*let them answer*) You are looking so you will be ready if you do see him or hear about him from someone else who has seen him.

We want to be ready since we do not know when he is coming. We want to be looking for Jesus we that we can be ready to welcome him into our hearts as well as our homes.

Happy Easter!

Mark 16:1-8

They had been saying to one another, "Who will roll away the stone for us from the entrance of the tomb?" (v. 3)

Object: a gravestone marker (or a picture of one)

Good morning, boys and girls. I should have said, "Happy Easter!" Happy Easter, everyone. Why do we say Happy Easter? (*let them answer*) Is there a special reason why Easter should be happier than any other day? (*let them answer*) That's right, because this is the day that Jesus was raised from the dead. Who raised Jesus from the dead? (*let them answer*) Right, God raised Jesus from the dead.

Do you remember the story of how Jesus was taken down from the cross where he died, and then taken to a garden? (*let them answer*) Do you remember how a man by the name of Joseph gave a special place to bury Jesus that he had once saved for himself and his family? (*let them answer*) Did you also know that after Jesus had been put in the tomb, a big stone was rolled in front of it so that no man could get inside? (*let them answer*) That is exactly what they did. It must have been a very big stone because as Jesus' friends came to take care of his body the way they always did for dead people, they worried about how they were going to get into Jesus' grave.

Today things are a little different. We don't bury very many people in the way that Jesus was buried. Most of us are buried in the ground, and once we are buried you can't open the grave anymore. How many of you have been to a cemetery? (*let them answer*) If you have been to a cemetery you have seen things like this. (*show them the gravestone marker*) It has the name of the person on it; when the person was born, and when he died. It is also made out of stone. But the stone that covered Jesus' grave was much bigger. It was ten times bigger or maybe even 100 times bigger. You can understand how worried the women were when they thought of how they would move this big stone that covered Jesus' tomb.

But think of their surprise when they got to the tomb and found the stone already moved. They could see right into the tomb where the dead body of Jesus was put.

But then another surprise. Jesus wasn't there! An angel told them that Jesus was no longer dead. He was risen. It was the first time this had ever happened, but it was what Jesus had promised would happen time and time again. Jesus had told them that when he died he would be raised from the dead by his Father in heaven. No one really believed it before he died, but now they had to believe it. Jesus Christ is risen today. That's why we say, "Happy Easter!" and we mean it.

You too will be raised from the dead. It is a promise of God and we are happy to know that we shall share in the resurrection of Jesus.

69

His Name Is John

Luke 1:57-67

He asked for a writing tablet and wrote, "His name is John." (v. 63)

Object: a baptismal certificate and a birth certificate

Good morning, boys and girls. Today is a time for us to remember the story of when John the Baptist was born and how he got his name.

How many of you remember when you were born or how you were named? (*let them answer*) None of us remember the day that we were born, but all of us have a piece of paper that tells when we were born and another piece of paper that tells when we were named. Let me show you mine. (*take out your birth certificate or a birth certificate of someone*) This is a birth certificate. (*read the information*) That proves that I was born. Here is something else that I think all of you have somewhere at home. (*show them a baptismal certificate*) This was given to me the day I was baptized. I was given my Christian name that day. My parents promised God that they would raise me as a Christian and then they gave me my own special name. (*show them your name on the certificate*)

The reason that I wanted to share this with you is because there is a greater story about John and his father. John's father was a priest at the temple and really quite an old man. He and his wife had prayed to God for years for a child, but they never had one. One day an angel promised John's mother and father that they were going to have a child, a special child, who would not only be their child but also someone who would help God tell the world about the Messiah. When John's father heard this he was so happy, but he also lose his voice. He could no longer speak. He tried, but he could not talk. All of the other people were amazed at how he lost his voice. For nine months he did not talk.

Then one day John was born to his parents. All of the people were so happy for his parents, Elizabeth and Zechariah. They knew how proud Zechariah was of the little boy and they were sure that he would want to give the baby his name. But God had also told Zechariah what to call the child, and Zechariah kept his promise to God. When the people asked Zechariah what the name was going to be, he took a tablet and wrote on it the name "John." Everyone was amazed, but of course they did what Zechariah wanted and named the baby boy John.

Then something else very strange happened. As soon as John was given his name, Zechariah was able to talk. What a happy day it was for everyone! John, the servant of God, was given his name and Elizabeth was now a mother, something she wanted all of her life. Zechariah was not only a proud father, but he also received his voice back. That is the story of how John the Baptist got his name, and it is one for you and me to remember.

Soft Blankets For A Baby
(Appropriate for use at Christmas)

Luke 2:1-20

"This will be a sign for you: you will find a child wrapped in bands of cloths and lying in a manger." (v. 12)

Object: receiving blankets for a baby

Happy birthday, Jesus! Would you all like to sing happy birthday to Jesus? (*lead them in a chorus of Happy Birthday*) Does anyone know on what day we celebrate Jesus' birthday? (*let them answer*) That's right, on Christmas Day. Of course, nobody knows when Jesus' birthday really is, but Christmas Day is when most of us celebrate it. I love Christmas and all of the things that it means to me. I am sure that all of you love it too. Is there anyone who does not like Christmas? (*let them answer*) I didn't think so, but I thought I would ask.

I have some very soft cloth with me today, and I wonder if you know what it is used for? (*let them answer*) Have any of you ever held a tiny baby in a cloth or blanket like this? That's good. I am glad that all of you have held a tiny baby, because I think it is one of the nicest things in the world to hold. When you see a blanket like this you must know that somewhere there is a baby who belongs to it.

An angel of God appeared to the shepherds and told them to go to Bethlehem and find a stable where there was a new baby born in a manger. The baby was going to be wrapped in a soft cloth like the one that you are touching. A baby was usually born in a house in those days, and very seldom, if ever, was a baby born in a stable. The angel told them to go and find a baby born in a stable that was wrapped in soft cloth, and when they did they would also find the Savior, Jesus Christ.

Can you imagine how excited the shepherds must have felt? I know they were excited. First of all, I am sure that it was the first time that they had ever seen an angel. People usually don't see angels. Secondly, they were told to go and find a baby wrapped in a soft blanket that was lying in a manger. You know that a manger is something that animals eat out of, and that it was not a baby bed. So the shepherds knew that they were going to see something very unusual. But the angel wanted them to look for something unusual because Jesus was not an ordinary baby. He was the Son of God, and he was meant to save the world. The angel said that this was the sign. Of course, the shepherds did what they were told, and they went to Bethlehem and found a baby lying in a manger wrapped in soft cloth. That baby was Jesus, and Jesus is our Lord.

Maybe the next time that you see some soft blankets like this or when you see a baby wrapped up in them, you will think about the shepherds and how they found Jesus on that first Christmas Day.

Save The Good Part

Luke 3:15-17, 21-22

"His winnowing fork is in his hand, to clear his threshing floor and to gather the wheat into his granary; but the chaff he will burn with unquenchable fire." (v. 17)

Object: a banana

Good morning, boys and girls. How many of you like bananas? (*let them answer*) A banana is one of my favorite fruits. I like to eat it on cereal, or I like to eat it all by itself. I guess my favorite way to eat a banana is in a banana split, but I don't have those often. I brought a banana along today to see if you eat it the same way I do. Is there anyone here who would like to eat the banana for us? Let's all watch very carefully to see how she (he) does it. (*watch her for a moment until it is apparent that she is not going to eat the peeling*) What are you going to do with the peeling? Does that mean that you are not going to eat it? (*let her answer*) Are you going to throw it away? (*you may act a little shocked*) In other words, you are only going to eat the inside of the banana, and you are going to throw the peeling in the garbage or do something to get rid of it. (*let her answer*) Is that the way the rest of you would eat a banana? (*let them answer*)

All right, I think that everyone knows that we do not eat banana peelings, because they are not good to eat. They are bitter, not tasty, and so we get rid of them.

The Bible says something like this when it talks about the way that God works with the people who obey him and the ones who do not. The Bible teaches us that, after our lives are lived here on earth, God makes a choice between the people who do obey him, and those who don't. The ones who obey him, love him, and live the way he teaches are forgiven for any wrong that they do, and are asked to share his life in heaven. The ones who are wrong, have hate in their hearts, and are unforgiving, are done away with about the same way that you get rid of a banana peeling. There is no place for them in heaven.

I don't want to scare you. You should not be scared, but instead, you should be pleased to know that God wants to share his life with you. People who love God, and there are many, are going to have a wonderful life on earth and forever after with God in his heaven. That is what the Bible teaches, and it is what we believe. But if you want to know what happens to the people who do not love God, who hate what he teaches, then you can remember the way we care for a banana peel, and you will have the answer.

So the next time you eat a banana, I want you to remember that there is a good part and a bad part, and that the two parts are the two kinds of people who live in this world and how both of them know God.

It's Tempting

Luke 4:1-13

Jesus answered him, "It is said, 'Do not put the Lord your God to the test.' " (v. 12)

Object: a television schedule

Good morning, boys and girls. I brought something along with me this morning that I think all of you will recognize immediately. (*hold up the television guide*) What is it? (*let them answer*) Right, it is the television guide from the Saturday paper. If you want to know what is going to be on this week, or what the special programs are going to be for each day, you can read all about them in the television guide.

How many of you like television? (*let them answer*) Do you watch it often? Do you wish that you could watch it more? (*let them answer*) How many of you think that you watch television too much? (*let them answer*) Not many of you think that you watch it too much. How many of your parents think that you watch it too much? (*let them answer*) I thought so.

If you had some homework to do and you also wanted to watch a special program on television, which would you do? (*let them answer*) Does the television ever tempt you to lie? (*let them answer*) I know some boys and girls who tell their mothers and dads that they don't have any homework, so that their parents will let them watch the television.

Anything we like as much as television is bound to be a temptation. It causes us to act differently than we should, and say things that we should not, because we like television so much that we do not want to give it up for anything.

We call that temptation. Jesus knew about temptation. As a matter of fact, he told the devil one day that he should not tempt God or ask anyone else to tempt God. Temptation is a bad thing. The devil tried to get Jesus to tempt God by asking Jesus to jump off a high building, so that the angels would catch him before he hit the ground. Jesus said that there was no reason for him to jump off a high building. If you jumped from a high building, you would be hurt. If you do not study, but watch television instead, you could flunk your school tests. We can't blame the television. We have to blame ourselves instead. God says that we should not tempt ourselves or other people. When you do the wrong thing, you should not expect it to turn out right. We know how to act for God and with God, and when we don't do what we should, we have problems. When we do right and share our lives in the right way, we have right things happen to us.

Maybe the next time you decide to watch television instead of doing your homework, you will remember how Jesus told the devil to leave when he tried to get Jesus to tempt God. Then you will turn off the television and do what is expected of you. The television can be good, or it can be a temptation for you. Only you know when it is right and when it is wrong. Use it the right way and you will be pleasing to God and to yourself.

A Good Custom

Luke 4:14-21

When he came to Nazareth, where he had been brought up, he went to the synagogue on the sabbath day, as was his custom. (v. 16)

Object: praying hands and bowed head

Good morning, boys and girls. How many of you know what a custom is or what I mean by the word *custom*? (*let them answer*) A custom is something that you do at a particular time. You always do it no matter how many times it happens. Putting up the Christmas tree is a custom in most homes at Christmas time. Even when there are no children at home, many people still have a Christmas tree in their house. It may be large or small, but they have a tree.

Praying is a custom. I pray before every meal. I am sure that most of you pray before you eat, to thank God for the food and all of the good things he has done for you. You probably also pray before you fall asleep at night and when you get up in the morning. It is good to talk to God and to share all of your thoughts with him. It is a custom to pray. We even make it more of a custom when we fold our hands like this, and then bow our heads in this way. (*demonstrate the posture of prayer*) It is a custom, and a wonderful custom, and it has been done by people and families for thousands of years. If you don't do it, I hope you will begin today.

Jesus prayed. It was a custom of Jesus to pray, and he also had other customs which I would like to share with you. The one custom that the Bible tells us about this morning is the custom that Jesus had of going to church on the day of worship. The Bible tells us that it was his custom to go every week to worship God.

Isn't that wonderful? Jesus did the same thing that you and I do. He did not think that he was so good that he didn't have to go to church. As a matter of fact, Jesus loved to go to worship and be with all of his friends and family, and sing the Psalms, and read the scriptures. The story we hear today is that when he went back home to the church where he was raised, he also went to church with his neighbors, and read the scriptures, and preached to the people about who he was.

You don't have to preach, but I am sure that it is good when you take your turn in Sunday school and help to read from the Bible, and share your prayers with your friends. It is a good custom to pray, and also to attend church every Sunday in the same way that Jesus followed his custom and prayed and went to church.

I hope you remember the word "custom" and that you will make it a custom to come to church every Sunday.

Jesus In The News

Luke 4:21-30

He said to them, "Doubtless you will quote to me this proverb, 'Doctor, cure your-self!' And you will say, 'Do here also in your hometown the things that we have heard you did at Capernaum.' " (v. 23)

Object: a newspaper

Good morning, boys and girls. How many of you have read the newspaper that was delivered to your house yesterday? (*let them answer*) Tell me what you have read. (*let them answer*) You read the funnies and what else? (*let them answer*) Most of you do not read the rest of the paper yet, but before long you will. When you do, you will read about some very interesting people and the things that they have done. You also will read some interesting things about people who live in other towns and cities. When someone does something that is very interesting in another city, the newspaper prints it in our town and we read about the things that person has done. (*read such an article in the newspaper that you brought with you*)

This is the way that it was with Jesus. When Jesus came into a town, the people had already heard about the things that he had done in other places. They wanted him to do the same things for them. The news traveled fast.

But Jesus was not just doing things so that people could write about him in the newspaper, or talk about him to friends and neighbors. That was not the reason. Jesus did what he wanted to do for people who were ill because they were ill, and because they believed in the power of God to make them well. Jesus called that kind of belief "faith."

When Jesus came to his hometown, the people did not believe that he was the Son of God. Instead, they thought that he was just like all of the other boys who had grown up there, but with some special magic. They knew him as the son of Mary and Joseph, and not as the Son of God. They did not have faith or believe that God wanted to make them well. Because the people did not believe Jesus, he could not cure them. He could not cure someone who did not believe that it was God who was doing the healing.

We have read a lot about Jesus and talked a lot about Jesus. You can find something in your newspaper almost every day about him. If you do not believe that his power comes from God, then Jesus is not something special to you. Reading about him, or talking about him doesn't make him our Savior. Believing in him does, and that is what the people of Nazareth did not do.

We want to believe in Jesus and believe that he can do what he says, so we must have faith that Jesus is the Son of God and that he has great power. When you read about him in your newspaper, then you can say that you also know him in your heart. God bless you.

Strange Fishing

Luke 5:1-11

Then Jesus said to Simon, "Do not be afraid; from now on you will be catching people." (v. 10b)

Object: a badminton net

Good morning, boys and girls. I read in the Bible today that Jesus said he was going to make people like Peter and John fish for other people. Do you know what that means? (*let them answer*) I think it means that they would catch people just like they caught fish.

Did you know that Peter and his brother Andrew, and also James and John were fishermen? That was their job and they were pretty good at it. Every morning they would get in their boats and go out on the lake to catch fish and bring them home to sell. Some days they would catch a lot, and some days they would catch very few. There are not many people who still fish the way they did in those days.

But can you imagine catching people in a net like you catch fish? Do you think that this is what Jesus meant when he said that he would make them fish for people? (*let them answer*)

Let's suppose that this is what he meant. I have a big net here and I am going to catch some boys and girls. (*take the net and throw it over the children*) Now, what do I do with you? I don't think this is what Jesus meant.

What Jesus did mean was that he was going to teach the disciples about God's love, so that they could teach other people. Jesus wanted the disciples to learn as much as they could from him so that, when they began teaching other people about God, those people would also become disciples of Jesus as well. That is what Jesus meant. He didn't want to catch people in a net. He wanted to make them disciples. But he knew that Peter and John would understand him better if he told them that they were going to stop catching fish and instead start "catching" people.

Jesus would like to make you fishers of people also. He wants all of his disciples to look for ways to teach people about the wonderful things that God can do for us. If people are going to learn about God, they must first be "caught," or spoken to, by other people like you and me.

Maybe the next time you see a big net, you will remember the time that Jesus told Peter how he was going to make him a fisher of people, and what that really means. I hope you remember also to be a fisher and to teach someone about the good things that God does for you.

Jesus The Healer

Luke 6:17-26

And all in the crowd were trying to touch him, for power came out from him and healed all of them. (v. 19)

Object: some chicken noodle soup

Good morning, boys and girls. How many of you have ever eaten chicken noodle soup? (*let them answer*) When do you like to eat it the most? (*let them answer*) At lunch, when you want a snack, when it is cold outside and you have been in a snowball fight, are all good times, but I have a favorite time to eat chicken noodle soup. I like my chicken noodle soup when I have a cold or some aches and pains. Nothing makes me feel better than chicken noodle soup.

Why do you think that helps me when I feel bad? (*let them answer*) Have you ever had chicken noodle soup when your ear aches or your nose runs or your throat is so sore you can hardly talk? (*let them answer*) Is it because it is warm and the noodles are so soft they just slide down your throat and into your tummy? Is it because your mom or dad made it special just for you as a sign of their love? (*let them answer*) Is it because it is filled with vitamins? (*let them answer*) I think it is because of all of those things, especially Mom's or Dad's love.

Jesus was kind of like chicken noodle soup. No one was sure how he did it, but they knew they felt better when they were around him. He talked about faith, but they just knew that they had touched him or spoken to him or he was nearby talking to others. Jesus was very special and filled with love. He wants all of his people to feel good and to get better when they feel bad.

I remember several times in the Bible stories when people would see Jesus in a crowd and they would get close and reach out and touch him. Now the power that Jesus had came from God. He would tell everyone that it was not he that was doing the healing but his Father in heaven. The power was not in the clothes he was wearing or in his fingertips. Jesus did not carry around a special stick that he used to heal people. The healing came from God and Jesus told them so.

The same thing is true about the chicken noodle soup. The healing comes from God, but the soup makes us feel better, especially when Mom or Dad makes it.

So the next time you don't feel too good and you want to feel better, ask your mom or dad to fix you a bowl of chicken noodle soup. While you are eating the soup, say a short prayer and ask God to heal you in the name of Jesus. The next thing you know, you will feel a lot better. Thank Mom or Dad for the soup and Jesus for the power of healing.

A Dog Named Sport

Luke 7:1-10

"Therefore I did not presume to come to you. But only speak the word, and let my servant be healed." (v. 7)

Object: an invisible dog named Sport

Good morning, boys and girls. I brought along with me this morning a friend who is invisible. Sport just loves to come to church, and being an invisible dog, he comes quite often. But he is kind of shy, and I only use him in children's sermons once in a while. Sport is a beautiful dog. What color would you say he is? (*let them answer, and whatever color they give, he can be; they can describe him as a dog with short ears, long ears, tall, short, or whatever they want him to be*) I told you he was a beautiful invisible dog. I want to let you each pet him once, and then I am going to have him go over and sit down for a moment. (*let them each pet him and then send him to a certain spot*) The thing I like most about Sport is that he will do whatever I say. (*tell Sport to do some tricks and compliment him on his obedience*) Thank you, Sport.

Now the reason that I brought Sport with me this morning was to help me tell you another story that we find in the Bible. It is the story about a time when Jesus was asked to come to the home of a soldier. He was not a private, but he wasn't a general either. This soldier had a man who worked for him who was very sick. The soldier loved this man and wanted more than almost anything else for him to be well.

He heard about Jesus, and he sent some friends to ask Jesus if he would come and heal the man. Jesus was so impressed about the soldier because of the nice things that other people said about him that he went immediately. Before Jesus arrived at the soldier's house, there was someone sent to meet him and tell him that he did not have to come any farther. The soldier knew that whatever Jesus said would be done. Jesus did not have to be in the soldier's house to make this man well. The soldier knew that Jesus could do the same thing with healing that he could do with other things. When the soldier gave an order to one of his men, the man did it. When he gave an order he considered the job done. The soldier knew that if Jesus would only command that the man be healed, he would be healed.

This is a great lesson for all of us to learn. It is called "faith." The soldier knew that if Jesus wanted to heal the man, he would and could heal him, even from a distance. All Jesus had to do was to ask his Father in heaven to do it and it would be done.

That is the way Sport is with me. I tell him to do something, and I know that Sport will do it. Maybe the next time you think about my dog Sport you will remember the faith that I have in Sport to do anything that I ask him to do, and when you think of that, then you will also think about what our faith in God means, and how much we must trust him to have all things done.

Compassion

Luke 7:11-17

When the Lord saw her, he had compassion on her and said to her, "Do not weep." (v. 13)

Object: a nurse's ID badge (borrowed from a nurse)

Good morning, boys and girls. How many of you have ever been hurt so badly that you had to go to the hospital to be cared for by the doctors and nurses? (*let them answer*) Some of you have been there. Do you remember how afraid you were? (*let them answer*) First of all, you hurt pretty badly, and second, you were not sure what was going to happen to you. That would make anyone afraid. Do you remember how nice the nurses were to you that day and every day that you were in the hospital? (*let them answer*) They were really something special and they made a lot of the worry and fear go right out of you.

I brought along a nurse's ID badge with me this morning so that you could think about nurses when I tell you a big word. The word is *compassion*, and that is what the nurses feel for you when you come into the hospital. They have compassion for you. That is another word, only a nice powerful word, for caring. They not only feel strongly for you, but they also take care of what is hurting you. And the nurses will be there to keep taking care of you until you are well enough to go home.

Jesus was a person who was filled with compassion. He had compassion for all who needed him, and that includes everyone. I remember the story in the Bible about a woman who was walking to the cemetery to bury her son. She had already buried her husband after he died, and now she was all alone. The people who walked with her were carrying the body of her son, and they were all very sad. Jesus watched the people coming toward him, and the Bible said that he had compassion for her. That means that he not only felt sorry for her hurt, but that he was going to do something about it.

First, he told her not to cry any more, which is another way of telling her that she would soon have nothing to be sad about. Then he went over to the place where the body was being carried and told the son to wake up, to come back to life. And I am sure that you know what happened. The man who was dead was brought back to life.

That was just one sign of Jesus' compassion. Jesus has compassion on lots of people. He cares about us, and he does something about it. Nurses have compassion, and, when you see a badge like this, you can remember that the nurses, like many other people, learn their compassion from God.

We should all have compassion, which means that when we see someone who needs us, we should care and do what we can to help them.

Learning To Forgive A Lot

Luke 7:36-50

"Therefore, I tell you, her sins, which were many, have been forgiven; hence she has shown great love. But the one to whom little is forgiven, loves little." (v. 47)

Object: a small bag of potatoes and a twenty-pound bag of potatoes

Good morning, boys and girls. Today we are going to have a little experiment that I hope will prove something about the way that God loves and takes care of us. I need two volunteers to help me. (*choose two, one of them a lot smaller than the other if possible; give the larger sack of potatoes to the smaller child*) Now the only thing that you must do to help in this experiment is to each hold a sack of potatoes. (*hand out the sacks*) Now I want you to hold these sacks while I tell a story about Jesus.

A long time ago, Jesus ate dinner in the house of a very important person. While he was there, a woman who did not have a very good reputation showed up at the place where they were eating, and began to pay a lot of attention to Jesus. She washed his feet and dried them with her hair, and she did other things that showed how much she believed in him as someone special. The people who were eating were shocked that Jesus would let someone with such great sin care for him. They said some pretty nasty things to Jesus, and about the woman. Of course, she could hear what they said, but they never talked to her. Instead, they just pretended that she was not there as a person, but only as a bad thing.

Jesus then said to the important man that he had done none of the things for Jesus that she had done, even though Jesus was a guest in his house. It was true that the woman had sinned a lot, and it would take a lot of forgiveness to forgive her. But Jesus said that when you forgive a person a lot, then they also love a lot.

I want to prove that last point. I am going to take away the potatoes from this person and see if he (she) is really glad that I have taken them away. (*take away the potatoes from the large child with the small bag*) Do you feel really happy that I have taken away the potatoes so that you do not have to carry them any longer? (*now take away the big sack from the little person*) How do you feel now that I have helped you? (*let this one answer*) You seem a lot happier than the other person. Do you think it's because you had the bigger sack? (*let them answer*) I think that this has something to do with it.

I think that this is what Jesus was trying to tell the people that day. The woman knew that she had sinned a lot. She was so glad for the forgiveness of Jesus that she wanted to do something to show it. The others felt that they had not done much wrong, and therefore they did not appreciate what Jesus did for them. It is a hard lesson to learn, but an important one to know that the forgiveness of Jesus is the most precious gift we have.

Eric Eraser

Luke 9:18-24

"For those who want to save their life will lose it, and those who lose their life for my sake will save it." (v. 24)

Object: a well-worn rubber eraser

Good morning, boys and girls. Today we are going to talk about one of the teachings of Jesus that changed the world. It changed the way that people think and act.

I brought along a little friend of mine to help me show you how important that teaching is. I hope that it will help you to think and act as Jesus taught us to. My friend's name is Eric. His whole name is Eric Eraser. How many of you have a friend who looks just like my friend Eric? (*let them answer*) Take a close look at Eric and you will see that he is not the same as he used to be. (*show them the well-worn rubber eraser*) Does he look kind of worn out and used up? (*let them answer*) He is. That's the way that Eric likes it. Eric would not have it any other way. The best thing that can happen to Eric is for me to use him to correct one of my many mistakes.

I guess there are some erasers that would like to stay neat and clean and never be used. But that is not the way that Eric feels. Eric knows that the only way he knows that he is alive is to be used, and that is the way that he wants to live. I want you to know that this is the way that Jesus taught us to live.

Some people always want to save themselves, just like some erasers. They never want to be used, and so they never really live. They just lie in a box somewhere and are completely forgotten. But live erasers are ones that are used every day for every mistake until they are all gone. They love life and can hardly wait until they are all used up.

Every Christian should feel this way about the special promise made to us by Jesus. Jesus promises us that when we use up this life by living it the way that he teaches us to live, he will give us a new life that is even better than the one that we have now.

That is why I want all of you to be like Eric. He is not all used up yet, just like many Christians are not used up yet, but when he is used up, he will be happy. You will be happy, too, if you live for Jesus and share your life in love with all of God's people.

That is the story of Eric Eraser, and I hope you remember it today and every day, as you share the things that Jesus taught you with your friends and all of the people that you meet. Will you do that? Good. God bless you.

What A Change!

Luke 9:28-36

And while he was praying, the appearance of his face changed, and his clothes became dazzling white. (v. 29)

Object: a very dusty mirror and some glass cleaner

Good morning, boys and girls. Things have a way of changing, don't they? The weather changes, the time changes, we change our clothes and our friends and almost everything else that we can think of around us. Can you think of one thing that does not change? (*let them answer*) I guess the only thing that I can think of that does not change is God's love.

I want to tell you about a time that Jesus changed and some of the disciples saw it happen. They were with him when this change took place, and they watched Jesus become dazzling white. That is the way that the Bible described Jesus when he made this change.

I brought along a mirror of mine to help you see what I mean when I talk about something changing. This mirror is pretty dusty and clouded. You can see yourself in it, but if you had your choice, you would want it different. Most of the time we do not even notice a mirror when it is dusty, but let me show you what happens when we clean it. (*proceed to clean the mirror and make the glass shine*) Now you can really tell the difference between the way that it was and the way that it is now. The mirror has changed.

Jesus changed from his normal-looking self to a dazzling white. It happened one day when Jesus took Peter, James, and John up a mountain to pray, and to be alone with God. While they were there, they had a very strange experience not only of Jesus changing, but also of being visited by some men who had died many years before. Right there, where they stood, appeared Moses and Elijah.

Peter was so excited that he could hardly speak. And then to make it one of the most unusual days in the disciples' lives, they heard the voice of God saying, "This is my Son, my Chosen; listen to him." You can imagine how impressed Peter, James, and John were when they saw what they saw and heard what they heard. They knew for certain that Jesus was something special, not only to them, but to the Father in heaven.

Maybe the next time you are standing in front of a mirror, or maybe when you watch someone clean a mirror, you will remember the day that Jesus changed. It was an important day for Jesus, and an important day for everyone who believes in Jesus.

Hoe Jesus' Row

Luke 9:51-62

Jesus said to him, "No one who puts his hand to the plow and looks back is fit for the kingdom of God." (v. 62)

Object: a garden hoe

Good morning, boys and girls. Today we are going to learn something about farming or having a garden, and while we are doing this, we hope to learn something about the kingdom of God. Let's see if we can do this.

I brought a hoe with me this morning. How many of you have ever used a hoe? (*let them answer*) If you have used one, then tell me how to use it. (*let someone explain or demonstrate the way that he or she uses it*) You must be a very good farmer. If you use a hoe like this, you should not have any weeds in your garden, and your plants should be growing very well. Sometimes you must use a hoe to plant a garden, and that means having straight rows. Have you ever seen someone try to make a straight row with a hoe? (*let them answer*)

I am going to show you two ways to use a hoe, and I want you to tell me which way is the best way to have a straight row. (*demonstrate lining up the hoe with a supposed marker straight ahead, and then hoe by looking back over your shoulder; as you walk, you should make it fairly obvious that looking over your shoulder produces a crooked path*) Which way seems best to you? (*let them answer*) That's right; the best way is to look straight ahead so that you know where you have been, if you want to keep on going in a straight line. If you look over your shoulder, you will make a crooked path.

The same thing is true about being a member of God's kingdom. Jesus knew that there were some people who wanted to be a part of the group who believed in Jesus, but that they also wanted things to be like they used to be for them. In other words, they liked what Jesus said and did, and hoped that it would happen to them, but they did not want to give up some of their sins. They always wanted to be able to go back and do the things that they used to do, like telling a lie if they needed to, instead of telling the truth. Jesus said you can't be a part of God's world one day and wish you were part of the other way another day. That won't work. You can't have it both ways. It is like hoeing your garden and looking over your shoulder; you never get to the place that you want to be, and instead you always get somewhere where you don't want to be. If you make up your mind that you want to be a Christian, then you must forget about the other things, and just keep looking forward to the time when you shall be with God in God's world.

Yummy Good Spinach

Luke 10:1-9

"Whenever you enter a town and its people welcome you, eat what is set before you." (v. 8)

Object: a package of spinach

Good morning, boys and girls. I hope that all of you love spinach, because that is what I want to share with you today. How many of you just love spinach? (*let them answer*) None of you like spinach? Isn't there someone here who would like it if I put some vinegar on it with salt and pepper? None of you like vinegar? Suppose I invited you to my house and I served you spinach on your plate, and I just expected you to eat it. What would you do? (*let them answer*) Would you make faces and not eat it if you knew that it would hurt my feelings? (*let them answer*)

I had to ask you these questions because Jesus told his disciples a lot of things when he sent them out to teach others about Christianity, and one of the things that he told them was to eat whatever the people offered them in their homes. Jesus told them that it was very important to have good manners about what they ate and how they lived, so that people would not have an excuse not to like them. Jesus did not care what it was that the people offered his disciples to eat while they stayed in their homes. They were supposed to eat it and be thankful for it. Do you think that you could have been one of the disciples of Jesus? (*let them answer*) Why do you think that Jesus told them to act this way? (*let them answer*)

People think that what they eat is what all people eat, and they also think that it is very good. If you tell them that you don't like what they serve for food, then the people also think that you don't like them. If you came to tell me about Jesus and to show me how much you love him, and I gave you spinach to eat, and you said you didn't like the spinach, then I might think more about the spinach, and how you don't like the way that I cook it, than I do about what you are trying to tell me about Jesus. Does that make sense to you? (*let them answer*)

Having good manners is always important. I am not talking about only when you are teaching about Jesus. But it is very important that you do not make people feel bad about other things when you are trying to teach them about Jesus.

The next time that you are a guest at someone's house and they share their food with you, I want you to remember this and how Jesus taught his disciples to be polite and never to make someone feel bad. That is something that all Christians must learn if they are going to teach the whole world about Jesus.

You Need All The Pieces

Luke 10:25-37

He answered, "You shall love the Lord your God with all your heart, and with all your soul, and with all your strength, and with all your mind; and your neighbor as yourself." (v. 27)

Object: a jigsaw puzzle

Good morning, boys and girls. How many of you know what the word *all* means? (*let them answer*) Is it an important word? (*let them answer*) The word *all* means a lot and it is a very important word. Sometimes if you don't have it all, you don't have anything.

Let me show you what I mean. I brought along a jigsaw puzzle. It has a lot of pieces and it will take all of the pieces to make the whole puzzle. If one of the pieces is missing, the puzzle is ruined, and you cannot have a whole picture. I want you to know that there is one piece of the puzzle missing. Isn't that awful? (*let them answer*)

This is the way Jesus felt about the way that people should feel about God. When someone asked him how they should be toward God, he asked them what the Bible said. They knew what the Bible said, and so they repeated the words that they had heard so often. The Bible says that you should love God with all of your heart, all of your soul, all of your mind, and all of your strength. It did not say part of your mind or part of your soul or part of your heart or part of your strength. It just isn't like that. You have to give God "all" that you have if you want to give him anything.

Loving God is like making a puzzle. You have to do it all, you have to give it all, because that is the way that God wants it. Part of a puzzle is not good enough. If you put it all together and you were missing one part, you would search and search until you found the one piece that was missing, and then you would put it in and be very happy.

That is the way it is with loving God. If you are saving some of your love for something else instead of giving it to God, you will find that you are always looking for the part that you have not given him. You are looking and looking and looking for whatever is missing and keeping you from loving God. But, when you find what you have been hiding even from yourself, and you give it to God, then you are really happy. Give all of your love to God and you will know why Jesus taught us to do what he wanted us to do.

The word *all* is a very important word, and, if you do not believe me, then hide one piece of the next puzzle that you do and see how much you miss it. Find that piece and put it together, and then you will know why it is important to love God with all that you have to share.

Do You Choose Marge Or Chris?

Luke 10:38-42

"Mary has chosen the better part, which will not be taken away from her." (v. 42b)

Object: a candy bar and a glass of milk

Good morning, boys and girls. Today we are going to talk about the way that people spend their time with Jesus. It is a good lesson and one that all of us should learn. Sometimes we have to learn this lesson over and over again.

I brought along some friends of yours that I am sure all of you like. I have with me Marge Milk and Chris Candy Bar. Both of them are good, and, if I told you that you could have as much as you wanted of each or both, I am sure that you would choose both of them. But if I told you that you could have only one of them, and the one that you chose would be the one that you would have for the rest of your life, I wonder which one you would choose. Let me see your hands, and then I will know which one you like the most. (*let them vote for one or the other*)

Some of you have chosen the milk, but most of you have chosen the candy bar. I wonder which was the good choice. The one is going to build you into a strong boy or girl, while the other one is going to give you cavities if you eat too much of it. Do you know which one is which? That's right; the candy bar is not really good if you have too much, but the milk is good for you no matter how much you drink. We have to make choices all of the time and our choices are important.

Today we find that Jesus was asked to settle an argument between two sisters. One of the sisters felt like she wanted to have a clean house and serve a good dinner, while the other sister wanted to know all that she could learn from Jesus. Having a clean house is important, and cooking good meals is important, but I wonder which is the most important. If you had your choice between listening to Jesus and serving him a good meal, which one would you take? Both of them thought that they were making the right choice. But Jesus said that the sister who learned was making the right choice. Spending time learning and loving God is the most important choice, and it should come above everything else. The rest of the things that we do or have to do should come after our loving and learning about God.

Some people put working around the church ahead of worshiping God. They think that they are serving God, but really they are serving themselves. Jesus said it is better to worship and share our lives with him than it is to do anything else. It is a hard lesson to learn, and one that we must learn many times; but it is a good lesson, and one that we should never forget.

86

Snakes On Your Plate

Luke 11:1-13

"Is there anyone among you who, if your child asks for a fish, will give a snake instead of a fish? Or if the child asks for an egg, will give a scorpion?" (vv. 11-12)

Object: a plastic or rubber snake and spider

Good morning, boys and girls. How many of you like snakes and spiders? (*let them answer*) Some of you like them, but a lot of you don't like them. The older they get, the less most people like them. I don't know many older people who like snakes, but when we are young, we do seem to like the things that crawl and slither in the grass.

But now I have another question for you. How would you like to come to dinner or breakfast and ask for an egg or a fish, and, when your mother brought you your food, see a snake or a big spider on your plate instead of the fish or egg? (*let them answer*) Can you imagine having a plate full of snakes or spiders? (*let them answer*) I can't either. Do you think that your mother or father would give you snakes and spiders if you asked for a fish or an egg? (*let them answer*) Fathers and mothers are not like this. We trust our mothers and fathers to give us what we need, and they would never trick us by giving us something that could harm us or scare us.

Jesus told us that our Father in heaven is a lot like our mother and father on earth are in this way. God is not going to trick us with something that would be bad for us or scare us in a terrible way. If we ask for love, he will give us love, and not hate. If we are wanting help, he will give us help, and he will not trick us with something else. Jesus says that we can trust God to give us whatever we need, when we need it.

You would never expect your father or mother to scare you or break a promise to you. Parents are not like that to their children. When they promise something they keep the promise. God is like that also because he never breaks a promise. Of course, we must ask him for the things that we want. We can't just wait and hope that God gives us everything. God wants us to ask for the things that we need, so that he can decide how to give them.

Jesus compared our parents to the Father in heaven often, because they act a lot like the way that God acts toward us. But I want you to know that God loves us even more than our parents, and that means that he loves us a bunch.

The next time that you have something to eat, and you know your mom did not give you a snake or spider, I want you to think about the way God wants to share his life with all of us and answer all of our prayers.

What Do You Do With The Leftover Jelly Beans?

Luke 12:13-21

And he thought to himself, "What should I do, for I have no place to store my crops?" (v. 17)

Object: a large bag of jelly beans

Good morning, boys and girls. I need a volunteer this morning, someone who is really something special. This person must love jelly beans. Is there anyone here who really likes jelly beans? (*let them answer, and pick a child who will participate in an enthusiastic way*) Do you think that you really like jelly beans? (*let the child answer*) I know that you cannot eat all of the jelly beans that I have brought with me, so I am going to give them to you, and you can save them in any way that you want. (*begin handing the child the jelly beans, and, after he has eaten a few, you might suggest that he fill his pockets, take some back to his parents, fill his hands, or try anything so that he can take all of the jelly beans he can carry*) Now that you have all the jelly beans that you can carry, what should I do with the ones that I have left? (*let the child answer*) Should I just throw them away, or wait until you come back next week, or what should I do? (*let him answer*)

Did I ever tell you the story about the man in the Bible who had such a wonderful year growing his crops that he filled up all of his barns and still had things left over, so the only thing he thought he could do was build some bigger barns? Did I ever tell you this story? He didn't know what else to do but to keep it all for himself. He never thought of sharing it with the people who were hungry. He thought that God just gave it all to him, and that God did not care if all of the rest of the people went hungry or not.

Our own friend did not think of the rest of you either. He (She) was like the rich farmer. Our own friend kept all of the jelly beans to himself, just like the rest of you may have done. When his pockets and hands, and even his mouth were filled, he still wanted more if he could find another place to put them. The rich farmer tore down his barns that were filled and built bigger barns.

Jesus taught us something different. He said that God gives us all that we need, and it would be more than enough if we would share it with others.

Our friend could have shared his jelly beans with each of you, and would probably like to do so now. While he is sharing with you and feeling good about it, I hope that you will remember that you cannot take what God gives to your death, and that it is better if you share when you can.

What Is Your Treasure?

Luke 12:32-40

"For where your treasure is, there your heart will be also." (v. 34)

Object: a pocket knife, a baseball glove, and a doll

Good morning, boys and girls. How many of you have a treasure? (*let them answer*) Very good, a lot of you have some treasure. What kind of treasure do you have? (*let them answer*) I brought along some things that I thought might be a treasure to you. A treasure is something very important to you, something that is worth almost more than anything you can think of, when you think of things that you want or have.

When I was a boy, I always thought that my baseball glove was the most important treasure that I had, and I would not have given it up for anything. My brother always wanted a pocket knife that he could carry with him. When he was old enough to have a knife, he got one, and he still carries it with him today. My sister was not too interested in ball gloves and pocket knives, but she loved her doll. That was really "it" for her, and she would take the doll with her wherever she went, even to bed when she went to sleep at night. She loved that doll with all of her heart, just like my brother loved his knife and I loved my ball glove.

Jesus knew how people love things, and he thought that this was all right, even good, as long as we remember what love is really meant to be. Jesus told us that we should not love gloves, knives, money, dolls, gold, cars, or anything more than we love people, and especially God. Loving our treasure can be wrong if we love it more than we love God and people. When we love our things more than we love God and people, it makes us greedy and unkind. Nothing is as important as God, and we should love him the most. Next to God is our love for each other, and when we share our love with each other instead of loving things, then we are also doing right. But if we love money or whatever is special to us, we end up trying to hurt others so that we can have more things. If we try to keep things such as food and clothes to ourselves, even when others need them, then we have wars or fights. But when you love God, it means that you want to share things that you have. You may even share your most important treasure, even if it is your ball glove or your knife or your doll.

When you learn to share your treasure at your age, you will then be ready to share your money, your food, and whatever else is important to you when you grow older.

A Big Problem

Luke 12:49-53

"Do you think that I have come to bring peace to the earth? No, I tell you, but rather division!" (v. 51)

Object: a blackboard, some chalk, and a division problem

Good morning, boys and girls. Today we are going to get back to school a little early. I want to work a math problem on this board, so that I can teach you something about the way God feels about the people of this world. All of us have wondered why everyone does not believe and trust in God. Why do certain people seem to do all of the things that God says are wrong when God tells us that he loves all of us?

That is a big problem, but an old problem. I have a big problem, too, and I want to figure it out, so I have brought along my blackboard, my chalk, and my problem. This is my problem. I can clean about four rooms at the church in an hour. It must be done by tomorrow. The church is a big place, and I think there are about 32 rooms in the whole church. Some of the rooms are much bigger than others, but some are also much smaller. I want to know how many people it will take to clean the church. Can you figure that problem out for me? (*let them answer, but go over the problem again*)

The way to find the answer is to divide the number of rooms that must be cleaned by the number of rooms that I can clean in an hour. (*do the problem*) That means that I need eight people if I want to do it in one hour, or four people if I want to do it in two hours. To find the answer I must divide.

Jesus talked about dividing also. Some people thought that Jesus just came to earth to bring us all together, and that it did not make any difference what was right or wrong. They thought Jesus was supposed to be like glue. But Jesus said that this wasn't true. Some things are more important than this, and so Jesus said he would be dividing us. There would be some people who would follow what he taught, and some people who would not follow what he taught. That means that they will be divided. It is the answer to the problem. Jesus is the divider. He teaches us right from wrong. He teaches us what is true and what is untrue. He tells us that we must follow him. If we do follow him, we are on one side. If we do not follow him, we are on the other side. Of course, the church is teaching us that we should do what Jesus teaches and follow him, but we all know that there is another side, and Jesus is not going to change to make the people who do wrong and believe wrong a part of his side.

Maybe the next time you are working a big problem that has to do with dividing, you will remember that Jesus is the big divider, and that we must choose which side we are going to be on.

Bearing Fruit For God

Luke 13:1-9

"If it bears fruit next year, well and good; but if not, you can cut it down." (v. 9)

Object: some fertilizer

Good morning, boys and girls. How many of you have ever tried to grow a plant or a tree? (*let them answer*) Did it live? (*let them answer*) How did you take care of your plant? (*let them answer*)

There is a story Jesus tells in the Bible about a man who had a fig tree planted on his farm. He asked another man who worked for him to take care of the tree. After a while, he came back to pick some of the fruit that had grown on the tree, but he was surprised to find that the tree had no figs. The owner was disappointed, and he told his worker to cut it down. But the worker asked him to give the tree one more chance. So the owner told him to give the tree some fertilizer, and that if it did not grow in one year, then he should cut it down.

Fertilizer helps plants to grow strong so that they will produce fruit, flowers, or whatever they are supposed to produce. If you want a strong plant, one that grows and grows, you must fertilize it. Fertilizer is very important for plants and trees.

Jesus told this story so that we would learn something very important about ourselves, too. Sin makes us weak. We all sin. Every one of us is a sinner. Sin makes us very weak and keeps us from living the way that God wants us to live. When we are weak, we cannot even do the good things that we want to do.

There is only one way to make things better so that we can get over our weakness. We must tell God how sorry we are for our sin. This is called repentance, and it is as good for us as fertilizer is for a plant.

Tell God that you are sorry, and ask him to forgive you, and you will get rid of your sin. When you do not have the sin, then you can grow strong and be the way that God wanted you to be.

The next time you see someone feeding a plant some fertilizer to help it grow strong, I hope you will remember how telling God you are sorry for your sin will also help you to grow strong. Will you do that? (*let them answer*) Good. God bless you very much.

Charley Becomes Happy

Luke 13:22-30

"Indeed, some are last who will be first, and some are first who will be last." (v. 30)

Object: a folding chair

Good morning, boys and girls. Today I have a story to tell you about one of my favorite friends. His name is Charley, and I want you to know that Charley is a really good friend. It hasn't always been easy for Charley, because, you see, Charley is a folding chair. (*show them a folding chair*) How many of you have ever sat on a chair like Charley? (*let them answer*) Aren't they great? You can take a friend like Charley almost anywhere and sit on him. I have had Charley in the yard, in different rooms of the house, and all over the church. Charley certainly is a good friend.

Now let me tell you why it hasn't always been easy for Charley. When people are through with Charley, they fold him up and put him away. Many times, I guess almost all of the time, Charley is on the bottom of the stack. All of the other folding chairs are on top of him, and you can imagine how that must feel. It isn't too bad if they stack the other chairs right, but when they are put down on him the wrong way, it really hurts. But the worst part of all is that Charley is always the last folding chair to be used.

I tried to tell Charley that this wasn't so bad, but he didn't agree. I told him that he would not wear out so fast, but Charley likes to be used and sat on, since that is the reason why he was made. Charley really felt bad. But then one day that all changed.

He was still at the bottom, and that meant that he was the last chair used, but he was put up at the far end of a big hall. He heard it was going to be a very big dinner, and he was glad that they had to use all of the chairs, because it meant that he would be used also. When Charley was finally set up, he noticed that he was all alone at a very beautiful table. He was glad to be used, but now he was all alone and that made him sad. But he wasn't sad for long. Because into the hall came the president of our country, and he was taken to the front where the beautiful table was set. Then after everyone had clapped their hands until they hurt, the president sat down on Charley, and Charley felt good all over. There he was — the president's chair. What a wonderful day for Charley.

That is a good lesson for all of us who sometimes feel unnoticed and not very important. Jesus told us that his kingdom is going to be made up of the people who may not have been very important in this world, and who, most of the time, felt that they were the last. But Jesus said that the last will be first in his world, and the first in this world will be last. The most important thing is to be loving and to want to be used like Charley the folding chair. Then some day you will have the most important place in the world, a place called the kingdom of God.

What's In A Name?

Luke 13:31-35

"See, your house is left to you. And I tell you, you will not see me until you say, 'Blessed be he who comes in the name of the Lord!'" (v. 35)

Object: two brands of soda crackers like "Krispy" and "Zesta"

Good morning, boys and girls. Today we are going to talk about Jesus and how he came to share his life with us. Jesus represented God on earth. The Bible says that Jesus came in the name of the Lord. I want to show you what that means.

How many of you like crackers? (*let them answer*) Do you like your crackers in soup, or with peanut butter on them? (*let them answer*) Sometimes I like to eat my crackers just plain with nothing on them. I just like the salty taste. But that is not the important part of these crackers today. I want these crackers to teach you something about Jesus.

There are a lot of people who make soda crackers, and everyone who makes crackers thinks that these crackers are the very best crackers in the world. I have two kinds of crackers with me today. (*show them the crackers*) This cracker is called a "Krispy" cracker and it comes in a beautiful box that looks like this. (*show them the box*) How many of you have ever eaten a "Krispy" cracker? (*let them answer*)

Now here is a second soda cracker. It is called a "Zesta" cracker, and it comes in a box like this. (*show them the box*) How many of you have ever eaten a "Zesta" cracker? (*let them answer*)

Each of the crackers comes with a name. One is called a "Zesta Cracker," and one is called a "Krispy Cracker." You could say that this cracker comes in the name of "Krispy," and this one comes in the name of "Zesta."

Jesus said that he came in the name of the Lord. Jesus came because God sent Jesus to represent him on earth among all of the people. Jesus comes in the name of the Lord, like a soda cracker comes in the name of "Krispy" or "Zesta." Of course, representing God is a lot more important than representing a cracker company, but I hope that you understand the idea.

When you eat a certain cracker, you think of "Zesta" or "Krispy." When you think of Jesus, you should think of God our Father in heaven. Is that who you think of when you hear about Jesus? (*let them answer*) If you do, then you know what Jesus meant when he said that he came in the "name of the Lord." God bless you.

The Humble Teddy

Luke 14:1, 7-14

"For all who exalt themselves will be humbled, and those who humble themselves will be exalted." (v. 11)

Object: a tire jack

Good morning, boys and girls. How many of you have ever been with your father or mother when they had a flat tire on their car? (*let them answer*) Did it seem like a good time to them? Did they enjoy changing the tire? (*let them answer*) It isn't much fun, is it? As a matter of fact, it is an awful experience, and I don't know anyone who likes to change a tire. But if you think that it is bad for your father or mother, wait until you must do it. As bad as it is, though, I want you to know that it helped me to come to know one of my very best friends.

How many of you have met my friend Teddy Tire Jack? (*let them answer*) I am sure that you have a friend like my friend Teddy, but I want you to know that he isn't easy to get to know. As a matter of fact, Teddy has been with me ever since I bought my car, and I did not get to meet him until the other day when I had a flat tire while driving in the country.

There I was driving along and having a good time, when, all of a sudden, I heard this funny noise and the car started to run funny. I knew that I had a flat tire. It seemed awful at first, but then I went to the trunk of my car and got out the spare tire, and began to think of what a dirty job it would be. As I told you, I had not met my friend Teddy until that moment, and when I got him out he looked like a lot of hard work for me. But Teddy was a surprise. Imagine how he worked to lift that heavy car so I could take the flat tire off and put on a new tire. It was wonderful the way he raised that car and did almost all of the work for me. It wasn't so bad after all, and I owe it all to Teddy the Tire Jack.

Jesus says that there are a lot of people who are his followers just like Teddy. We call them humble people, and they work hard, though very few people notice them. Teddy rides around in my trunk and never says a word. He is almost unnoticed until I have something awful happen like a flat tire, and then he is ready to help, even to lift a heavy car. That is something I cannot do, and look how much bigger I am than Teddy is. He lifts the car up and, when he is done, I put him back in the trunk. I would say that Teddy is very humble.

That is the way that we should be. We don't have to ride in the trunk of a car, but we should remember how great our God is when we think of ourselves, and that will make us humble also. When God wants you, he will use you, and he will make you great just like I used Teddy and made him great. It is a hard lesson to learn when we talk about being humble, but it is the way that every Christian should feel when he thinks of his Lord Jesus Christ and his loving God.

It Costs To Follow Jesus

Luke 14:25-33

"For which of you, intending to build a tower, does not first sit down and estimate the cost, to see whether he has enough to complete it?" (v. 28)

Object: a bank statement

Good morning, boys and girls. Do any of you ever go to the bank with your mother or father? (*let them answer*) What do they do at a bank? (*let them answer*) That's right, they put money in the bank and they take money out of the bank. The bank is a place where they save their money, or a place where they can borrow money. I brought along a bank statement that tells me how much money I have saved at this bank. It tells me how much I can spend if I want to build a new house, or buy a house or a car, or anything else that I think that I need to use my money for. That is very important because you do not want to spend more money than you have in the bank.

This little statement tells me exactly how much I can spend. Just think how awful it would be if you decided to build a house with the money that you had in the bank, and then you made the house so big that you could not pay for it. The house would never get finished. You might only have three walls, or a house with no windows or doors. You must plan what you are going to do, and spend the right amount of money on it, but not too much.

Jesus told us that the same kind of thing is true about being his disciple. He says that being his disciple is not free. It is going to cost you something, and you must decide if it is worth it. It will cost you time. You must worship Jesus, if you are going to be his disciple. You can't stay home and read the funny papers and still be in church at the same time; but being a disciple says that you must worship Jesus. You must share your things with others, too. You cannot be a disciple of Jesus and be selfish. Jesus makes you promise him that you will be ready to share what you have with others. And you must be forgiving. That means when someone does something wrong to you and it makes you angry, you cannot stay angry. You must be ready to forgive the person who hurt you, and show him how much you love him. These are some of the things that you must do if you want to be a disciple of Jesus and follow him. We call these things "counting the cost." It is like building a house. If you want to build a house, then you must have some money in the bank. If you want to be a follower of Jesus, you must have love and be ready to share it with all of the people of this world. Being a Christian isn't cheap. It is very expensive because you must spend yourself, and follow the teachings of Jesus.

The next time that see your mother or father look at their bank statement, I hope that you will think about what it is costing you to be a Christian, and that you will be glad that you have your life to spend for Jesus. God bless you.

Happiness Is Finding The Lost

Luke 15:1-10

"Or what woman having ten silver coins, if she loses one coin, does not light a lamp, sweep the house, and search carefully until she finds it?" (v. 8)

Object: a coin

Good morning, boys and girls. How many of you have ever lost some money? (*let them answer*) Was it a lot of money? (*let them answer*) I think that people really are upset when they lose money, because it is usually money that was needed to spend for food, or clothes, or maybe a gift for somebody that they loved. Money is very important to all of us because we use it to buy the things that we need. Our fathers and mothers work very hard for their money and, if they lose it, they usually hunt for it.

How many of you have ever hunted for money? (*let them answer*) Did you find it? (*let them answer*) If you found it, I want you to remember if it made you happy? I know the answer to that question, because I have lost money and then found it, and it made me very happy.

Jesus knows how important money can be to all of us, and he told a story about a woman who lost some money, to show us how important people are to God. He said that when a woman lost some money, she hunted all day and night until she found it, and then when she found it, she celebrated by inviting all of her friends in to her home.

Jesus said that this is the way that God feels about people who become lost from him. He is sad that he lost them, but when he finds them he has a great celebration. Jesus did not mean that he forgot where he put one of us. Jesus did not mean that he dropped one of us in another country and did not bring us back home. Jesus talks about people being lost when they forget to worship him or decide that they want to be their own gods or when they hate others instead of loving people the way they were taught. These are the lost people, and God is very sad when he loses people.

If you would decide to stop coming to Sunday church school and church, or if you started to live differently by cheating your friends and lying to your parents, then God would think that you were lost from him. That would make him very sad. But if you also remembered what God had taught you, and decided that you wanted to be forgiven, and you asked God to be with you, then you would know how happy it made him feel to find you again. That is the thing that makes God the happiest: finding his children and bringing them back home to live with him and Jesus.

The next time that you lose a coin or any amount of money, and you feel bad, remember how bad God feels when he loses a person; but then when you find your money you will also know how much God loves bringing back the people who were lost.

96

Call In The Clowns!

Luke 15:1-3, 11-32

"For this son of mine was dead and is alive again; he was lost, and is found!" And they began to celebrate. (v. 24)

Object: some horns, drums, and other party items

Good morning, boys and girls. How many of you like a good party? (*let them answer*) Do you remember the last party that you went to? (*let them answer*) I brought along some things that I thought might help us think about a party. (*pass out the party toys*) If we were planning a really special party, we might even call in some clowns. Wouldn't that be an exciting way to have a party? (*let them answer*)

When do we have parties? (*let them answer*) That's right, birthdays and other times when we want to celebrate something that is really happy or important.

Jesus told a story about a father who had two sons. The older son was always good to his father and worked hard on their farm. But the younger son did not like to work and asked for his share of the family's money, then ran away to have a good time. It wasn't too long until he had spent all of the money, and he was broke. He got a job taking care of some pigs, but he also had to live with the pigs. Finally, one day, he made up his mind to go back and ask his father to forgive him. So he went back, but before he could say anything to his father about how sorry he was, his father ran out to greet him and tell him how much he had missed him. Finally, the father had a big party to celebrate his son's happy return.

Jesus told this story to show us how glad God is when we change our minds, and come back to tell him how sorry we are for our sins. God is so happy to have us back that it is almost like a party in heaven.

God loves us a lot, and he misses us when we leave him to go off in another direction. But God is so happy when we come back, that it is like a very happy and wonderful party.

It isn't easy to come back to God. Sometimes we are afraid, or we think that God doesn't want us when we have been bad, but this isn't true. God always loves us and is really pleased when we change our minds and come back to him.

Remember, going back to God is like being a part of a party in heaven. We don't know whether there will be any clowns, but we do know we will have a wonderful time there!

A Candle With Two Wicks

Luke 16:1-13

"No slave can serve two masters; for a slave will either hate the one and love the other, or be devoted to the one and despise the other. You cannot serve God and wealth." (v. 13)

Object: a candle with the wick exposed at both ends

Good morning, boys and girls. Today we are going to try something that we have heard about, but have seldom seen. I brought a candle along with me that is a very special candle. I want to show it to you. (*show them the candle*) What is different about this candle? (*let them answer*) That's right; there is a wick on each end. Have you ever heard about burning the candle at both ends? Older people talk about burning the candle at both ends when they are doing too many things and not getting enough rest. But I want to show it to you today for another reason.

Suppose your electricity went out at home and you wanted or needed some light. You could light this end of the candle as I am doing now and it would give you light. Do you like candlelight? (*let them answer*) That's nice, but it isn't bright enough for me, so I have this special candle, and I think I will light the other end as well. Now I have twice as much light from the same candle. How do you like the candlelight now? (*let them answer*)

But all of a sudden I have a terrible problem. First of all I cannot set the candle down, and second, it is dripping all over me. I mean this is terrible. Now I don't know which end to put out. It gets so confusing. I know that it is the same candle, but this end seems brighter then the other end. But the other end seems to burn more evenly. What should I do? I just hate to make decisions like this. As a matter of fact, I am beginning to hate one end of this candle. I just don't know which end I hate and which end I love. It is confusing.

The same thing is true of you and me that is true of the candle. We were made by God, to serve and love God. But the devil seems like so much more fun sometimes that we think maybe we should be on the devil's side. Of course we can't be on both sides. That is when everything seems so confusing.

Jesus tells us that we must choose one side or the other. There is no way that we can serve both God and someone else. It is Jesus' advice of course, that we make up our minds to serve God and to forget the other side. If we don't, Jesus says, we will end up hating one and loving the other, or hating the other and loving the one.

Each of us must decide who we are going to love. I am going to love God, and I hope that he is your choice also. Remember what happened to the person who burned the candle at both ends, and then choose who you are going to serve.

Warning!

Luke 16:19-31

"He said, 'Then, father, I beg you to send him to my father's house — for I have five brothers — that he may warn them, so that they will not also come into this place of torment.'" (vv. 27-28)

Object: a warning device, like a siren or buzzer

Good morning, boys and girls. (*sound your warning device*) What was that? How many of you have heard something like that before? (*let them answer*) Do you know why we use a siren? (*let them answer*) That's right; we want to warn people to get out of the way, to tell them someone is coming who needs to get somewhere in a hurry, and that they want everyone else to get out of the way until they get there. Ambulances use them, fire departments use them, and sometimes the police use them. A siren is a very important thing, and it keeps us from having big wrecks and hurting other people.

Of course, you must listen to the warning and pull over if you are driving. A warning is not any good if you don't pay attention to it. Some children do not pay attention to the warnings that their fathers and mothers give them, and they get hurt. I know a child who was warned not to play with matches, and he did. Do you know what happened? (*let them fill in the answer*) That's right, he was burned.

Jesus tells us about the warnings that we have gotten in the Bible from God about the way that we should behave, and what will happen to us if we do not listen to the teachings. He said that the reason these things were written was not to scare us, but to warn us so that something terrible would not happen to us. I think that this is a very loving thing for God to do. He warns us about the bad things so that they will not hurt us and cause us great harm.

Jesus told stories like this to the disciples and to everyone else who wanted to listen. Some people listened and did what he told them not to do anyway. Those people did not listen to the warning. They suffered what they thought was an awful accident. But it was not an accident, because they had been warned.

If you hear a siren and still try to drive down the middle of the street where the fire engine or ambulance is coming, you will have a terrible accident and cause other people to get hurt as well. The same thing is true about not listening to God's warnings that he gives us in the Bible. If we hear the warnings and still cause the trouble, then it is not an accident. We will be hurt, and others will be hurt also because we did not listen. When you read the Ten Commandments, and they warn you about how to live, then you should pay attention to them the same way that you do to a siren. They are God's warning to teach us how to live safely.

Will you remember that? (*let them answer*) Good!

Homework Is A Duty

Luke 17:1-10

"So you also, when you have done all that you were ordered to do, say, 'We are worthless slaves; we have done only what we ought to have done!'" (v. 10)

Object: some homework papers

Good morning, boys and girls. How many of you are glad to be in school? (*let them raise their hands*) Most of you like to go to school, but some of you are not too happy about it. Not all of us like the same things, but I am glad that most of you like to go to school. School is really very important, because it is there where we learn to read and write and work with numbers. All of those things and many others are really very important, and school is the place where we learn them.

How many of you have homework to bring home with you after school is out? (*let them answer*) Do you like to do homework? Most boys and girls like to play outside or watch television, or use the computer, or do something else when they come home instead of doing their homework. But still we must do it. It is our duty.

How many of you know what the word *duty* means? (*let them answer*) Most all of you know the word *duty*. It is when we have something to do that is our responsibility, something that we do not receive special thanks for doing. It is something that is expected.

I think that there are things like that between us and God. There are some things that are our duty to God, and we should not expect God to send us a special message of thanks, or have one of his workers pat us on the back, for doing it.

I know some people who think that they are doing God a favor when they come to church or Sunday school. That is not a favor, or something that you should be thanked for doing. That is your duty. Some people think that they should be thanked for telling the truth or helping someone who needs help. If you see someone who needs you, then you should help them because you are a Christian. We don't need to be thanked and patted on the back for doing good things, because that is what we are supposed to do.

No one thanks you for doing your homework. Doing homework is your duty. No one should thank you for doing Christian things, either, because you also have Christian things to do. That's what Jesus thought, and he told the disciples that very thing one day when they asked him about doing special things to be special people. Do what is right, and you will be doing your Christian duty.

The next time that you do some homework and you think about it, I hope that you think about your Christian duties, and then remember to do them.

Ten Broken Pencils

Luke 17:11-19

Then Jesus asked, "Were not ten made clean? But the other nine, where are they? Was none of them found to return and give praise to God except this foreigner?" (vv. 17-18)

Object: ten pencils with broken points and one pencil sharpener

Good morning, boys and girls. How many of you like to write with pencils? (*let them answer*) Good pencils are hard to find. Whenever I am looking for a pencil, I either cannot find one, or when I find the pencil, it either has a broken point or has never been sharpened. Do you have that problem? (*let them answer*)

I have a little story to tell you about ten pencils that I found around my house, and every one of them was either broken or had never been sharpened. This is their story.

I found these pencils in different places. One of them was on my dresser, several of them were in a kitchen drawer where they had been for several years. I even found one of them on the kitchen floor beneath the refrigerator. It seemed like everywhere I went I found a pencil, but all of them were broken in one way or another. On a shelf in a beautiful tea cup, I found some paper clips, rubber bands, and another pencil. Of course it was broken also. There were others in different places, like on top of the washer, since someone had forgotten to empty his pockets before sending his slacks to the laundry. There was another on my workbench, one in the garage, and a couple behind the cushions of the couch. Every one of them was broken, and they looked sad in their terrible condition.

A pencil is meant to have a sharp point and to write; to leave them in this kind of condition was awful. So I decided to do what I thought should be done. I got out my special pencil sharpener and went right to work. Soon each pencil I sharpened looked happy and relieved to be back at work again. I could hardly work fast enough, I felt so good. But as I finished sharpening one and putting it down, it would disappear before I could pick up another. All ten pencils were sharpened like they had never been sharpened before, and not one of them who left even said thank you. Excuse me, that isn't true. There was one that said thank you. The one that I found on the floor under the refrigerator. It came back to tell me how grateful it was for what I had done for it.

You know the story of my pencils is not original. Jesus told a similar story about something even more important. He told about healing ten men, only one of whom thanked God for what happened. I hope that you remember the story, but I hope even more that you remember to thank God every day for the wonderful things that he does for you. That is one of the most important parts of our life — to be grateful to God, and to praise him for all of the glorious things that he does to help us.

Jesus And The Beggar

Luke 18:31-43

As he approached Jericho, a blind man was sitting by the roadside begging. When he heard a crowd going by, he asked what was happening. (vv. 35-36)

Object: a cup or bag or something that a beggar might use for begging

Good morning, boys and girls. How many of you have ever seen a beggar? Do you know what a beggar looks like or what a beggar does? (*let them answer*) That's right, he begs for money or food or clothing. Some of them do this because it is the only way that they can live. They may be hurt or sick or have something else wrong with them so they cannot work, so they must beg.

Have you ever thought of how the beggar must hold his cup or bag? Watch how I hold a begging cup. (*let them see it*) I hold it out and up so that people can put what they have into it easily. If I turned the cup upside down or put it behind my back they would have a hard time finding it and some of them would not even notice. That means that I would not get the kind of things that I need for my living.

There is a reason why I am telling you this. People are like a beggar's sack or cup. Some people hide from God or make it so difficult for God to find them that they look like a hidden cup or sack. In a way we are all like beggars before God. None of us ever earns or works for the things that he gives us. God gives us what we need and we are glad. We tell him in our prayers what we would like, but we are always sure to say that we will take whatever he gives us without a complaint. That is a little bit the way it is with a beggar. Every day he waits for people to bless him with some of the things that they have, and he takes the gift that is given and gives thanks.

There is a story in the Bible about a blind man who heard of the coming of Jesus. He began to call for Jesus to come and heal him. At first Jesus did not hear him, but he called out louder and louder until Jesus heard him and came over and talked to him. When Jesus found out that the man wanted to be healed of his blindness and believed that only God could do it, he healed him and made his eyesight brand new. That is the way God works with people. There are a lot of things you cannot do for yourself and need God's help. Ask God and ask him again and again. God will do only good for you.

You will find, as many other Christians have found, that God loves you and wants to share with you all that he has for all that you need.

102

Jesus Is A Ladder To Us

Luke 19:1-10

Then Jesus said to him, "Today salvation has come to this house, because he too is a son of Abraham." (v. 9)

Object: a ladder

Good morning, boys and girls. Today we are going to talk about rescuing someone whom we love very much. Let's pretend that there is someone caught in a house that is burning and she cannot get out by the door, but she is too high to jump without getting hurt. What will we do to rescue this person? (*let them answer*) Those are good answers. We could do a lot of those things, but maybe the best answer is to put our ladder up against the house and either climb up the ladder and help her out, or let her just climb down the ladder. Either way we have helped to rescue her.

Let's pretend again. Suppose that someone has fallen through the ice while he was ice skating. You want to help him but the ice is too thin to walk on, so what can you do? (*let them answer*) That's right, you can put the ladder down on the ice and let the person grab hold of it and pull himself to the shore. Sometimes you can even crawl out on a ladder to rescue someone in the water when you can't walk on the ice.

Those are just two ways that you can save someone or rescue them with your ladder.

Jesus is like a ladder to us. Jesus rescued us, or saved us, from death when he died on the cross. That was the biggest saving job that anyone ever did. When Jesus came to earth to save you and me from our sins, we never knew what a great job he did until after he died on the cross. We knew that we had committed a few sins here and there, and that we were not the kind of people that God wanted us to be. But we were not sure that we were as bad as we were until we knew how perfect Jesus was. Jesus did not have any sin, and still he loved us so much that he died for us so that we could live with God forever.

That is a great love, and a real rescue job. Jesus saved us from our sins and made us good enough to live with God forever.

The next time that you see a ladder or hear about someone rescuing someone else with a ladder, perhaps you will think about today and how Jesus is like a ladder. He comes to us, stretches out, and saves us from whatever our sins are. Jesus is a great Savior, which means that he rescues us from our sin.

The Shouting Stones
(Appropriate for use on Palm Sunday)

Luke 19:28-40

He answered, "I tell you, if these were silent, the stones would shout out." (v. 40)

Object: enough small stones so that each child may receive one

Good morning, boys and girls. Today is Palm Sunday and it is one of the very biggest days in our church year. Can you imagine how excited you would have been if you had been one of Jesus' disciples and walked beside him while he rode a small donkey into the great city of Jerusalem? (*let them answer*) The crowds were cheering, and waving their palm branches, and throwing their coats on the road, so that the road looked like it had been carpeted. You would have loved it.

Of course not everyone was happy about Jesus coming into Jerusalem. There were some of the people who called themselves the leaders of the Jews, who thought Jesus was dangerous and working against them. They wanted Jesus to go away and be silent. If Jesus would become king like the people wanted, then they knew that they could no longer be the leaders.

But the people kept shouting and waving their banners. Everywhere you went you could hear things being said like, "Blessed is the king who comes in the name of the Lord." Those were dangerous words and frightening words to the people who disliked Jesus. These men told Jesus to tell his disciples to be quiet. But they would not be quiet. The disciples had waited a long time for a day like this and they loved it. Other people who had only heard of Jesus began to shout and sing the same things that the disciples were shouting.

Now the leaders were really angry, and they commanded Jesus to quiet the disciples. But Jesus was not afraid of these men, and he knew that this day belonged to God. He looked at the men who were angry with him, and told them that even if they could make his disciples silent, the stones on the ground would begin singing and shouting the same things that the disciples were singing and shouting. Stones just like these stones were all over the road, and they would have made a mighty sound if they could have spoken. The leaders knew that there was nothing they could do that day. It was the day for Jesus and for the people who believed in him.

I want each of you to have one of these stones, so that you will remember Palm Sunday as the day that Jesus rode into Jerusalem and his disciples made a great chorus, proclaiming Jesus as "the king who comes in the name of the Lord." It will also help you to remember that even if not one human voice said that Jesus was the Christ, God would make sure that we still would know it — even if he had to make the stones shout that Christ was the King.

More Important Than We Thought

Luke 20:9-19

But he looked at them and said, "What does this text mean: 'The stone that the builders rejected has become the cornerstone'?" (v. 17)

Object: a garage sale item such as a picture or a lamp

Good morning, boys and girls. How many of you have ever been to a garage sale? (*let them answer*) Did you have fun? (*let them answer*) Did you buy anything? (*let them answer*)

A couple months ago I bought a picture at a garage sale. (*hold up picture*) It is a nice picture, but nothing really special. Someone wanted to get rid of it and did not think it was very special either. After I bought it, took it home, and cleaned it up, I found that it was really very special. A lot of people would really like to have this picture, because it is painted by a very famous artist and is quite valuable. Here I have something that no one thought was important, and now I find it is very important.

That is the way that it is with Jesus. When Jesus was on earth and teaching, there were some people who thought that he was just another man and nothing special. There were other people who thought that they could get rid of Jesus and no one would ever miss him. As a matter of fact, there were some people who wanted to get rid of Jesus and were even willing to murder him if they could. They really hated him.

But after Jesus died on the cross, the people found out how important he really was to this world. Jesus was the most important person who ever lived, but most people did not know it until after he had died.

Jesus is like a picture that no one knows is important until after it is gone, or sold to someone else. Jesus became so important to us because, when he died, he saved us all from our sins.

Some people wanted to get rid of him, and they never knew how important he was until after he died. Then they knew that Jesus was the most important person who ever lived.

Jesus Is Coming
(Appropriate for use in Advent)

Luke 21:25-36

"There will be signs in the sun, the moon, and the stars, and on the earth distress among nations confused by the roaring of the sea and the waves." (v. 25)

Object: some signs such as "Beware Of Dog" and "Garage Sale"

Good morning, boys and girls. Today is the first Sunday of the new church year. It is also the first day of Advent and a time for all of us to get a fresh start.

I like the first of almost anything. I love the first bite of my favorite sandwich, the first time I wear new clothes, and the first part of every new day. I like to finish first when I run a race or if I have to take a test. So being first or celebrating the first day of Advent is a pretty natural thing.

Advent is a time for us to get ready. We are supposed to be preparing ourselves for a pretty important something that is going to happen to all of us someday. How many of you know what we are getting ready for when we celebrate Advent? (*let them answer*) You are right when you say we are getting ready for Christmas but even more important is that we are getting ready for the return of Jesus, his Second Coming.

The Bible tells us about the time that Jesus talked to his disciples about how and when he would come back to earth again. Jesus said there would be signs that we would understand. I usually understand signs and I think you probably do also. I brought along a couple to see if you could tell me what you thought a certain sign meant. (*hold up your "Beware Of Dog" sign*) What does a sign like this mean? (*let them answer*) That's right; it means that there is a dangerous dog that may bite you if you trespass or go on someone's property where you don't belong. The people are warning you that their dog may bite. Here is another sign for you to tell me what you think it means. (*hold up your "Garage Sale" sign*) What does this sign mean? (*let them answer*) That's right; it means that someone is having a sale of things that they want to get rid of. It isn't a store or a supermarket, but the people sell their things out of the garage.

Signs tell us a lot about what is going to happen. Jesus said that when he came back there would be signs in the sun and moon and stars. He also said that we would be able to tell that something special was going to happen because of the noise of the sea and the great waves that rolled in the sea. These were signs, and people who knew what to look for could expect to see Jesus come back to live among them once more.

Advent is a time when we look for the signs that Jesus may be coming, and we prepare ourselves to welcome him back into our hearts and into our homes. The next time you see a sign that tells you something like my signs did this morning, I hope that you will think about the signs that Jesus is going to send out before he comes back to be with us.

Who Cleans You Up?

Luke 22:24-30

"For who is greater, the one who is at the table or the one who serves? Is it not the one at the table? But I am among you as one who serves." (v. 27)

Object: a mop, a bucket, and a silver candlestick

Good morning, boys and girls, and how are you today? Did any of you tell anyone about Jesus this week? Some of you did tell others about him, didn't you? That's good. Jesus enjoys it when you tell others about the things that he did.

Today I want to show you a different kind of Jesus. Do you know what I have in my hands? (*hold up the mop and bucket*) That's right. I have an idea that Jesus might think he was like a mop or a bucket. (*hold up the candlestick*) Some people would like to think that Jesus was a fancy candlestick, but I think that Jesus would rather be a mop or a bucket. What do you think Jesus would like to think that he was? (*let them answer*) Jesus never reminds me of something fancy, even though he was the greatest man who ever lived. I never think of Jesus in some beautiful suit or eating in some fancy restaurant. Jesus is something else. One time, Jesus said that while the big shot ate at the table, he — Jesus — would probably be the one who was serving the man at the table. Jesus thought of himself as a servant to people. That is why I think Jesus reminds me of a mop or a bucket. Other people make the dirt, but Jesus cleans it up and makes it a good place to live.

Sometimes I see people walk down the street and throw away the paper from their gum or candy bar and it lands in the street. I think that Jesus would pick up that paper and put it in a trash can. Sometimes I hear people talking with kind of a dirty mouth trying to be funny. I think that Jesus never talked dirty, but instead he would take what was being said and clean it up.

That is the way that Jesus is to people. He cleans us up, and to do that he must work for us. That is why Jesus called himself a servant, and why I think that, if there is anything around the house that reminds me of Jesus, it is my mop and bucket. I know that Jesus is not a candlestick or something fancy like that in my house. Jesus came to serve people and save them from their sins. He also left us an example to follow.

If you want to be a follower of Jesus, then you must be more like the mop and bucket, and less like the candlestick, because to do the work of Jesus means doing the hard work of cleaning things up and not just sitting around looking pretty. That's what Jesus reminds me of. What is there around your house that makes you think of Jesus? I hope that you will think about it.

A Different Kind Of King

Luke 23:35-43

The soldiers also mocked him, coming up and offering him sour wine, and saying, "If you are the King of the Jews, save yourself." (vv. 36-37)

Object: a cup of vinegar

Good morning, boys and girls. We refer to Jesus as a king, and he was a kind of king different from the king of a country. Jesus was king over all the earth. People did not always know what kind of king he was. Some people thought that he would make a good king of the land in which he lived. They tried to make him a king who lived in a palace, made laws, and collected taxes. But Jesus was not that kind of a king.

The people who were kings and were close to kings were afraid of Jesus because they thought he wanted their jobs, or would give their jobs to his friends. They did not know that Jesus was sent by God to start a new kind of world over which he would be king. Jesus is the King of Peace and Love on earth, and of the new world where all of the people who believe in him will live after they die. That is the kind of king that Jesus was then and is now. But the people did not know it.

You have heard how they hung him on a cross and killed him. While he was hanging on the cross, they thought that he could not hurt them, and, though they were a little bit afraid of him, they mocked him terribly. One of the things they did was make fun of his being a king. They gave him a crown that was made out of thorns. That was awful and it hurt when they shoved it down on his head. One of the other things they did was to give him something to drink.

I have something like what they gave him that day, and I thought that you might want to smell it. (*give them the cup to pass around and ask them what they think it is*) That's right; it is vinegar. Can you imagine drinking vinegar? (*let them answer*) Jesus was thirsty, but they thought in their own evil way that they were having fun with a dying man whom many called their king. It was awful at that moment.

But things got better. Jesus died and you know he was buried, and many thought that this was the last they would ever hear about him. But he fooled them by coming back to life and starting the kingdom that he always promised would happen. We are part of Jesus' world, and citizens of his kingdom. We are so happy that Jesus is not a king like other kings, but instead, is a king forever. This was God's plan, and it is the best plan for a king that anyone ever had.

Gum!
(Appropriate for use at Easter)

Luke 24:1-11

But when they went in, they did not find the body. (v. 3)

Object: some packs of gum with the sticks of gum removed and the wrappers replaced in the packages and a plate with the sticks of gum to be handed out

Good morning, boys and girls. How many of you know what today is and what it means? (*let them answer*) That's right; it is Easter, but what is Easter all about? (*let them answer*) Right, today is the day that we celebrate to remember when God raised Jesus from the dead. We all remember how awful it was when Jesus was crucified on the cross, and we were sorry that he died. But now we know that God did not forget him. Instead, he made him come back from the dead. What a wonderful day Easter is for all of us!

Do you remember the story of how the women who were friends of Jesus came up to where he was buried, and how they met an angel who talked to them? Do you remember how surprised they were to find out something that they did not expect? I have something with me this morning to help you remember how the women felt when they came to the tomb. I know all of you like what I brought, and I am going to share it with you. (*begin to pass out the empty wrappers of gum*) How many of you know what this is? (*let them answer*) Gum. Do you like gum? (*let them answer*) Well, I am going to let you chew your piece of gum if you want to, as soon as you get it unwrapped. (*as they discover that there is not any gum inside the wrapper, share their amazement with them*) Isn't that a shock! When you get a piece of paper wrapped like that, you expect that there will be a piece of gum inside it, don't you? (*let them answer*) That is the way it is supposed to be.

That is also the way that the women felt when they arrived at the place where Jesus was buried and found that Jesus was not there. He had died, they saw him die. He was buried in the tomb. They had seen him being taken to the tomb. When dead people are put in tombs, they stay in tombs. But Jesus was not there, and the women were surprised.

Now an angel of God met them in the place where Jesus had been buried and told them that Jesus was living, and that he was no longer in the tomb. What a wonderful surprise! Jesus was dead, but now he is alive.

I have a surprise for you also. (*bring out a plate with the missing sticks of gum*) Here are the sticks of gum that you thought were buried in the paper wrappers. As you can see, they are alive and well. This is just a reminder for you, so that you will never forget that while Jesus was not in the tomb, he was alive and well, and still lives today as the Christ, the Son of the Living God.

You Can't Hide The Light

John 1:1-18

The light shines in the darkness, and the darkness did not overcome it. (v. 5)

Object: a box with a hole in one end and a blanket that will shut out the light attached to the other end

Good morning, boys and girls. Today we are going to have a little fun and also learn something about Jesus. I brought a special box with me that I want to share with you. I want you to put your head in the box and shut out all of the light with the blanket. I want you to see how dark it is inside of that box. Then when you tell me that it is dark, really dark, I am going to open up this tiny hole in the other end of the box and see if you can see the light, and also if the light lets you see the inside of the box. (*begin the experiment with several of the children*)

The whole box is dark. We have a lot of darkness and only one small bit of light. What I want you to learn is that all of the darkness in the whole world cannot shut out a little bit of light. The little bit of light can be seen in the biggest amount of darkness. Do you understand what I mean? (*let them answer*)

The reason that we shared this little experiment is because it is what the Bible teaches us about Jesus. Jesus is like the light. He is only one person in the world, but he is such a strong person that he can overcome, or be stronger than, all of the rest of the people in the world. Jesus is light, Jesus is good. There is nothing wrong with Jesus at all, and wherever Jesus is, he will bring his goodness with him.

Let's say that there is a lot of sin in the world. All of us make sin, and are a part of sin. There is so much sin in the world you might think that we could not get rid of it. But that is not true. Jesus is like the light in the darkness. He gets rid of the sin by just being there. When you have sin in your heart, and you can have a lot of it, then ask Jesus to share your life with you, and your sin will go away. Jesus will forgive you your sin and you will have no more.

That is why I want you to put your head in the box. The box is like a world full of sin. We don't think that we will ever get rid of sin, but the Bible teaches us that when Jesus came into the world, he was like a light, and wherever he went he made the darkness, or the sin, leave so that people could live without living in sin.

Maybe you want to make your own box when you go home. Then you can remember how glad we are to have Jesus in our lives so that we don't live in the dark, but rather in the light. God bless you all.

You Shall See Great Things

John 1:43-51

Jesus answered, "Do you believe because I told you that I saw you under the fig tree? You will see greater things than these." (v. 50)

Object: an airplane model — the earliest model available — and a moon rocket

Good morning, boys and girls. Did you know that about 100 years ago the Wright brothers flew their first plane? That seems like a long time ago to you, doesn't it? (*let them answer*) Just think, 100 years ago, people flew for the first time! That was something that most people had always thought could not be done.

Jesus lived on earth over 2,000 years ago, and he had never seen anyone fly in an airplane. Abraham Lincoln lived almost 150 years ago, and he had never seen anyone fly in an airplane. People thought that this was the most fantastic thing that they had ever heard of in their lives. Nothing could ever top that idea that people could fly in a machine.

Not too many years ago people saw something even greater. They watched some men get in a rocket and fly away from our earth and land on the moon. No one thought that anyone could leave earth and land somewhere else. That was too much! Now some people think that nothing will ever happen that will be greater than watching Neil Armstrong land on the moon. But you wait and see. Someday it will be something else that we never expected will happen that we will think is the greatest.

That's the way it is and Jesus knew it. Once there was a man by the name of Nathanael whom Jesus called to be one of his disciples. When Nathanael met Jesus and Jesus told him something that he did not think anyone else knew about him, he was amazed. He thought that this was one of the most amazing things that he had ever seen. But Jesus was not amazed and he did not want Nathanael to be amazed. Jesus told him that this was nothing compared to what he was going to see. There were a lot of things that Jesus would do, like healing sick people, walking on water, telling about the love of God, things that were far greater than what Nathanael saw that day. Jesus was like the first airplane when he saw Nathanael, and later, when he came back from the dead, he was like a rocket ship. No one could believe that Jesus could come back from the dead. But there are still things happening that are even more amazing that God does every day.

So, the next time you see an airplane or space ship, just think about the day that Nathanael met Jesus and was impressed with the things that Jesus did and then think about all of the other things that Jesus did and is still doing. Then you will be amazed about Jesus just as Nathanael was.

Now What Do We Do?

John 2:1-11

When the steward tasted the water that had become wine, and did not know where it came from (though the servants who had drawn the water knew), the steward called the bridegroom and said to him, "Every one serves the good wine first, and then the inferior wine after the guests have become drunk. But you have kept the good wine until now." (vv. 9-10)

Objects: some wine and some water in containers, to show the children

Good morning, boys and girls. I want to tell you a story this morning, and I hope it will help you to believe something wonderful about the person we know as Jesus.

Jesus was invited to a wedding in a town called Cana. The people to be married were either close friends of Jesus, or of his family, because we know that his mother was at the wedding, too. Jesus went to the wedding with his disciples and met his mother there. The disciples were fairly new, since Jesus had just begun his ministry a short time before. They had not been at the wedding very long when the people who were in charge ran out of refreshments. No doubt some of the people had been there a lot longer than Jesus and the disciples, so they did as people do today. They ate and drank almost everything that was given to them.

What do you do when you run out of refreshments at your parties? (*let them answer*) That's right; you get some more refreshments. The only problem was that the people at the wedding were drinking some very good wine and there was no place to get more. Mary knew that her son was someone very special, and that he could take care of almost any problem. She also knew that Jesus was not a magician. He did not trick people, or switch things so fast with his hands that people could not see what was happening. Jesus solved problems in only one way, and that was through his Father in heaven. Mary did not know what Jesus would do, but she was certain he could do something if it was wanted by God.

It takes a long time to make wine. There are good wines, and bad wines. Jesus told the people who were working at the party to take some very large jars and fill them with water. They did as they were told and then brought the jars back to the party. (*show the children the water*) When the people went over to the jars to fill their glasses, out came wine! (*show the wine*) No one knew what had happened, except Mary, the people working at the party, and the disciples of Jesus. But I want you to know that, from that time on, those people knew that Jesus was someone very special with a power that no one else had.

Do you think that you could change this water (*hold up the water*) to this wine? (*hold up the wine*) That's right; you could not. Maybe the next time you hear of someone running out of something to eat or drink, you will remember the day that Jesus took some clear water and turned it into the best wine that anyone had ever drunk.

God's House Is Special

John 2:13-22

He told those who were selling the doves, "Take these things out of here! Stop making my Father's house a marketplace!" (v. 16)

Object: some items that appear to be for sale with prices marked on them

Good morning, boys and girls. I am certainly glad that you came to church this morning because I am looking for customers. I have some of the most wonderful things for sale today, and I hope that you have brought your money with you so that you can buy whatever you like.

First of all, I have this lovely sweater. It was made by a wonderful knitter who took lots of time and loving care to make it for a person just like you. This sweater is only $11.99 and I hope you will choose it. I also have delightful stocking caps to go with the sweater. Since we are going into spring and the winter is over, these stocking caps are on sale today. If you buy them now you can save money for next year. These hats are a special buy, and you can have one for only $1.39. That is a real bargain. What else do I have with me today? I have beautiful jewelry that I would be willing to sell at the right price. Would anyone like to make an offer for my jewelry? (*let them answer*)

What do you think of this? Is this what you expected to find when you came to church this morning? (*let them answer*) When was the last time you came to church and found yourself shopping in a store? (*let them answer*) It doesn't seem right, does it? What's wrong with selling clothes, jewelry, or anything else in church? (*let them answer*)

That's right; this is God's house and it is not a place to do business. Jesus found people selling animals and other things in the temple when he was in Jerusalem, and he drove them out of the temple telling them that God's house was not a store. It is a place to worship and pray and not to make bargains.

There is nothing wrong with buying and selling in a store. That is where it should be done. But we should never buy and sell in God's house. This is a special place where we can share our lives with God. We come here to listen to God's word, to sing hymns of praise, to pray quietly with God, and to tell him of our problems and ask for his help. We can't do that if we are selling and buying.

Jesus actually took off his belt when he went into the temple to pray and waved it in the air and told the people to take their goods and leave the temple. Jesus was very angry with what he found in the temple. We need always to remember what God's house is meant to be and make sure that we are here to worship and not here to do anything else.

The next time you hear about a special bargain I hope it is in the store and not in God's house.

Live In The Light

John 3:14-21

"For all who do evil hate the light and do not come to the light, so that their deeds may not be exposed." (v. 20)

Object: a burglar's disguise and a sack for "loot"

Good morning, boys and girls. I brought with me something today that is very frightening, but I hope will not be afraid. We must remember that we are only pretending, but this is something that happens and we must know about it. How many of you have seen a robber or burglar? (*let them answer*) We see them on television but we don't see them many other places.

I brought along some of the things that a robber wears and I am going to put them on. (*take out a mask or a stocking and pull it over your face; then take a cap and put it over the stocking; hold up the sack in which to put your loot*) Many times, burglars try to hide their faces and hands. They also do most of their robbing at night in the dark.

Do you know why they do it like this and at that time? (*let them answer*) That's right, so that no one will know who they are and so that no one will see them. They are not very proud of what they do, are they? They are ashamed of themselves. People who do evil are not only afraid of being caught, they are ashamed of themselves. They don't like themselves and they will hide even when they are alone. When people do evil things, they like darkness.

Jesus is called the Light of the World. Jesus is light because he is good and he does good. He can even forgive the evil because he is good. When you do something wrong and you are ashamed of it, you feel like hiding. If you tell Jesus about it and ask him to forgive you and promise that you won't do it again, then Jesus will forgive you. When Jesus forgives us it is like having a bright light come to you. You feel clean and wonderful and you can stop being ashamed.

I know little boys and girls who have told a big lie. They are afraid that their mother or father will find it out. They try to hide. They don't want to talk. They have their feelings hurt easily. They are in bad moods. Then they think about Jesus and how he doesn't like lies, and they are ashamed. When that happens, they ask Jesus to forgive them and promise him that they won't lie about such a thing again. Pretty soon they feel better and they can tell their mom and dad what they did and how badly they feel that they lied. Now their mom and dad can forgive them also. Everyone is happy. They don't feel like hiding in the dark. They want to live and be happy in the light of Jesus.

You remember that Jesus is the light. Evil wants to hide from light. When you feel like hiding you know that you have done wrong just like the robber. But when you live in the light, then you are living with Jesus and that is the best feeling in the world.

114

The Woman At The Well

John 4:4-42

Many Samaritans from that city believed in him because of the woman's testimony, "He told me everything I have ever done." (v. 39)

Object: none

Good morning, boys and girls. When you are taking a long trip, how many of you like to make little stops along the way? (*let them answer*) Do you like to stop and get a cold Coke, stretch your legs, and just look at the strange town that you are in for the moment? (*let them answer*) I know that you do because almost everyone I know likes to do this.

I want to tell you about a day that was like that in the life of Jesus. The writers of the Bible remembered it so well that they could tell almost every detail. Jesus did not have to stretch his legs because he walked everywhere he went, but he had to do the opposite — rest. When Jesus wanted a break, he would find a well where he could get a cold drink of water (they didn't have Coke in those days) and a shady tree to sit under.

That's what he did one day when he and the disciples were on a long trip from Jerusalem north to the Sea of Galilee. They took a short cut through a land called Samaria where Jews did not go very often because they did not like Samaritans. But Jesus did not feel that way about the Samaritans, and so he made it a point to go through Samaria. After they arrived at the well, he sent the disciples into a town called Sychar to get some food to eat and some to take with them. The well was a famous one, named after a Bible hero, Jacob.

Jesus had just sat down when a woman approached the well and Jesus asked her to give him a drink. The woman had noticed Jesus and knew that he was a Jew. She was shocked when Jesus spoke to her. Many Jews in those days thought that they were too good for Samaritans. The woman knew this, so she could not believe that Jesus would talk to her. Jesus and the woman had a conversation that was so helpful that I want to tell you about it.

First of all, Jesus convinced her that he had special powers because he told her things that no one else knew about her. He also told her in the conversation that he was the Messiah, the Son of God, and as far as we know, she was the first one to know that fact. He also told her that the differences between people were not the same as the differences between God and humans. Jesus wanted the woman to change and be a good woman not only to God, but to all of the people in Sychar. The woman at the well was so amazed at what she heard about herself and about Jesus that she believed in him immediately.

Just then the disciples returned and saw Jesus talking to her. They were shocked that he would speak with a Samaritan, but they did not say anything about it. The woman left, and while the disciples ate, they listened to Jesus tell about how God was going to work through him to bring an end to the hatred. They tried to get Jesus to eat but he was so filled with the Spirit of God that this kind of food meant nothing to him at the moment.

Pretty soon the place was filled with other Samaritans who had heard about Jesus from the woman and had come to see for themselves. For two days Jesus stayed in Sychar and taught the people and made them followers. The woman at the well had become one of the best followers Jesus ever had.

I hope you remember Sychar and the way that Jesus turned an enemy into a friend and a follower. Talking with Jesus can change a lot of things and make everything better than it was before we knew him.

School

John 5:39

"You search the scriptures because you think that in them you have eternal life, and it is they that testify on my behalf." (v. 39)

Object: a sign resembling a road sign with "School" printed on it

Good morning, boys and girls. Today I have brought with me a road sign. In every city or town there are very special places where people come together, and these places are specially marked. For instance today I have brought with me a very special sign that says _____. (*let the children read it aloud*) That's right; school. Every day boys and girls from all over town get up in the morning and walk or ride to one place called the school. It's a good place to go and the sign tells our parents who drive cars to slow down a whole lot because all around them are children going to school.

Now the sign saying "School" is not where the children meet. How would you all like to sit under a sign or eat your lunch by a sign? Sounds kind of silly, doesn't it? But the sign tells everyone that a school is nearby.

This sign that I have here this morning kind of reminds me of the Bible and the way it tells people about heaven. The Bible says that heaven is nearby and that we don't want to go so fast that we miss it. The Bible isn't heaven. You can't go to Bible or live in the Bible, but it tells us some important things about where we want to go and where someday we want to live with God.

I hope you can remember what I tell you about my friends and especially about this friend that I've spoken about today, the school sign. The next time you are driving along in your car and you see a sign that says "School," you can remember that that sign is like the Bible. And when you think of the Bible, you will think of how it tells you about heaven.

A Little Black Dot

John 6:1-15

He said this to test him, for he himself knew what he was going to do. (v. 6)

Object: a large white piece of paper or poster board with a black dot on it

Good morning, boys and girls. I'm going to give you a test today, and you are going to just love it. This morning I brought with me something that I want you to look at very carefully to see if you can find the answer. (*hold up a big white piece of paper or poster board with a black dot on it and do not make any reference to the words "white," "white paper," or "poster board"*) Tell me what you see. (*let them look very carefully*) Do you see anything that will show me that you know the answer to my test? (*keep asking the children until someone says they see a black dot on a white piece of paper*) All of you see the black dot, but didn't any of you see the white paper? I knew that you would tell me that you saw a black dot, and I also knew that not very many of you would say that you saw a white piece of paper even though all of you really did see it. Sometimes we miss the things or the answers that are the easiest because we are looking for something else.

Jesus asked his disciple Philip one day what they should do about feeding 5,000 people who had come to hear him teach and preach. Philip had never seen so many hungry people in one place. He didn't think it was possible to feed that many people, so he told Jesus to send them all away to find some place else to eat. Philip knew that he didn't have enough food, nor did any of the disciples or Jesus himself, to feed 5,000 people. What did Jesus do? (*let them answer*)

Some of you know, and you are right. Jesus borrowed some fish and bread from a little boy and blessed it. Then he asked the disciples to begin passing it out to others. The disciples could hardly believe their eyes. As they went from one group to the next, they still had plenty of fish and bread. They fed 100 and then they fed 500 more.

Before long, the disciples had fed not 1,000 or 2,000 or 3,000 but they had fed all 5,000 people with just a few fish and some bread. Can you imagine how excited Philip must have been when he brought back to Jesus a basket filled with bread and fish after feeding all of those people? Philip must have remembered the question Jesus asked him about what they should do with all those hungry people. Philip also now knew that Jesus had the answers to questions that other people never dreamed about. This was one of the miracles that Jesus did because he believed that God could see beyond what people could see.

When you and I look at my paper, we could only see the little black dot. When God looks, he sees the whole page. The next time you see a piece of paper with a little dot on it, I hope you see everything and not just one little speck down in the corner. If you do, then you will remember the story of the day Jesus fed a crowd of 5,000 people with just a few fish and a couple of loaves of bread.

What's Your Prize?

John 6:24-35

"Do not work for the food that perishes, but for the food that endures for eternal life, which the Son of Man will give you".... (v. 27)

Object: a bag of garbage

Good morning, boys and girls. Today I want to share with you a prize that I just know you are going to love. The prize I have is in this bag and it will go to the person who wins the big race. Some people may want to know what's in the bag, so I think I should tell you ahead of time. It's a bag of garbage. How many of you would like to win a prize like this? A great big bag of garbage. (*let them answer*)

None of you want to win the prize? I don't understand. I thought everybody liked prizes. Why don't you want to win this big prize? (*let them answer*) You don't like garbage, not even if it's in a beautiful bag like the one I have it in? You probably don't even want to be in a race if you are going to have a chance at this prize then.

Your life and my life are like a race. We are all in it and the only difference between the way that some people run their lives from the way that other people run their lives is the prize that they get. Some people run the race of life for a prize that is just like my bag of garbage. Their prize is worthless. It doesn't mean anything. These people have lived for only themselves and for what is bad. They live bad, they do bad things to other people. They either do not know God or they hate him. Their prize at the end of their life will be worse than a bag of garbage. What they will get will be just plain rotten. They have lived their whole life and when it is over like the end of a race, the prize is just plain rotten.

But God says that there is another way to live our lives, another way to run the race, for a different kind of prize. In this race of life, you fill it with love, share yourself and the things that you have with others, try to be helpful, and the prize you get at the end of life is something that never rots but goes on forever. This prize is called eternal life. It is living with God in a wonderful world that he makes for us. The prize for living with God and according to God's ways is something that never breaks or wears out or rots. It is something that will last forever.

You have a choice as to which way you live or which race you get in. I hope you do not end up with a bag of garbage, but instead I want for you to end up with a wonderful life that goes on forever with God.

The Bread Of Life

John 6:51-58

"I am the living bread that came down from heaven; whoever eats of this bread, will live forever; and the bread that I will give for the life of the world is my flesh." (v. 51)

Object: an unsliced loaf of bread

Good morning, boys and girls. Have you ever thought of the things that Jesus said he was, or what he called himself? Jesus wanted everyone to understand why God had sent him, and so he called himself some very interesting names. He said that he was like a "vine," the main vine. He called himself the "groom" like in the bride and groom. He said that he was a "shepherd," and one time he called himself "living water." Another time he talked about being the "Lamb of God," and once in a while he was the "teacher" and "master." Jesus wanted people to know who he was, when he talked to them and each name meant something special to him and to the people whom he was talking to.

I brought along with me something that Jesus called himself one day, something that all of us know a little bit about. (*show them the loaf of bread*) What do you call this? (*let them answer*) That's right. Bread. Did you know that Jesus called himself "bread"? (*let them answer*) He did. It might not surprise you that he called himself bread when you know that he also called himself a vine or water, but let's think about being bread.

What do you like about bread? (*let them answer*) You like the taste of it. Do you like it in the morning? (*let them answer*) You like toast, don't you? And do you like bread in sandwiches for lunch? How about with butter and jelly on it when you eat your dinner? Some people eat a peanut butter and jelly sandwich before they go to bed at night. One of the things about bread is that it is good at any time. Jesus is good for us all of the time. Bread also fills you up, doesn't it? (*let them answer*) It sure does. Bread can make you feel so full that you can't eat another bite. Jesus is also enough for anyone. When we have Jesus, we don't need anything else, but of course when we have Jesus, we are wanted and shared by everyone.

But Jesus said he was a different kind of bread. You eat this bread and by lunch you will be hungry again. (*show the bread*) You eat some bread at lunch, and you will be hungry again by dinner. The food we eat here, even the bread, only lasts a little while. Jesus said that he was different because he said that once we have had him, we would not need any other kind of Lord or Savior. Jesus said that he was the kind of bread that would fill a person up with the Spirit of God so much, that once we had him, it would be enough for our entire life. That is the kind of Savior that we want. We want a Savior that will fill us up forever.

Do you all agree? Good. God bless you.

Who Can Fill You Up? Jesus!

John 7:37-39

On the last day of the feast, the great day, while Jesus was standing there, he cried out, "Let any who is thirsty come to me...." (v. 37)

Object: a bucket of cold water, a dipper, and some small cups

Good morning, boys and girls. How many of you have ever been outside on a hot, really hot, afternoon and all of a sudden realized that you were thirsty? (*let them answer*) There isn't any water anywhere. You have to go home to get the water. You think about the water and you get thirstier and thirstier and thirstier. Your legs are tired. You don't want to walk any further but you have to because you want that drink of water. Everywhere you look you see dust, rocks, weeds, and trees, but there is no water. You walk faster but you are so tired you just want to lie down. Have you ever felt like this? (*let them answer*) I have felt like that lots of times. Finally you get home and the first thing you want is some cold, cold water. Is anyone thirsty right now? I brought along a bucket of cold water for anyone who is thirsty. I even have cups so that you can get a good drink of you like. (*let anyone who wants a drink have a cup of water at this point*)

When you are thirsty, nothing tastes as good as water. People have other kinds of thirsts. Lots of times we wish that we could just find someone who cares about us. Have you ever felt lonely and wished that you could find one friend to play with? All of your friends are gone or they seem mad at you. I remember once when I was on vacation and I didn't know anyone. I would have given anything to have one of my friends to play with. We are lonely sometimes. Jesus says that he would like to be our friend. When we are all alone, he would love to share the day with us. We are thirsty for a friend and Jesus gives us friendship.

Sometimes we are sick. Really sick. Our heads, stomachs, backs, legs, and arms all hurt, and hurt bad. We want to get well, but the medicine doesn't seem to help. Jesus says that he wants to be with us then to help us get better. We are thirsty to get better, just like we are thirsty for a drink.

Sometimes we have done something awful to a friend and we feel bad. We need to be forgiven. We want to tell our friend what we did but we are afraid that the friend will not understand. We are thirsty for forgiveness. Jesus gives us strength to ask forgiveness and to make up.

Those are other ways of being thirsty. Jesus is like a long, cold, drink of water. He changes us from not feeling so good to feeling terrific. The next time that you are thirsty and you want a drink of cold water, think of Jesus who told us that he is always ready to help us when we need his help.

Combination Locks And Freedom

John 8:31-36

"And you will know the truth, and the truth will make you free." (v. 32)

Object: a combination lock

Good morning, boys and girls. Does anyone have a combination lock? (*let them answer*) If you have a combination lock, that is, a lock that has a lot of numbers on it, tell me what you use it for. (*let them answer*) A lot of boys and girls have a combination lock to use on their bicycles. They ride their bikes to school or to the park, and while they are in school or playing, they know that their bikes are safely locked. Once you lock your bike up with a lock like this, then it cannot be moved or taken.

Of course, you must remember the combination so that you can open the lock after you have used it. That means that you must have the right numbers and know how to turn the lock in the right directions so that it will open. Knowing the combination is very important, and it is the only thing that can make something locked be free again.

I think that a combination is like the truth. Combinations open locks or free things that are locked up. The truth makes things free also, according to Jesus. When we know the truth about anything, we work with it and get the right answers to whatever problem we have. For instance, when we know the truth about Jesus and that he is the Savior of the world, then we know a truth that is very important.

It means that we can stop worrying about a lot of things. We can stop worrying about dying. How many of you ever have worried about dying? (*let them answer*) That is a big worry to a lot of people who do not know that Jesus promises us a much longer life in his new world than in this world. Once you know the truth, then you are free from worry. The truth is that Jesus forgives sins. If you are worried about your sins, like the time that you told a lie to your mother or brother, and you ask Jesus to forgive you for the sin, and he does, then you can quit worrying about the sin.

The truth makes you free. You do not have to worry or fuss about something when you know the truth. Jesus says that he is the truth. There is nothing about Jesus that is a lie. Whatever he does or says is the truth.

That is why I like to think about the truth as being the combination. It is the right combination, and it makes us just as free as if we have a bicycle lock with a combination and we spin it to the right numbers. If we do it right, then the bicycle lock will come free just as you and I do when we follow Jesus. Jesus is the truth, and Jesus makes us free.

Prissy Plant

John 9:1-41

Jesus said, "I came into this world for judgment so that those who do not see may see, and those who do see may become blind." (v. 39)

Object: an attractive artificial plant

Good morning, boys and girls. I brought along with me this morning a little bit of a problem. Her name is Prissy Plant and she has me in a fit. She won't get along with any of the other plants that I have in my house. Let me tell you a little bit about her.

This morning she was making all kinds of noise telling the other plants in my house how perfect she was. Prissy can never keep her mouth shut, and she has a large one. She told my one little plant over in the corner what a shrimp he was and how big and beautiful she was by comparison. That wasn't a nice thing to say. That little plant is small, but that is the way he was made, and he is growing. Yesterday Prissy was complaining to another plant that hangs in the window that she smelled, and of course Prissy is right about that. Prissy doesn't smell at all. The other night when I was eating dinner, I heard Prissy criticizing a plant that sits on the piano about his odd shape. She said that all of her leaves are perfect, each one is the right size and none of them are brown or nicked in any way. That was disgusting. Of course Prissy is perfectly made, but that is the problem. Prissy is artificial. She should be perfect.

I finally took Prissy aside this morning and told her that she was coming to church with me and that I was going to teach her a lesson. Prissy thinks so much about herself that she cannot see the truth or the beauty in anything else. What is more than that, is that she will never grow. She is false all of the way through.

I hope that you can learn something by listening to Prissy. There are a lot of people who think they know everything, and you can't teach them even the simplest truth.

Jesus ran into people like this all of the time. They didn't believe in him because they were afraid that if they did, they would be less than what they thought they already were. They were blind to the truth, and they didn't want to know the truth. They were artificial people just like Prissy is an artificial plant. Real people listen to Jesus and learn the truth about themselves and about God. If you are going to be a real person, then you must also follow the teachings of Jesus and be a real person.

Give Your Life To The Lord

John 10:11-18

"For this reason the Father loves me, because I lay down my life, in order to take it up again." (v. 17)

Object: a doll or teddy bear

Good morning, boys and girls. How many of you have a very special doll or stuffed animal that belongs to you? (*let them answer*) Almost all of you. What do you call your friend? (*let them answer*) A lot of people have a friend that looks like this. (*hold up your teddy bear, hopefully one that is well worn*) I call him Teddy. Do any of you call your bear "Teddy"? (*let them answer*) A lot of you have Teddy bears. That's wonderful. How many of you sleep with Teddy? (*let them answer*) Does your friend ever eat with you or watch television with you? (*let them answer*) A Teddy bear can be a very good friend and a lot of fun to share good times with.

I guess the best part of having a Teddy bear is that the teddy bear belongs to me. No one else owns Teddy. Teddy does what I want him to do, goes where I want him to go, sleeps when I want him to sleep and eats when I want him to eat. That's what I mean when I say that Teddy belongs to me. Since Teddy belongs to me, I can share him with you if I want to. I can even give Teddy away if I want to. Of course, if I gave him away, then he would belong to someone else and that person could do the same things with him that I do with him now.

God the Father loved Jesus even more than I love Teddy or more than you love your friend. Jesus belonged to the Father and the Father belonged to Jesus. They shared life together. The Father and Jesus had a plan about how they were going to share the life of Jesus with all of the people in the world. It was their life and they could do whatever they wanted to with it. Just like you can do whatever you want to with your friend Teddy. God decided to offer the life of Jesus for our sins. It was God's plan to have Jesus die for our sins and use up his life so that we would not die forever. God could do this with Jesus' life because it belonged to him. Now there was more to the plan than just dying. God also decided that after Jesus suffered and died he would give him back his life. God could do that also because even when Jesus was dead he belonged to God. So God gave back to Jesus his life.

The same thing can happen to you and me. If God owns your life like he owned Jesus and you own Teddy, then he can give you back your life after you die. God is so good that he will only do what is best for you. So you can belong to God like Jesus did and just like Teddy belongs to me and your friend belongs to you. That is a super plan and one that all of us should follow.

Remember, God will take even better care of your life, if you give it to him, than you take care of friends like Teddy.

Do You Know His Voice?

John 10:22-30

"My sheep hear my voice. I know them, and they follow me." (v. 27)

Objects: some blindfolds

Good morning, boys and girls. How many of you think that you know the voices of other people? I wonder if you would know your mother's voice or your father's voice, or even my voice if you could not see me. Would you like to try? (*let them answer*) I have some blindfolds that I want you to put on and wear for a few minutes. While I am helping you put on your blindfolds, I want to invite some of your parents to come up front with us. We are going to let them talk to one another while you are blindfolded, and when you hear your mother or father speak, and you are sure that it is your parent talking, then you should walk toward them and hold out your hand. We will see if you know their voices as well as you think you do. (*help them put on their blindfolds; invite the parents to gather around and begin to talk about anything; suggest that they talk about what they did this morning before they came to church; it might help if you took each child by the hand and walked him close to the parents; when they have all found their children, or their children have found them, you can invite them to remain for the rest of the sermon*)

That was a lot of fun, and we really learned something. Most of us really do know the voices of our parents, don't we? We did this experiment for a very good reason which I am going to share with you right now.

Jesus liked to talk about himself as being a shepherd. He thought that this was a good way to explain how God and people worked together. God is the shepherd, and we are like the sheep. A shepherd takes very good care of his sheep, but the sheep are allowed to do a lot of things on their own. A good shepherd is so close to his sheep that the sheep recognize the shepherd's voice. If there were a lot of sheep and a lot of shepherds together, the sheep would always know the voice of their shepherd, and gather around him.

That is the way it is with Christians. Jesus is our shepherd and we belong to him. When Jesus speaks, we should hear his voice and do what he tells us to do. We should also follow him and behave ourselves in the way that we know that Jesus would behave himself. The voices of the people whom we love are very important to us, and we like to hear them because they make us feel safe and loved.

Jesus has a voice like that, and, though we cannot hear it in the same way, we are sure that he speaks to us in our prayers and through the Bible. That means that we must pray and listen to the Bible; and when we do, we know that Jesus will be just like a shepherd.

The next time that you hear the voice of someone whom you cannot see, I want you to think about today and remember that Jesus speaks to us in many ways to show us how much he loves and cares for us.

One Flower Or Many?

John 11:1-53

"You do not understand that it is better for you to have one man die for the people than to have the whole nation destroyed." (v. 50)

Object: a flower with some seeds that will shake out when the petals are removed

Good morning, boys and girls. I want to tell you a story I hope you will never forget. It is about a man who was an enemy of Jesus and who helped to plan Jesus' death. But first I want to show you something that I think will help you to understand the story better. I have a beautiful flower with me. (*show them the flower*) Inside of the petals on this flower there are seeds. Did you know that when the petals drop off of this flower and it looks like it has died the seeds fall to the ground? (*let them answer*) What happens to the little seeds? (*let them answer*) That's right; they are buried in the ground and next year you have a bunch of flowers growing where there was one growing last year. The seeds of the flower that died make many new flowers. If you know this, then you can listen to the story better.

There was a man named Caiaphas, and he was the chief priest of Israel. He was afraid of Jesus. The chief priest thought that he should know more about God, and what God wanted, than anyone else in the whole world. He was so sure that he was so important that he could not listen to what Jesus said or taught. Whenever he listened or was told something that Jesus did or said, he forgot about that and thought only of how other people would think that Jesus was greater than he was. He was also afraid that the Roman armies that lived in his country might think he was a follower of Jesus or that his people were followers of Jesus and they would become angry and kill all of the people. At least that is what he told his friends. He said the only way that he could take care of Israel was to kill Jesus. If Jesus were dead, then the people would forget about him and come back to listen to them. Then the armies of Rome would not be nervous and afraid and everything would be better. In other words, Caiaphas said that it was better for one man to die than a lot of men. If they killed Jesus, then everyone else would live.

God also had a plan. It was not the same plan that Caiaphas had, but it worked out in the same way. Caiaphas said if you kill one flower, then all of the other flowers that are living will go on living. But God knew that everyone was going to die someday, and God wanted people to live forever with him. So God let Jesus die on the cross. But when Jesus died, it was like the flower I showed you a little while ago. When he died, his seeds, who are people like Peter and John and also like you and me, had a chance to live. We belong to Jesus like the seeds belonged to the flower. We can live, because Jesus died.

Caiaphas told a truth, but he didn't know what he was saying. It is an interesting story and a very true one. I hope that you will remember this story when you see a flower and the seeds of the flower. Jesus died so that we can live.

Jesus Is No Joke

John 12:20-23

"Very truly, I tell you, unless a grain of wheat falls into the earth and dies, it remains just a single grain; but if it dies, it bears much fruit." (v. 24)

Object: some grains of wheat

Good morning, boys and girls. Do you know what April 1 is? We call it April Fool's Day. How many of you have ever said, "April Fool!" (*let them answer*) What does that mean when you say, "April Fool"? (*let them answer*) That's right; you play a trick on someone and then you tell them, "April Fool."

Jesus didn't play April Fool with us but he said some things that made people wonder if he was trying to trick them. He talked a lot about how you had to die before you could really live. Dying and living are two different things, but Jesus made it sound like they went together.

One day Jesus told some people about a grain of wheat and how it had to die so that it could really live. He took a piece of wheat that looked like this and told them if they kept it on a shelf it would just lay there and do nothing. One piece of wheat on a shelf is worth almost nothing. But Jesus said to put it in the ground and let it die and see what happens.

Do you know what happens to a piece of wheat if you bury it in the ground? (*let them answer*) That's right; it grows. But before it grows, it must die. That piece of wheat comes apart, it sort of disappears, but from it grow some roots and then a stalk and finally a whole bunch of things begin to appear that look like this one piece of wheat. From one seed comes hundreds of other wheat seeds. In other words, when one piece of wheat dies, it comes alive in a hundred different pieces of wheat. Does that sound like April Fool? It isn't, that's the truth.

Jesus was trying to tell us that the same thing is going to happen to us. We are going to die. He knew it and we know it and he isn't trying to fool us. But when we die and we believe in God, then our lives become a hundred times better. We call that "hundred times better" heaven. Being with God in heaven is a hundred times better than we know it here, but we have to wait for the time to die. None of us know when we are going to die. Only God knows when he wants us to die, and we can't hurry that time. We should live on earth as God wants us to live and then wait for the time when we are planted in the ground according to God's plan. We are going to die for sure, just like the piece of wheat dies, but when we do, the promise of God is that it will be at least a hundred times better with him than it is now. That's a promise that God is going to keep and one for you to remember.

A Light Bulb And God

John 13:31-35

When he had gone out, Jesus said, "Now the Son of Man has been glorified, and God has been glorified in him." (v. 31)

Object: a light bulb inside of a light globe

Good morning, boys and girls. Today we are going to talk about the way Jesus and the person whom we call God are the same. Sometimes this is a very hard thing to explain, but I hope I can make it somewhat easier with the object that I have brought with me this morning. How many of you think that Jesus was part of God's plan? (*let them answer*) Very good, Jesus was part of God's plan. But Jesus was more than just another man who loved God and did what God wanted him to do. God was in Jesus in a very special way, so special that we must say that God and Jesus are one person.

Now let me show you what I mean. I brought a light bulb with me, and I am going to call the light bulb "God." As you can see, the light bulb is a very bright light, and it shines in a very special way. Wherever this light shines, the darkness goes away. I also have a globe that fits over the light bulb, so that when the light shines you cannot see it shine, but you can see the light through the globe. I am going to call the globe "Jesus." Let's put the light inside of the globe and turn it on, so that you can share with me the idea that when the bulb is turned on, both the bulb and the globe are shining.

Now I told you that Jesus and God are one, and that is true. When we talk about one, we are talking about the other; and when we talk about the other, we are talking about one. It is the same with the light. When I tell you to turn on the light, I do not tell you to turn on the light bulb so that the globe will give us light. I just tell you to turn on the light, and I know that we are talking about the bulb and the globe.

Jesus wanted us to know how close he and God were to one another. He said that when we talked about one, we talked about the other. He also said that when one of them did something wonderful, the other one shared in the wonderful thing that happened because they were one. God came to us in the form of Jesus, but when Jesus went back to God, they were the same again.

I know that this is a very hard thing to understand, but I also hope that the next time you see a light, it will help you to remember that there is only one light, even though there is one bulb and one globe on the ceiling or on the wall. Just remember that Jesus and God are one, and that we worship our Jesus as our God. Will you do that? Good. God bless you very much.

Jesus Is Our Map

John 14:1-7

Jesus said to him, "I am the way, and the truth, and the life. No one comes to the Father, except through me." (v. 6)

Object: a map with the location of some surprises for the children. This could be given out to the children at the time of the children's sermon, to be hunted for after the service is over. The surprise could be some candy or oranges or whatever you would choose

Good morning, boys and girls. Today I have a surprise for you. I will tell you what the surprise is in a minute, but I want you to know what made me think of the surprise.

In the Bible, there is a verse that almost everyone who is a Christian remembers. It is something that Jesus said. He told his disciples that he was the way, the truth, and the life, and anyone who wanted to know the Father had to follow him and what he taught. In other words Jesus is the map to the Father. If we follow Jesus, we will know God and be with him. Did you know that Jesus was like a map? All of you have seen maps that show the cities and roads and rivers. If you want to find your way from one city to the next city, you follow the map and it will get you there. That is why Jesus wanted us to understand the importance of our following him. Jesus is the way to God the Father, the truth about God the Father and the life of God the Father. If we want these things, we must follow our map of Jesus.

The way that I can show you the importance of a map is to give you a map. I have made you a map that you can follow after the service. If you and your parents follow this map that I am giving to you, then you will find a wonderful surprise. This surprise is somewhere in the church, but you must take the map and go where it tells you to go.

I hope that you enjoy the surprise that I have left for you. Remember to share your love from Jesus with someone else.

Do You Believe What He Said?

John 14:23-29

"And now I have told you before it occurs, so that when it does occur, you may believe." (v. 29)

Object: some nut cups, some wet cotton for each cup, and a package of dry lima beans

Good morning, boys and girls. We are going to do something exciting today, but we will not know what a great day it is until a week or so from now. How many of you have ever heard the saying that "seeing is believing"? (*let them answer*) That means that it is very hard to believe something unless you see it with your own eyes. A lot of people feel like this, and they have a hard time believing you, unless you can show them the proof.

People have always been like this, and they were this way even with Jesus. It did not make any difference that Jesus healed people and did all kinds of other miracles; they still wanted the proof over and over again before they would believe him.

That was the reason that one day he told them how much better life would be for them when he left them and sent the Holy Spirit to take his place, while he went back to the Father in heaven. People found that rather hard to believe, but he told them anyway. He told them then, so that when the things happened that he said were going to happen, they could remember that this was a promise of Jesus. Then they would think, "Jesus told us it was going to happen and now we know that he was right."

I have an experiment that I want to share with you this morning that you are going to love. I have some beans with me that I am going to give you to take home. By this time next week they are going to be plants. That's the truth, and to show you how fast they are going to grow, I am going to have you grow them in this little nut cup with some cotton. Now you don't have to put them in water, plant them in the ground, or anything like you usually do. All I want you to do is to put them inside the wet cotton in the cup, and then come back and tell me next week if they did what I said they would do. Remember, I told you that they would grow into plants. I am doing this because I know that some of you will not believe me until it happens, but I know it will happen. This is the way that Jesus told the disciples and others about his great promises. They just had to wait until the things happened that he said were going to happen before they could find out if he was telling the truth. I can tell you now that whatever he promised was going to happen did happen. Jesus knew exactly what was going to take place, and it did.

I think that you will remember how much Jesus knew when you try our little experiment and watch your bean grow this week into a plant. When that bean becomes a plant, then I want you to remember the day that Jesus told everyone what was going to happen before it did, so that they would believe that Jesus was the Christ, the Son of the Living God. If you remember that, then you, too, will also believe that he was the Son of God.

Stay Close To The Vine

John 15:1-8

"I am the vine, you are the branches." (v. 5a)

Object: some ivy in a pot

Good morning, boys and girls. How many of you like to grow plants? (*let them answer*) Working with plants is a wonderful hobby because you're working with life. You plant something and you help it grow. Some plants have flowers, some have leaves, some have fruit, and some have nuts. If you have a garden at your house, you are a very lucky person, and if you help take care of it, then you are even luckier. Working with plants teaches you a lot of things.

Jesus must have loved plants. He talked a lot about flowers, trees, and other kinds of plants that grew where he lived. One time he talked about how some plants grew and made homes for the birds. You can almost see Jesus looking in one of the big bushes that grew on the hillsides and showing his friends a bird's nest. Another time Jesus talked about how beautiful the lilies were and how God made them special. Maybe you remember all of the lilies that we had in our church on Easter to remind us of Jesus.

Jesus mentioned another plant, and he talked about it so that we could understand how we belonged to him. I brought along some ivy because it is a vine. Jesus was talking about vines and branches of the vine. He said that he was the vine.

Let's take a look at the vine. (*show them the vine and how it goes from one end to the other*) The vine is the main part. But look at all of the branches. (*show them, or even count the branches*) Now if you can imagine a very big vine that has millions and millions of branches, you can see why Jesus called himself the vine and us the branches. The branches cannot live without the vine. All of the food for the branches comes from the vine. Jesus was telling us that we cannot really live without him. He is the one who gives us life.

Maybe the next time you are working in your garden with some tomato plants you will see the vine and all of the branches. As the vine gets bigger and bigger, there are more and more branches. They also grow like the vine grows. But if you take one of the branches away from the vine it will quickly die. It cannot live without the vine.

That was a good story by Jesus and it tells us a lot about how important he is to our life. We need to keep close to Jesus so that we can grow and live very good lives together.

131

It's Not On Any Map

John 15:26-27; 16:4b-11

"But now I am going to him who sent me; yet none of you asks me, 'Where are you going?'" (v. 5)

Object: a large map of the world, any map of Israel, or a globe of the world

Good morning, boys and girls. Today we are going to take a look at a large map that I brought with me, because I read something in the Bible that I thought we should answer. You will remember that some time ago we talked about how Jesus was crucified and buried, and how three days later he came back to life in what we call the Resurrection. How many of you remember us talking about that time? (*let them answer*)

After the Resurrection, Jesus walked and talked with his disciples for almost seven weeks. One time he met some of them on a road while they were walking. Another time he met with them in a room in Jerusalem. Then, once, he actually cooked their breakfast on the shore of the lake and invited them to come and share not only the food, but also some talk with him. Jesus was very much alive after the Resurrection. But this day he asked them a question, and I think that it is a good one to ask you also. He said to them that he keeps telling them that he is going away, but that not one of them asked him, "Where are you going?" When you hear that Jesus is leaving, do you ever think about asking him where he is going?

I brought along a map today to ask you if you know where Jesus went when he left the disciples. (*let them answer*) Do you think you could find on the map the place where Jesus went after he left the disciples? (*have some of them look at the map to see if they will point out a place*) Do you think Jesus went to America or Egypt or Germany, or to any of the towns close by in Israel? (*let them answer*) Where do you think that Jesus went, and why is it important for us to know where he went when he left the disciples?

I will tell you why it is important. The reason that Jesus told the disciples that he was going away was because he wanted them to know where he was going. He did not want them to think that he was hiding, or just going to another town. He wanted them to know that the place he was going was the most special part of the whole plan of God. Now do you know where Jesus went when he left the disciples? (*let them answer*)

Yes, he went back to live with God in the place we call heaven. I don't mean the sky, but a real world where God is making a place for us to live after all of us die. Jesus is here on earth, but we cannot see him or touch him or feel him. Jesus is not in a body like ours any longer. But Jesus is alive and well and living with the Father. You can't find the place that he is staying on a map, but someday we will join him wherever he is, and we are going to love it more than anything we have ever loved. You can't find Jesus on a map, but you can be sure that Jesus knows where we are and what we are doing. Someday we will be with Jesus, and then we will be the happiest people that you ever knew. I can hardly wait. Can you?

The Funnel Of God

John 16:12-15

"When the Spirit of truth comes, he will guide you into all the truth; for he will not speak on his own, but will speak whatever he hears, and he will declare to you the things that are to come." (v. 13)

Object: a funnel

Good morning, boys and girls. Have you ever tried to pour something from one bottle into another bottle? (*let them answer*) Do you usually spill some of it when you try to do this? (*let them answer*) Do you know how to keep from spilling whatever you have in the bottle? (*let them answer*) You can be extra careful, but I have a better way.

How many of you have ever used a funnel? (*let them answer*) Tell me how you use one of these things that we call a funnel. (*allow someone to give an explanation*) That's right, you put the funnel into one of the bottles and then pour whatever you have into that bottle. The funnel acts like a guide, and it puts whatever you are pouring in just the right place so nothing is spilled or lost. A funnel is a very helpful tool.

I would like us to think that the funnel is like the Spirit of God. We can try to do things on our own. We can look at the trees and the birds and bees, and see how God has made them, and the way that he takes care of them, and we can try to understand how God wants us to live. We can read books and talk to other people, but that does not really tell us how God loves us as people. We want to feel love from God, and not find it out in any other way.

The Bible tells us that the Spirit of God is like a funnel. The Spirit is a guide who brings the love of God right to us without spilling one drop. The Spirit does not change a word of what he hears when he speaks to us. He is really like a funnel. Whatever God wants us to know, the Spirit of God tells us. The Spirit of God works with us as children of God to help us learn every day something new about God and God's church. The Spirit teaches us how to forgive and how to be honest with each other. The Spirit does not make this up, but rather he brings it to us from God, without losing one part of what God wanted us to know. This is why I tell you that the Spirit is like a funnel.

The next time that you see someone filling the gas tank on their mower with a funnel, or you see your father or mother using a funnel in the kitchen, I want you to think about all of the different ways that a funnel is used. Then I want you to think about the way that the Spirit of God is like a funnel, and the very many ways that the Spirit is used by God in teaching us. You must remember that the funnel does not make the stuff that it helps to pour. It comes from somewhere else. The same thing is true of the Spirit. The Spirit does not make up what he teaches us. The things that the Spirit pours into us are the good stuff that comes from God. The Spirit is like a funnel carrying the good news from God to us.

Stick Together For God

John 17:11b-19

"Holy Father, protect them in your name that you have given me, so that they may be one, as we are one." (v. 11b)

Object: some sticks or pencils held together with some string or rubber band

Good morning, boys and girls. I want to share a very favorite story with you this morning. My story is about how God makes us strong when we stay together. It is really an old story, but it is a good one.

First of all I need someone very strong to help me with the story. (*select one of the biggest children*) You look very strong, and I know that you are the perfect person to help me this morning. I brought along some pencils, wooden pencils. Do you use pencils like this in school? (*let him answer*) I want you to take the pencil and use all of your great strength to break it. (*give him the pencil and watch how easily he breaks the pencil*) My, you are strong. You broke that pencil so fast that I could hardly keep up with you. Do you know if you could break the rest of the pencils just like you broke this one? (*let him answer*) I think you could if I let you.

I am going to let you try, only this time we are going to make it a little different. Instead of having you break them one at a time, I am going to put them all together and put this rubber band around them as tightly as I can. Now I want to see if you can break the pencils while they are put together as one. (*give him the pencils and let him try several times*) That was a good effort but the pencils are too strong when they are tied together. You broke one pencil by itself, but when the pencils are put together, they are stronger than you are.

Jesus said a prayer to God asking him to keep his disciples together so that they would stay strong. Jesus knew if they stayed together they could do a lot of things that they could not do by themselves, individually. He prayed that God would keep them together in his name. Jesus prays the same thing for us each day. To keep us together. That is why we call ourselves Christian. We are Christians together. We are strong together. We would not be strong if we each tried to do what Jesus asked us all by ourselves. We need to come together like we do every Sunday and worship God. We need to study together in Sunday school and many times we need to work together.

When we are alone, we can be broken in two just like the first pencil. But when we work together, study together, and worship together, we are strong and no one can break us.

Jesus knew how to make us strong, and he prayed that God would keep us together. It was a wonderful prayer and one that none of us should ever forget.

You Are Jesus' Magnifying Glass

John 17:20-26

"I ask not only on behalf of these, but also on behalf of those who will believe in me through their word, that they may all be one." (v. 20)

Object: a magnifying glass

Good morning, boys and girls. How many of you have ever worked or played with a magnifying glass? (*let them answer*) A lot of you! I brought one along with me so that we could look through one and see how helpful it is for seeing something that would be hard to see without it. (*take out the magnifying glass and read some very small print or look at the particles that make up a page of paper*) Isn't that something, that a piece of glass can help us see so much that we might miss if we did not use it? For some people a magnifying glass is really important in their work. I know that jewelers use them to work on watches, and doctors use them in some operations. Other people find them just as important.

A magnifying glass is something that you look through to see something else. A disciple of Jesus is like a magnifying glass. Did you know that? (*let them answer*) That's right, a disciple is someone who helps us to see God and believe in him a lot better than we could, without the disciple.

Let's think about Peter or Paul, or any of the other disciples, and remember how much we have learned about Jesus and the teachings of God because of the way that they were and what they said. Jesus knew how important they were, and one of his very last prayers that he said on earth was a prayer for his disciples, saying how thankful he was for those who helped others believe in God. Jesus was telling us that he knew that his disciples were like magnifying glasses for other people, and that they helped the people in Jerusalem and other cities believe in the true God.

You can be a magnifying glass for Jesus also. When you tell your friends how much you love Jesus and why you love him, you are being a magnifying glass. That's right. And when you do this you are just like Peter or Paul or any other disciple. You can tell people how God loves you, forgives you, and makes a place in heaven for you to share with him at just the right time.

Did you ever think that someone would call you a magnifying glass? (*let them answer*) You are, every time that you show someone else Jesus and what he means to you.

The next time you see a magnifying glass, I hope that you will remember what we said today, and that you will always he a disciple of Jesus Christ.

Christer The King

John 18:33-37

Then Pilate entered the headquarters again, summoned Jesus, and asked him, "Are you the King of the Jews?" (v. 33)

Object: a crown and a map of the world or a globe

Good morning, boys and girls. How many of you have ever heard of a king? Do you know a king? (*let them answer*) You know the name of a president, don't you? (*let them answer*) But you probably don't know the name of any king. We have the Queen of England whose name is Elizabeth, and there is also a king from the land of Jordan. There is a king of Sweden and there are kings in other places. At one time, each country had a king. There was a king in France and one in Italy and another in Russia. Take a look at the map and see all of the countries that there are on the earth. See how the colors change from one place to another. Each time you see the colors change, there is another country. At one time all of those countries had kings.

In our scripture lesson today, the representative of the man the people called the king of Rome asked Jesus if he were the king of the Jews. He meant, was Jesus the new king of Israel. He knew that there already was a king of Israel by the name of Herod, but Pilate wanted to know if he was starting a revolution or a fight to take the kingship away from Herod.

Jesus knew what he was thinking and he also wanted to show Pilate that he was a different kind of king. Jesus was surely the king of something, but it was not of one little country like Israel or France or Russia or the United States of America. Jesus is the king of people and not countries. Jesus is the king of God's kingdom. Jesus does not have armies with guns like Herod and others had. He does not have palaces and places filled with gold. He doesn't wear fancy clothes and have people to wait on him. Jesus is the king of people's minds and their hearts. He is the king of love and joy. He is the king over death and disease. Jesus is the king of the world. Jesus is not the king of one country or one planet, but instead he is the king of the entire universe.

So when you hear about kings — any kings — I hope that you will think of Jesus Christ, the real king who lives forever and rules over everything. That is what Jesus was telling Pilate that day, and the message remains for everyone who wants to ask. Jesus is not just the king of a country, one country, but all countries and all worlds.

The Spear

John 19:31-35

But when they came to Jesus and saw that he was already dead, they did not break his legs. Instead, one of the soldiers pierced his side with a spear, and at once blood and water came out. (vv. 33-34)

Object: a spear

Good morning, boys and girls. Perhaps you remember the moment that we spoke of when the soldier came up to Jesus, climbed the ladder and put a sponge with sour wine to Jesus' lips. Jesus died very shortly after that moment. I don't know how many people who were there that day heard Jesus say it, but after the soldier lifted the sponge to his lips Jesus said, "It is finished." He was dead. It seemed impossible that only a few hours before, he was eating with his disciples and now he was dead.

This was a Friday and only a few hours away from the Sabbath which was the Jewish holy day, like our Sunday. The Jewish leaders didn't want any sign of a dead body or any sort of trouble showing on the Sabbath, so they asked the Roman governor, Pilate, to have the legs of the men who were still on the crosses broken so that they would die sooner. Not only were they beaten and nailed to the crosses, but now they were going to have broken legs.

The soldiers didn't mind. At least most of them didn't care, because they thought this was part of their job. The two thieves who were on crosses on each side of Jesus' cross were not dead, and when the soldiers came to their crosses, they struck them several times across their legs until they were sure that their legs were broken. How cruel, how terribly cruel.

But when they came to Jesus they stopped and looked at him carefully. They could see no sign of breath or any other movement. He was dead. There was no need to break his legs. He was not going anywhere. For a moment it seemed as if they were not going to do anything, just pass him by. But just as the last soldier had taken a step away from Jesus, he stopped and turned, and then he lifted his spear and shoved it into the side of Jesus. As the spear pierced the skin there was a rush of water and blood that covered the point and rushed down the handle. There was no sound, no moan, and the soldiers were satisfied that the one with the sign "King of the Jews" was really dead.

The soldier pulled back his spear and joined the other soldiers who were walking ahead. The friends of Jesus were now also very sure that Jesus was dead. They could think about all the things that he had said and the healings that he had performed, but they could never again talk with him or share a laugh, or a piece of bread. Jesus was dead and there was no doubt about it.

In a little while a man named Joseph, who was a secret disciple of Jesus' and also part of the Jewish leadership, went to the Roman governor, Pilate, and very boldly asked if he

137

could have permission to bury Jesus in his tomb. Pilate agreed and told him to go ahead and do with Jesus what he wanted. Another secret disciple by the name of Nicodemus, asked if he could help Joseph, and when told that he could, he brought a hundred pounds of special ointment and spices to cover the body of Jesus before burial.

With those arrangements made and the time drawing close to the beginning of the Sabbath, Joseph and Nicodemus moved quickly to the tomb in the garden. They wrapped his body in a long linen cloth bathed in the ointment and spices. When that was finished they left quickly but with great sadness in their hearts. As they went out of the tomb there were some soldiers coming to take their place as guards. A heavy stone was rolled in front of the tomb to seal it closed. It was a stone of such great weight that not even several men could move it.

A spear had been the final proof that Jesus was dead. No one could live with a wound like that in his side. Jesus the Christ would never be the same again. The soldier who shoved the spear into Jesus' side never knew that he was piercing the side of the Son of God, but some day it would serve as proof to a disciple that Jesus lived again. Remember that even as Jesuse died, he did so with a prayer on his lips. He forgave everyone who had sinned against God and him. Now we should be ready to do the same. God bless you.

An Empty Box

John 20:1-2, 11-18

So she ran and went to Simon Peter and the other disciple, the one whom Jesus loved, and said to them, "They have taken the Lord out of the tomb, and we do not know where they have laid him." (v. 2)

Object: a new, empty crayon box

Good morning, boys and girls. Have you ever been really disappointed? (*let them answer*) I mean, have you ever thought that something wonderful was going to happen to you and then for some reason it didn't? Supposing that I gave you this brand new box of crayons and I told you that you could do anything that you wanted to do with it. What would you expect to find inside this box and what would you want to do with it? (*let them answer*)

You think there are crayons inside and you want to color with the crayons. That's what I would think, also, if somebody gave me a brand new crayon box. Well, let me give it to one of you. Open it and tell me how you feel. (*let one of the children open the crayon box and show you and everyone else that it's empty; then solicit his disappointment*) That's disappointing. A brand new crayon box and no crayons inside! I feel awful and so do you.

Maybe you know now how Mary Magdalene felt when she went to Jesus' tomb and found it empty. It was just three days after he was crucified and she expected to find Jesus dead and in his tomb. When she saw that it was empty, she ran to tell Peter and John that Jesus had disappeared. She was so sad and so disappointed. She wondered how someone could be so mean as to steal the body of Jesus. Why would anyone take Jesus away from his grave?

Mary felt a lot sadder than you felt when you opened your brand new crayon box and found it empty because Jesus is sure a lot more important than brand new crayons.

But the best part of the story is yet to come, because Mary found out that no one had stolen Jesus, but instead, he had been raised from the dead, brought back to life by God the Father.

Somewhere I have all of the crayons that belong in this box, but I'm not going to put them back because I want you to know that Jesus' tomb is still empty. They didn't find Jesus and put him back in the grave. They found Jesus alive and well and happy. The empty crayon box, like the empty grave, is a sign for us to remember that God showed people like Mary and Peter and John that life is God's wish for everyone. Jesus was the first person to be brought back from the grave, but all of us will someday have the same marvelous experience. We too, will have empty graves just like Jesus had an empty grave.

The next time you see a crayon box, take all of the crayons out of it and look inside and see if you can remember how Mary Magdalene felt on that first Easter Day. Then think how happy you are to know that someday you will know the same joy that Mary knew when she discovered Jesus was raised from the dead.

Are You Who You Say You Are?

John 20:19-31

So the other disciples told him, "We have seen the Lord." But he said to them, "Unless I see the mark of nails in his hands, and put my finger in the mark of the nails and my hand in his side, I will not believe." (v. 25)

Object: a driver's license, Social Security card, or an identification bracelet

Good morning, boys and girls. How many of you know who you are? (*let them answer*) If I asked each of you that question, could you prove to me who you are? How can you prove that you are who you say you are? (*let them answer*) Do you have a piece of paper, or are you wearing something that proves that you are who you say you are? (*let them answer*)

If you asked me to prove to you that I am who I say I am, I might give you my driver's license or my Social Security card. (*show them some of your identification*) There are lots of times when I am asked to prove that I am who I say that I am. People in the banks and stores want to know that I am who I say I am before they will let me cash a check or charge something.

But I want you to know that I am not the only person who has to prove that I am who I say that I am. Did you know that Jesus had to prove to one of his disciples that he was Jesus? (*let them answer*) He did. But Jesus did not have a driver's license, and he did not have a Social Security card. If he had something like this, he might have used it, but I doubt that he did.

Let me tell you a story. You will remember that Jesus had been crucified on the cross, and that he had died. When he was crucified, the people drove nails through his hands and his feet into the cross of wood. As you can imagine, it not only hurt a lot, but it also left big holes where the nails went through his skin. It was after Jesus had died and was also resurrected that he had to prove himself.

Jesus had visited with all of the disciples except one called Thomas. He had told them how much he loved them and what he was going to do for them. They could hardly wait to tell Thomas about Jesus being with them. But Thomas could not believe that someone who had died could come back to life and visit again. So Thomas told the other disciples that unless he saw the places where the nails went through Jesus' hands and feet, he would not believe their story.

It was almost a week later when Thomas was with the other disciples that Jesus came again. Jesus knew that Thomas did not believe, so he showed Thomas the marks and scars in his hands and in his side. Then he asked Thomas if he believed.

Of couse Thomas did, and that is the day that Jesus proved who he was.

We can't see those nails, but we must believe what happened, just as Thomas and others like him did. That is why we call our kind of believing "faith." The next time that you see someone prove who he or she is with a driver's license, you can remember the day that Jesus proved who he was with the marks of the nails in his body.

The Day Jesus Cooked

John 21:1-14

When they had gone ashore, they saw a charcoal fire there, with fish on it, and bread. (v. 9)

Object: some charcoal and a loaf of bread

Good morning, boys and girls. How many of you ever thought about Jesus cooking breakfast? (*let them answer*) Did you think that Jesus could cook? (*let them answer*) You probably knew that he was a carpenter, but there are not many places in the Bible that tell you about Jesus as a cook. I don't know how often he cooked, but the Bible tells of one time that he did, and it was one of the most exciting events in the Bible.

First of all, you have to know that Jesus had been dead and had come back to life. This story happened during one of the times that Jesus visited with his disciples after he was risen from the dead. As you can imagine, the disciples were lonely without him, and some of them had decided that they would go fishing rather than just sit around and think about the good times they used to have with Jesus. They fished all night and did not catch anything, but I guess they really did not care about catching fish. Then, as it became morning, they saw a man on the beach waving to them and asking them how they had done with their fishing. Some of them thought right away that it might be Jesus, but they were not sure. The man on the shore told them to put their nets down on the other side of the boat to catch some fish. They told the man that they had fished all night, but that they would cast their nets once more the way he told them to.

As you might guess, they caught more fish than the nets could hold. Peter knew by now that the man was Jesus. He jumped into the water and swam ashore. The others followed him in the boat, and when they got there, they saw that Jesus had already started a fire with some charcoal and had some bread ready for them to eat. (*show them the charcoal and the loaf of bread*) It may not have looked like my charcoal or my loaf of bread, but it cooked and tasted pretty much the same.

I suppose you can imagine how glad they were to see Jesus. They were thrilled to share breakfast and tell stories about all of the good times they had spent together. Most of all they were glad because they knew once more that Jesus was alive and well, and that he remembered them as people whom he loved and cared for every day, whether he was eating or walking with them.

Jesus is that way with us today. He doesn't have to cook for us to show us that he cares for us. We know it anyway, but for the disciples, who had spent so much time with him on earth, it was one of the best things that ever happened to them.

Maybe the next time that you have a cookout and you put the charcoal on the fire, you will remember the day that Jesus cooked breakfast for his disciples, and shared some bread and fish with them. I hope you remember it, because it was one of the best moments in the disciples' lives.

A Man With A Hard Name To Remember

Acts 1:12-14

... Peter, and John, and James, and Andrew, Philip and Thomas, Bartholomew and Matthew, James son of Alphaeus, and Simon the Zealot, and Judas son of James. All these were constantly devoting themselves to prayer.... (vv. 13b-14a)

Object: symbol of Jude

Good morning, boys and girls. How many times have you heard someone's name and still you forget it? You remember what he does and where he lives, but you can't remember his name. Some people you never know by name, but you just call them the mail carrier, police officer, teacher, and other names like that. These are important people, but we forget to learn their names.

Jesus had a disciple like this, and while he was a hard worker and very important to Jesus, other people could never remember his name. Jesus called him Jude or Thaddaeus. The Bible called him by both names. Maybe that is the reason people forget his name, since they never could remember what to call him. But just because they forgot to mention his name does not mean that he was not important.

The thing that it does mean is that Jude did his job so well that people remembered what he did rather than who he was. There are a lot of people like this and maybe you are one of them. I know some pretty important boys and girls who people call Sis, or Sonny, or Junior, other names like that because they forget what their real name is, but I want you to know that these boys and girls are really important.

Because people forgot his name, there are no stories in the Bible about Jude like there are about Peter and Paul or James and John. Jude is one of those people like you and me. I doubt if anyone will write a book about us so that people will remember us in 2,000 years, but I want you to know that you are important to a lot of people, and especially important to God. Jude was like you and me. No one will write about us, but the world knows that it takes a lot of people like us to make the big people big. We may not win an election, but it is our vote that elects people to office. Without any big fuss, Jude did the job that Jesus asked him to do. The job got done, and Jesus loved Jude for the way that he did it.

I know people today who find it hard to tell other people about Jesus even though they love him very much. They tell me that they are not a pastor and that people would not listen to them since they have not gone to special schools for ministers. But Jude is the kind of a person that most of us are. Jude told anyone and everyone about Jesus and no one thought that he was so big. Jude did just what Jesus asked him to do and it worked out fine.

Your name may be hard to remember, but it is a good name. Don't wait until people know you by your name to tell them about Jesus. Do it like Jude did, and tell the people first about God, and let them worry about who told them later.

Jude had a hard name to remember, but he did the big job for Jesus.

A Second Choice

Acts 1:21-26

So one of the men who have accompanied us during all the time that the Lord Jesus went in and out among us ... must become a witness with us to his resurrection ... And they cast lots for them, and the lot fell on Matthias; and he was added to the eleven apostles. (vv. 21, 22, 26)

Object: symbol of Matthias

Good morning, boys and girls. How many of you know what it is like to be second choice? I mean, how many of you know what it is like to never be the first one chosen. There is always someone else who comes ahead of you, and it doesn't make any difference if it is a game, a friend, or getting something to eat, you always end up with your second choice. It is probably is not that bad, but it seems like it sometimes.

I have a story to tell you today about a man who was a second choice but it turned out pretty well for him. His name was Matthias, and he lived at the same time that Jesus and his apostles lived. Matthias began to follow Jesus when Jesus first started to preach and teach, and very early he was called a follower of Jesus. Matthias knew Peter, James, and John, and all of the other disciples who were called apostles, but he wasn't one of them. When Jesus had private meetings with his disciples, Matthias was not invited. He was not one of the disciples to pass out the little's boy's bread and fish when Jesus fed a big crowd, nor did he go with Jesus and the disciples to the wedding at Cana. There were a lot of things Jesus did not ask Matthias to do, but Matthias still believed in Jesus.

When Jesus was crucified and died on the cross, many of the apostles ran and hid in a room where no one could find them. They felt unsafe and feared that if they were caught, the Roman soldiers would do the same to them that they did to Jesus. Matthias was very close to the disciples and knew how they felt. He also knew that Judas, one of the 12, had betrayed Jesus and then was so ashamed that he took his own life and died. That meant that there were only 11 apostles left. Matthias helped the disciples while they were in that upper room hiding from the soldiers by bringing them news and food and delivering messages.

One day, the Spirit of God swept down onto Jerusalem and forced the disciples out of hiding and onto the streets. The Spirit of God spoke boldly and gave the disciples new courage to go back to work for Jesus. It was amazing how unafraid they were when they felt the presence of God.

This was just the beginning. The apostles of Jesus held a meeting and decided that they must go not only back to work, but they also decided where they must work and what each disciple was going to do. One of the first things they had to do was find a replacement for Judas. This person, they decided, had to be someone who had seen a lot of the wonderful things that Jesus had done. They had the names of two people who fit that description. Both were good men. One of the names they presented was Justus and the other was Matthias. Matthias hoped and prayed that when the choice was made, he would be the one chosen.

The two names were written on paper and put in a jar. Then when everyone was quiet Peter reached into the jar and pulled out the name. Peter looked around the room and said in a big voice, "Matthias is the one to serve the Lord."

What a relief! Now he knew why he had not been chosen before. God had a special time and place for Matthias and this was it. He had a hard job to do, for taking the place of a man who betrayed Jesus was not easy, but Matthias knew that he could do it. All of his life he had prepared for his one moment, and he would not fail.

That is the way it is with us. Some of us feel that we will never be chosen first. It is always someone else. Sometimes we even feel that God has forgotten about people like you and me, but he hasn't. There is a time when God will need you, and he will choose what that time will be. But stick around and do what is asked, even if it means to help others do the big job. Some day your chance will come, just as it did for Matthias. They you will be glad that you waited.

Matthias was a second choice but what a choice it was. Matthias was a disciple of Jesus. He was second choice but he was glad he waited.

Happy Birthday, Church!

Acts 2:1-13

And suddenly from heaven there came a sound like the rush of a violent wind, and it filled all the house where they were sitting. (v. 2)

Object: a big electric fan, with the sound increased by use of a microphone (if a fan is not available, then let the children make the noise themselves)

Good morning, boys and girls. Today I want to tell you about Pentecost, which is the birthday of the Church. The Christian Church was born on Pentecost Day. How many of you know when you were born? (*let them answer*) Everyone knows his or her birthday, and today is the birthday of the Church. Let's say, "Happy Birthday," to the Church. (*lead them in saying, "Happy Birthday"*)

Pentecost is a great church holiday. On Pentecost we remember the very first day that the Church had life. It was a day like this. Everything was kind of quiet. The disciples of Jesus were together in an upstairs room when all of a sudden they heard a sound, a loud sound. (*turn on the fan*) It sounded like something they had heard before only louder than anything that they had experienced.

What does that noise sound like to you? (*let them answer*) It sounds like a wind, a big wind, bigger than any wind they had ever heard before. Whenever something like that happens to some people, it scares them. But when the disciples ran out of the house, it wasn't because they were afraid. It was because God's Spirit came upon them.

At that time of the year there were a lot of people in Jerusalem who came from other countries. You can tell when people come from other countries because they may dress a little differently and speak differently. Have you ever heard someone speak another language? (*let them answer*) You can't understand them, can you? (*let them answer*) Usually you can't. But on this day, as everyone was speaking his own language, God worked a wonderful miracle. As Peter preached his special sermon, everyone understood him. Peter told everyone about Jesus and the wonderful things that he had done. He told people about how Jesus taught us of God's love, died for our sins, and rose from the grave.

The people were just wild about the things that Peter said that day. Thousands of them decided to follow Jesus. They were baptized that day and made members of Christ's Church. That is why we call this the birthday of the Church. All of God's promises came true that day because the Spirit of God came to live with us. Pentecost is a day that all of us remember and the Church celebrates it today.

Let's all say this together. "God bless the Father." (*have them repeat it*) "God bless the Son." (*have them repeat it*) "God bless the Holy Spirit." (*have them repeat it*) "And God bless the Church." (*repeat it*) "Happy Birthday, Church."

Bringing People To God

Acts 3:1-16

"The God of Abraham, the God of Isaac, and the God of Jacob, the God of our ancestors has glorified his servant Jesus, whom you handed over and rejected in the presence of Pilate, though he had decided to release him." (v. 13)

Object: a digital camera and things that go together: letters, numbers, salt and pepper shakers

Good morning, boys and girls. Today is a wonderful day. I love Sunday mornings when we all get together and share our happiness with one another. How many of you are happy people? (*let them answer*) Good!

One of the things I like best about Sunday morning is knowing that we all belong together. I have asked our friend (*a member of the congregation*) to take our picture this morning. Afterwards, I will have it printed and I will give you a copy next week.

There are other things that go together. For instance, I brought with me today a salt shaker. What goes with salt? (*let them answer*) Pepper! Suppose I said the letters A, B, __. What would you say is next? (*let them answer*) Very good! The letter C is next.

If I counted 1, 2, 3, 4, 5, 6, 7, 8, 9, then what would you say is the next number? (*let them answer*) Super, the number is 10! We know that certain things go together.

The reason that I asked for your help with this is because Peter, the disciple of Jesus, met with a lot of people who either did not know or believe in Jesus. These men believed in God but they were part of the old church. They only knew about things from before the time Jesus lived in this world. Peter had to teach them, and when he did, he used names that they had heard many times before.

Jesus talked about Abraham. They already knew of God's promise to make a great nation of Abraham's descendents if Abraham would only leave his home and start a new life in a strange land. Abraham, even though he was older than your Grandpa, followed God and was the great leader of a great family. Peter also talked about Isaac, Abraham's son, and how he was so obedient to God that he became a great leader. Finally, in this message, Peter mentioned Jacob, the son of Isaac, who wrestled with an angel and received God's blessing. Abraham, Isaac, and Jacob were all great heroes of the faith and all were well known to the Jews. It was like mentioning A, B, C, or salt and pepper, or 1, 2, 3, 4, 5, 6, 7, 8, 9, 10.

Then Peter told them that if they liked the ancestors of Jesus, they would really like Jesus, too. Abraham, Isaac, and Jacob were great heroes but Jesus was the Savior. Jesus died for them that they might be joined to God. Peter knew what went together. Many of the people he talked to that day asked to learn more about Jesus and then became followers of Jesus.

The next time you hear someone say A, B, C, or the numbers 1 through 10, or even mention the words "salt and pepper," then you will remember how Peter brought men and women to Jesus by bringing all of God's people together.

Healing The Lame Man

Acts 4:1-23

"But to keep it from spreading further among the people, let us warn them to speak no more to anyone in this name." (v. 17)

Object: a glass of water, a flat surface, and a sponge to mop it up

Good morning, boys and girls. Have you ever tried to keep a secret? (*let them answer*) It's pretty hard, isn't it? (*let them answer*) If the secret is about something good, it is really hard to tell no one. How many of you know a secret about something really good? (*let them answer*) Would you like to share it with the rest of us? (*let them answer*)

Did I tell you about the man who was carried by friends to the temple in Jerusalem every day for many years? They would bring him to a special place by a certain gate where he would sit all day long and beg for gifts of money. When people passed by, they would give him some money. When Peter and John came to the temple, they probably saw him, too.

One day Peter and John heard the lame man begging for help, and Peter said to him, "Look at us." The man looked up at Peter and John expecting money. Instead, Peter said to the lame man, "I have no gold or silver, but what I have I give you; in the name of Jesus Christ of Nazareth, stand up and walk." Peter reached down and helped the man to his feet.

Imagine, he had never walked in his life and he was forty years old. But he could walk! He could jump! He could leap! He was so happy that he ran into the temple with Peter and told everyone about how good he felt. The people recognized him because they had passed him for years sitting at that certain gate to the temple. They were amazed! Everyone ran excitedly toward Peter and said wonderful things. But Peter said it was not his power that made the man well. It was the power of Jesus.

But not everyone was happy. There were some men who thought that this talk about Jesus was working against them. People were following new leaders instead of them. Peter was telling the people to believe in the power of Jesus. The leaders of the temple were trying to keep people from learning about Jesus. They commanded Peter and John not to speak about Jesus. But Peter and John told them that they were filled with God's joy and love and could never stop talking about Jesus. The old leaders threatened Peter and John, but it did no good.

Let me show you what I mean. Pretend that this glass of water is filled with the love and joy of Jesus. When I pour some of this water out of the glass onto this table, what do you think is going to happen? (*let them answer*) Let's see what happens. (*pour the water on the table; then tell the water not to spread but to stay there in one place*) What is happening? (*let them answer*) That's right; it is spreading. It is going everywhere, isn't it?

That is what happened with the good news of God's healing the lame man. No one could stop talking about the power of Jesus and his work through Peter and John. The same thing is true today for us. If we are excited about the good news of Jesus, we can't keep from spreading it everywhere.

Advice From Gamaliel

Acts 5:17-42

"So in the present case, I tell you, keep away from these men and let them alone; because if this plan or this undertaking is of human origin, it will fail...." (v. 38)

Object: a bent nail with a hammer and board, wet matches, and a balloon with a hole in it

Good morning, boys and girls. Have you ever tried to do something that you know isn't going to work before you even try it? (*let them answer*) If I asked you to jump up and sit on my shoulders while I was standing here, how many of you think you could do it? (*if someone wants to try, let him/her try*) See, I knew it wasn't going to happen even if you tried.

Or let me show you this. Suppose I asked you to drive this bent nail into this board, do you think you could do it? (*let someone try if they want to try*) It is almost impossible to drive a bent nail into a board. You have the same chance of driving that nail that you do trying to make fire with wet matches. Wet matches will not work. You must wait until they dry and that will take some time. It just doesn't work. If you really want to try something that will not work, try to blow up this balloon with a hole in it. (*let someone try to blow up the balloon*) There are some things that just don't work and we don't even try.

The reason I tell you this is that was the advice that Gamaliel, a very brilliant person and leader of the Jews, told many of his friends when they discussed Jesus and his followers. The friends of Gamaliel wanted to kill the followers of Jesus. They wanted to hang, stab, stone, and crucify people like Peter and John and the other disciples. They wanted to get rid of them because people were excited about their teaching of Jesus. It was like Jesus was there even after they crucified and buried him. They did not want to believe that Jesus had been raised from the dead and returned to heaven with the Father. They didn't want to believe that the Holy Spirit was working in the lives of Peter and John. But Gamaliel saw what was happening, and he knew a little about the way God worked.

Here is what he told them. Gamaliel said if the things that Peter and John were doing were not from God they would last about as long as a bent nail, or wet matches, or a balloon with a hole in it. If it were some trick or fancy talk, it would die quickly and fade away.

But Gamaliel said, "If it is of God, you will not be able to overthrow them — in that case you may even be found fighting against God!" Does anyone want to fight God?

Would you like to be in a fight with God? (*let them answer*) I didn't think so. Fighting God is more like hammering a bent nail, trying to strike a wet match, or blowing up a balloon with a hole in it than anything I know.

The people listened to Gamaliel and turned the disciples loose. Peter and John and all of the disciples went out and taught the love of Jesus, and thousands of people became followers of Jesus, just like the disciples were.

God's Good Worker

Acts 6:8-15; 7:1-2a, 51-60

While they were stoning Stephen, he prayed, "Lord Jesus, receive my spirit." (v. 59)

Object: some big stones

Good morning, boys and girls. How many of you know something about stones? (*let them answer*) Where do you find stones? (*let them answer*) What do you do with stones? (*let them answer*) There are houses built out of stone. I have seen people build fences of stone or used them in their gardens to make pretty flower beds. I have seen flat stones used to make a walk or a path. Some stones are really pretty and can be very useful. But this morning I am going to tell you a story that is not so pretty. It is the story about a man called Stephen who was a disciple of Jesus.

Stephen became a disciple when the church was just beginning. He worked hard in the church and a lot of people learned more about Jesus. He told everyone he knew about the love of God and the wonderful things that you could do after you began to follow the teachings of Jesus. All the other disciples of Jesus loved Stephen and thought he was a real man of God.

Some of the other people who were jealous of Jesus and his teachings just hated Stephen. They did not like the way he fed the people who were hungry and visited the lonely and sick people. They thought that Stephen made them look bad. And they were right. Stephen did make the jealous people look bad, when he did the kind of jobs that they were supposed to do but never did. These people hated Christians, but they especially hated people like Stephen who were leaders in the Christian church.

One day, when they thought they could not stand it any longer, they started arguing with Stephen while he was telling people the good stories of Jesus. Soon they became very angry and started to yell curses at him. Stephen never raised his voice. He even forgave them for what they were doing. But the jealous men could stand it no longer, and they threw Stephen to the ground. Even while Stephen was on the ground, he looked at the men with love because he knew what was going to happen next. Then Stephen looked up to heaven and prayed to God for the forgiveness of those who were standing over him with angry faces.

Soon the faces began to move as they raised their hands and began throwing big stones at Stephen. One stone after the other hit Stephen as he prayed to God and looked toward heaven. Stephen knew he was going to die from being hit with the stones, but he also knew that soon he would be with Jesus and his heavenly Father.

The Bible teaches us that Stephen was the first man to die for believing in Jesus and his love. Because of that, and what Stephen taught us, we honor him today as a great Christian and church leader. I hope that when you look at the next stone you see, you will remember Stephen and how much he loved God.

Open Ears

Acts 7:55-60

But they covered their ears, and with a loud shout all rushed together against him. Then they dragged him out of the city and began to stone him. (vv. 57-58a)

Object: some ear muffs, cotton, ear plugs

Good morning, boys and girls. Have your parents ever accused you of being deaf? I mean, does your mother or dad ever say something to you and you pretend not to hear what they say? (*let them answer*) I brought along a couple of things to show you how you can keep from hearing what you don't want to hear.

I suppose the least effective way is to wear ear muffs. (*put a pair of ear muffs over your ears*) When you have these on and they fit well, it keeps some of the sound out. Whatever someone says is harder to hear with ear muffs on than it is without them. But a lot of sound still gets in, and if you want to keep all the sound out you have to try something else.

The second thing I have is some cotton. That's better than ear muffs. When you have cotton in your ears, it's hard to hear what someone is saying. (*have the children talk and show them that this makes it harder to hear when they speak softly*)

The last item that I brought with me is a pair of ear plugs. I know that a lot of you have worn these when you have gone swimming. You can almost shout, and it sounds like you are far away. It is hard for you to understand what other people are saying when you have ear plugs in your ears.

But why do people do things like this? Why don't they want to hear certain things?

I can tell you a story about a man called Stephen who was one of the early followers of Jesus. He was one of the most devoted disciples. He preached and preached about the love of God and what Jesus had done for everyone. He also told the people about all the ugly things that they were doing, and he asked them to change. There were some people who could not stand to hear about the way they were or about the goodness of Jesus. Do you know what they did? They put their hands over their ears and started screaming and yelling so that they could not hear anything that Stephen said. Try it. Put your hands over your ears and yell and see if you can hear anything that I say. You can't, can you? That's what the people did, and after they could not hear Stephen they took him out and killed him. Stephen was the first man who died for Jesus. We call him a martyr. Stephen was the first Christian martyr.

It may be hard to listen to everything that is said, but closing your ears with cotton, ear plugs, or even your hands is the wrong thing to do. Listen to what is said and try to understand why someone is saying it, and you will be better for it. Only cowards try to shut out the world and the love that God tries to share with all of us.

Will you all keep your ears open and listen? (*let them answer*) That's wonderful.

The Man From Ethiopia

Acts 8:26-40

He replied, "How can I, unless someone guides me?" And he invited Philip to get in and sit beside him. (v. 31)

Object: a shoe without shoelaces and some shoelaces, a screwdriver and a screw, a coloring book and crayons

Good morning, boys and girls. Let's take a good look at some of the things I brought with me today. Who would like to name all of the things I brought with me? (*select a volunteer to name each one; do not hold up the things that go together in sequence, instead hold up some shoe laces, then the screw, then the coloring book, then a shoe, then the screw driver and finally the crayons*) Now, I am going to pretend you do not know very much about these things. You are seeing them for the first time.

The reason I am telling you this is that I want to make things right. That is why I am going to tie up my coloring book with these strings. (*begin to tie up the coloring book*) Then it looks to me as if this is something to use to carry something in, so I am going to put this tool into the shoe. (*put the screwdriver into the shoe*) Finally I think I will put these two round things together. (*start to put the screw into the crayon*) There is that the way these things should be used? (*let them answer*) Do you know a different way to put these things together? (*let them answer*) Okay, this is much better. The screwdriver goes with the screw, the crayons with the coloring book, and the shoelaces with the shoe. That works much better, but it takes someone who knows how things work to know all of this.

This reminds me of a story in the Bible. It was about the disciple Philip and a man who worked for a queen. One day the official for the queen was riding in his chariot and he was reading the scriptures. An angel of God said to Philip, "There is an important person riding in a chariot down the road from you. Get up and go meet him." So Philip did what the angel asked him and ran down the road. When he saw the important man coming, he noticed that the man was reading the scriptures. Philip asked the man in the chariot if he understood what he was reading in the scriptures. The man said of course not, since he did not have anyone to guide him or teach him what the scriptures said. The important man noticed that Philip seemed to be familiar with the scriptures, so he invited Philip to teach him. Philip jumped into the chariot and, in a way that the official really understood, Philip began to teach him what the scriptures said. Soon they began to talk about Jesus and how important it was to be baptized. When they passed by a river, the official asked Philip to baptize him.

Philip knew about Jesus and loved him. He wanted to share his love for Jesus with everyone he met. That's how he was able to help the queen's official. He knew the scriptures and how to explain them.

That is why it is important for you to come to Sunday school, read your Bible, and stay in touch with the Spirit of God. Then you will be like Philip and share the love of Jesus.

Fighting Fear

Acts 9:13-14

But Ananias answered, "Lord, I have heard from many about this man, how much evil he has done to your saints in Jerusalem; and here he has authority from the chief priests to bind all who invoke your name." (vv. 13-14)

Object: none

Good morning, boys and girls. Have you ever had to do something that made you afraid just to think about it? (*let them answer*) Maybe your teacher or the principal of the school asked you to stay after school and you were afraid because you didn't know why he wanted to see you.

Or do you know a big bully? (*let them answer*) A big bully is someone who likes to pick on people who are smaller and not as strong as he is. Those kinds of people can make us afraid when we just think about them.

There was a man by the name of Ananias who had a problem with fear. He was a Christian who lived in a town called Damascus. He had not been a Christian very long, but then no one had in those early days. One day he had a vision. A vision is like a dream only you have it while you are awake. In his vision the Lord spoke to Ananias. The Lord said, "Go over to Straight Street and find the house of a man named Judas and ask there for Paul of Tarsus. He is praying to me right now, for I have shown him a vision of a man named Ananias coming in and laying his hands on him so that he can see again!"

Ananias was petrified with fear. Paul of Tarsus was the man who was hunting Christians and killing them. He had the government and all of the religious leaders behind him, and they were looking for Christians everywhere and killing them. The very name of Paul of Tarsus made Christians tremble. Ananias tried to argue with the Lord, but the voice of the Lord told him to go to a certain house on a certain street where Paul was expecting him.

What can you do when you hear the voice of God speaking to you? You do as you are told. Ananias went to the house, and there he found Paul lying on a bed. Paul was blind. Paul had been blinded by a very bright light on the way to Damascus, and he had also heard the voice of Jesus speak to him. When Ananias reached Paul's bed, he was no longer afraid. Something had replaced his fear. He reached out and touched Paul with his hands and said, "Brother Paul, the Lord Jesus, who appeared to you on the road, has sent me so that you may be filled with the Holy Spirit and get your sight back."

An amazing thing happened. Paul was able to see instantly. He praised God and thanked Ananias over and over again for coming to see him. Then Paul made Ananias promise to baptize him a Christian. Now Ananias began to think of all of the things that he had heard about Paul. He remembered that this was the man who had been present for the killing of Stephen. He was the man who had caught hundreds of other Christians and made them suffer, and he had now come to the town of Damascus to make Christians suffer and kill them. When Paul could not see he looked so helpless, but now that he could see and move around again, it seemed a little different.

But Ananias remembered something else. The Lord had told him that Paul was going to be the person to teach the Gentiles. There were a lot of Christians who used to be Jews, but there were very few, if any, who had been Gentiles. God must have thought that Paul was something really special. What else could Ananias do but baptize Paul? He did it, and he was glad.

During the next couple of days Paul told other Christians who were friends of Ananias all that had happened to him. He went to the synagogue and preached and told the good news about Jesus and how Jesus was the Son of God. The Jews in the synagogue began to argue with Paul, but he was able to convince many to do as he had done, and they also became Christians. But there were many who did not believe, and they began to make plans to get rid of Paul. When the Christian friends of Paul heard about what was happening, they protected him and hid him. Then one night they put him in a large basket, and when no one was looking they lowered him over the city wall to freedom.

Those were the very first days of Paul's Christian life. Paul would go on to great things, and we will be hearing about him forever. But we should not forget about the man Ananias who had to fight his fears to do what God had commanded him to do.

The next time you find that you are afraid of something that is going to happen or that may happen, I want you to think about the man called Ananias who went to Paul, healed his blindness, and baptized him a Christian.

God Is Fair

Acts 10:34-38

Then Peter began to speak to them: "I truly understand that God shows no partiality." (v. 34)

Object: a referee's shirt and whistle

Good morning, boys and girls. Do you like to make other people happy? (*let them answer*) Here are some ways to do that. Every night you are going to do your homework, pay attention to what your teachers tell you, come to church every Sunday, help your parents with the dishes, and keep your room clean. If you do all those things you will make a lot of people happy. How many of you have decided to make other people happy? (*let them answer*) That's great.

Do you like people to treat you fairly? (*let them answer*) What do you think it means when you say, "Treat people fairly"? (*let them answer*) Most of us think that being fair means to treat everyone the same. How many of you think that God is fair? (*let them answer*) All of you think that God is fair.

I have a shirt and a whistle this morning that I hope you know something about. (*show them the shirt*) What do we call this kind of a shirt? Who wears it? (*let them answer*) That's right; a referee. What does a referee do? (*let them answer*) He makes sure that the game is played fairly. Does he have a favorite team? (*let them answer*) Does he root for one team against another? (*let them answer*) No! He'd better not. If he is a good referee, he does not have a favorite team, and he is fair to whoever is playing the game. The referee shows no partiality. That is a big word but an important one. Can you say it with me? Partiality.

The Bible teaches us that God shows no partiality. God is always fair. God treats you and all of your friends the same. God does not have favorites. He doesn't like you better than he likes others. God is the best referee in the whole world.

Peter found this out one day when he was thinking about God, and he told everyone that he knew about it. Some people used to think that they were special to God because they lived in a certain place or had a special father and mother. Peter said no, that isn't right. God treats all people the same and loves everyone and not some people more than other people.

The next time you go to a game or watch one on television and you see a referee with this kind of a shirt on and blowing his whistle you can think about how God is fair to all and loves everyone the same. That is something for us all to remember.

154

God's Hero

Acts 11:27—12:3a

He had James, the brother of John, killed with the sword. (v. 2)

Object: a sword

Good morning, boys and girls. I suppose that all of you know that not everything that happens in the world is good. Sometimes people do some very bad things to themselves and to others. Today I am going to tell you about one of those things so that you will learn how strongly some men and women believe in Jesus. Jesus is so important to many people that they are willing to die at earlier ages, so that people will not forget that Jesus is a loving God.

James was one of the disciples of Jesus, and the brother of another disciple called John. James and John had been teaching about Jesus for a couple of years to a lot of people. Many of the people who heard them speak believed that what they said was true, and they became followers of Jesus. There was nothing that made James so happy as when someone, who had never before believed that Jesus was the Son of God, became a follower and shared in God's love.

James taught here and there, and then one day, while James was with some of the people in the church, the king of Judea became very angry about the good things that people were saying about the disciples and Jesus, and he decided that he would put a stop to it. He did not like people talking about Jesus as a great king, and as the one who gave everything that people needed. The king thought that he should be the only one that people spoke about, so he sent his soldiers out to get the followers of Jesus.

One of the first ones they found was James. They did not just arrest him, but instead they took out their swords and killed him in front of all of the other people who were watching. The soldiers thought that this would be a good lesson. The soldiers knew how afraid the people were of swords, and they thought that everyone else would be just as afraid.

When James died with that sword through him, he did so still loving Jesus and forgiving the men who killed him. The soldiers could not believe it, but that is the way the followers of Jesus acted. There was no way that a follower could be frightened by a sword. They knew that when they died, no matter how they died, that Jesus would be there to welcome them into the same kingdom that he went to when he died.

No sword could stop people from being followers of Jesus. Herod learned that, and so had everyone else who tried to stop people from being Christians. Many Christians died as heroes as they tried to teach the truth about Jesus.

Maybe the next time that you see a sword, you will remember the day that James died and how he taught others about the way that he believed in Jesus.

Sticking Up For God

Acts 13:8

But the magician Elymas (for that is the translation of his name) opposed them and tried to turn the proconsul away from the faith. (v. 8)

Object: none

Good morning, boys and girls. Have you ever been tricked? (*let them answer*) When someone makes you believe that you can have something for nothing, and you agree to try it his way and end up losing everything, you have been tricked. Some people have some very good tricks. People who like to trick other people also like to have very powerful friends so that if something goes wrong, the powerful people will protect them.

It happened this way a long time ago to Paul and his friend Barnabas. There was a man called Bar Jesus who was a sorcerer. A sorcerer is someone who believes he can tell the future, and he practices magic. They were fun for rich and powerful people to have around. They always told the rich and the powerful people things that they wanted to hear about themselves. Bar Jesus was that kind of sorcerer to the governor of an island called Paphos. The governor's name was Sergius Paulus. Sergius Paulus was a different kind of man from most people because, besides liking fun and funny people, he also liked to hear the truth.

One day Governor Paulus heard about Paul and Barnabas, and he asked them to come and speak to him about their God. Paul could hardly wait to have the chance to preach and teach a governor about Jesus. But when they arrived at the palace the sorcerer Bar Jesus began to complain to the governor about Paul and told him to pay no attention or evil things would happen to the governor. He kept it up and kept it up so that the governor had to listen to what he said. Bar Jesus knew that if the governor began to believe what Paul said and trusted in the Lord, then there would be no place for a trickster like him. He had to stop Paul in some way with some kind of a lie.

There was no time to sit and argue with a man like Bar Jesus. Paul stood up and looked Bar Jesus in the eyes and told him that he was a son of the devil, full of every trick that the devil could teach, and that he was going against the goodness of God no matter what anyone said. With that, Paul told him that he was going to be punished by God and made blind for a short period of time.

Almost immediately Bar Jesus saw only grey and then black and finally he saw nothing at all. He was blind. The governor was stunned. He could not believe such power. This was a man of God, a man of a very powerful God, and the governor wanted to know more about someone as powerful as this. Paul took the time to teach this governor all that he could about the life of Jesus and how he had come into this world to save people from their sins. Sergius Paulus, the governor of Paphos, believed what he was taught and he became a disciple of Christ.

It was not easy for Paul to ask God to make Bar Jesus blind, but then those were not easy times. There were a lot of people who were trying to stop Paul in his ministry of teaching about Jesus. There are a lot of people like that today. They know that if people learn about God, some of their bad places will not be visited. They know that people will not read some of their bad books, and they will not buy some things that can be used to harm others. When Christians meet people who teach or sell bad things, they have to do something about it. They either have to pretend that they do not see the bad things or they have to speak out against the bad things.

Speaking out is not easy to do. It takes courage and faith that God is on your side and ready to protect you. Paul knew that he was right and that the man who spoke against God had to be told to be quiet. There are a lot of people who speak against God or say he doesn't count or that he will hurt people if they follow him. Paul could not let those kinds of lies go on. Christians love their God and they want everyone to know about him and believe in him. It may take a lot of courage the first time to stand up and speak for God against people who are trying to trick other people into believing in them, but if you try, God will be on your side. We need Christians who think that God is always right and that he is right because he loves us and does what is right for us.

The next time you hear or see someone who is trying to keep people from believing in God by trying to get them to do something that is wrong, I hope you will remember what Paul did. Stick up for God and tell everyone about the way that God loves them.

How To Settle An Argument

Acts 15:22a

Then the apostles and elders, with the whole congregation, decided to choose men from among their members and send them to Antioch with Paul and Barnabas. (v. 22a)

Object: none

Good morning, boys and girls. Have you ever had an argument with someone and you knew that you were right and the other person was wrong? (*let them answer*) The big problem is that the people you are arguing with believe that they do right and you are wrong. That's trouble. What do you do when things like that happen? Do you get angry and fight, or do you just leave and never see that person again? Some people do it one way and some people do it another way. I even know some who do it both ways.

Paul had a problem like this. He knew that he had to do something about it before it was too late. The whole idea of the church being for all people depended on Paul's winning his argument with some very powerful people. Let me tell you a little bit about it.

Paul lived in Antioch with his friend, Barnabas, where they taught men and women who were not Jews about Jesus, the Son of God. These people were called Gentiles. They had never learned the law as Moses received it from God, nor had they ever been made a part of the Jewish religion by a very unusual ceremony. This ceremony was called circumcision. All Jewish baby boys were circumcised. Gentile boys were not circumcised and most of them had never heard about it. Jews said that anyone who was a follower of the one God had to be circumcised. That meant that they had to have a special part of their body cut in a certain way. The Jews didn't think that only little boys should have this done, but also grown-up men who wished to become followers. That was the argument. The Jews said that every man who wanted to be a follower of Jesus had to be first circumcised and be a follower of Moses before he could be a disciple of Jesus.

Paul said that this wasn't true. He had been a Jew and it did not make him a better Christian. It wasn't being circumcised that mattered, but it was believing in your heart that Jesus died for your sins. They argued and argued. First one side would make a point, and then the other side would make a point. Finally it was suggested that they would have to let someone else settle the argument. That sounded like the fair way to do it if everyone would agree. The Jews agreed and Paul and the Gentiles agreed. Now the question was where should they go? Everyone knew the answer to that in those days. They should go to Jerusalem where some of the apostles of Jesus still lived and did their teaching.

Paul, Barnabas, and some people from the Jewish side went to meet with Peter and James, the brother of Jesus, to tell their side of the story. You must remember that Peter and James had been raised as Jews and they were circumcised. It started out to be a battle just as it had been in Antioch. Some of the men stood up right away and said that every man who

158

was going to be a follower of Jesus must first do the things that all Jews had to do. They sounded like they meant it.

But Peter stood up and told his story about how God had done away with all of those laws when he sent the Holy Spirit to bless them and baptize them in love. Christians did things because they wanted to do them, and not because a law said they had to. Peter told them how hard it had been for the Jews to believe since they had so many laws to keep. Why should a Gentile first become a Jew before he could become a Christian? It was the same Holy Spirit that blessed both the Jew and the Gentile. That was a good point.

Now Paul and Barnabas felt they should tell the Jews about the wonderful things that were happening to the Gentiles and how they loved Jesus. That seemed to do it. James, the brother of Jesus, stood up and said that he knew it was right for Gentiles to be Christians without circumcision. The only thing that he asked was that they did not worship idols, eat meat that was not prepared properly, and that they should have respect for their bodies and the bodies of all people. Everyone agreed to this, and the people congratulated Paul and Barnabas and sent them back home with a letter telling the people of Antioch how much they agreed with them and their leaders, Barnabas and Paul. They even sent a couple of men from Jerusalem to read the letter and live with the Gentiles for a while to show them that they meant it.

It was the end to an argument, and it was a good ending. They settled the problem by talking it out and reaching an agreement. Both sides could have insisted that the other side agree with them, or they could have gone right on fighting with each other. But instead they settled the argument and lived together in fellowship the way that Jesus wanted them to.

Teaching Trust

Acts 16:28

But Paul shouted in a loud voice, "Do not harm yourself, for we are all here." (v. 28)

Object: none

Good morning, boys and girls. Did you ever hope that someone would trust you no matter what happened? (*let them answer*) I think that this is the best kind of friendship. When people trust each other they are the best kind of people. There is a great story about trust in the Bible concerning Paul and some of his friends.

It all started when a woman who was a slave to some evil men followed Paul around a town called Philippi, making fun of Paul's preaching. As you might guess, Paul was very serious about teaching others to love and follow Jesus. Having this woman, who was a fortune teller, laugh about it did not make Paul happy. Paul knew that there must be something evil in her to make fun of Jesus, so one day when he had just about enough, he commanded the evil spirit to come out of her and go away. It happened so fast that no one knew it. One minute she was making fun of Paul, and the next minute she was not.

Her masters who owned her were furious. They had made a lot of money with this woman telling fortunes to travelers and strangers, and now she would never do it again.

These men who hated good men like Paul grabbed him and took him to the center of town where they asked the judges to find him guilty of teaching people to act against the Roman law. But that was just a game. They did not want a court trial. They wanted Paul killed. They got some rough men together and told the judges to have Paul beaten. Again and again Paul was beaten with sticks and poles until his back was covered with blood. But Paul would not die, and when the crowd grew tired of whipping him, the judges ordered him thrown into prison. As they were carrying Paul down the steps into the dungeon, the judges told the jailor that he had better not let Paul escape or he would be put to death in place of Paul. That kind of a threat is enough to scare anyone.

During the night, the Philippian jailor heard some strange sounds coming from behind the doors of Paul's cell. Instead of crying or asking for help, he heard Paul praying and singing songs of love to God. Not only was he listening, but he could tell that all of the other prisoners were listening as well.

And then it happened. Without any warning, there was a loud crash and the whole prison trembled. It was an earthquake, and everything seemed to be falling and jumping and shaking at the same time. All of the doors to the prison opened and all of the chains that held the prisoners came loose. The Philippian jailor took one look, and he thought everyone had escaped. That meant that Paul had left and that the jailor would have to die for allowing their escape. It was no use to live a moment longer. Just as he was ready to push his own sword into his body and kill himself, he heard a voice that said, "Don't do it! We are all here!"

160

The jailor could hardly believe his eyes and ears. The prisoners were there. Even though they could have escaped and run away, they did not. Paul did not want anyone to die for him except the Lord Jesus. He wanted people to trust him for what he taught and preached. That is why he stayed and asked the others to stay as well. The jailor was so happy that he could hardly believe it. All he wanted to know was what could he do to be like Paul? Paul told him to believe in Jesus Christ. He would be saved and so would all of his family. The Philippian jailor loved Paul and all of his friends. He invited them to his house where he washed Paul's wounds and fed him from his table.

Paul was right. The jailor did feel like a new man and so did all of his family. It was wonderful to have someone like Paul trust you and someone for you to trust.

Paul didn't teach trust with words. He taught trust with his actions. He could have run away and saved his skin for a day or so, but then what would happen? It would only mean being arrested by somebody else. Paul knew if he stayed, he would show at least the jailor that he could be trusted. Trust was too important to Paul. He knew that if he could get people to trust him. Then they would also trust his God. That is why Paul did it. He loved his God and trusted his God and he wanted other people to trust God as he did.

That is something that all of us have to learn. If we want people to believe in God as we do, then we must show them that we can be trusted as their friends. We must be ready to help them when they are in trouble, just the way we do when everything is going well. Trust is something that we learn, and it is something that we can teach to others.

What Is God Made Of?

Acts 17:29

"Since we are God's offspring, we ought not to think that the deity is like gold, or silver, or stone, an image formed by the art and imagination of mortals." (v. 29)

Object: a picture of a marble or bronze statue depicting a god, a rock, a rabbit's foot, a four leaf clover, or a lucky penny

Good morning, boys and girls. Today we have an especially difficult question for you and for everybody. We want to know what God is made of, and that is especially hard since no one has ever felt God. For instance, if I could tell you that God felt like steel or fur or mud, you would know what kind of material God is made of.

A long time ago, boys and girls, people thought that their gods were made of things like this statue I have here. (*show them the picture of the statue*) Do you know what I mean? People thought that this statue made of marble was a god. They put the statue on a shelf and everybody thought that their house was protected from any kind of evil spirits.

A really long time ago, there were people who believed that their god lived in a rock like this (*show the rock*) or in a tree or in a very fast running river. That's what people used to think.

Today some people have other kinds of gods, although they don't call them gods. Some people have to have something that they can feel.

Let me show you what I mean. Have you ever seen someone carry one of these? (*hold up a four leaf clover or a rabbit's foot*) What is it? (*let them answer*) That's right; a rabbit's foot. People think if they rub that rabbit's foot nothing will happen to them and that everything will be all right. They trust the rabbit's foot (or a four leaf clover). Or some people carry a lucky penny in their pocket and rub it whenever they need something to happen.

People like to feel their god and know what he is made of, but our God tells us that he is a spirit, something that you cannot see or touch or smell or feel. He is different than anything else that we know. And that is one of the reasons that he is God. There is nothing else like him in the whole world. He does not like us to make other things and call them god. When people trust in pennies or rocks or gold or anything else, then God gets very angry.

What is a spirit? That's a good question. You know that God is near and he speaks to you in prayer, but you can't reach out and touch him, nor can you hear him.

Do you remember what it's like when you go away from home and you get lonely and wish that your mother was very near, but you can't go and find her? When you think about her, it makes you feel better all over. In a way, that is a spirit. Even though you can't feel or see or hear her, you still know that she loves you and will be there when you get home.

God is a spirit and while we don't know what he is made of, we do know that the Bible teaches that he is not made of anything like rocks or pennies. God is a spirit.

162

Working Together

Acts 18:1-3

After this, Paul left Athens and went to Corinth. There he found a Jew named Aquila, a native of Pontus, who had recently come from Italy with his wife Priscilla, because Claudius had ordered all Jews to leave Rome. Paul went to see them, and they worked together — by trade as they were tentmakers. (vv. 1-3)

Object: none

Good morning, boys and girls. Has anyone ever told you that one of the best ways to learn about another person is to work with him? (*let them answer*) If no one has ever told you that, I want you to know that it is true. It is the same as playing together. Sometimes you may see someone who really looks good to you, but you find that he is hard to get along with when you play together. Sometimes you meet someone who looks just awful to you, but when you play with him you really get to know each other and you like him very much.

This was the situation with Paul. Paul had been living in the great city of Athens, teaching about Jesus when he found that it was time to move on to another place. That was the way a missionary had to live in the time of Paul. There were very few people who were missionaries, so those few had to move around often. Paul went to another Greek town by the name of Corinth.

Now Paul didn't have a salary, and he was not a rich man. He had to work for a living as well as teach about Jesus. That meant that Paul did something else besides preach. Paul was a tentmaker. He made tents for people to use as houses or for when they traveled and camped out under the stars. But Paul did not have his own business because he traveled from town to town. That meant that Paul usually worked for someone in the town he was living in while preaching.

On one such occasion he worked for some tentmakers by the name of Priscilla and Aquila. Priscilla and her husband Aquila had been told to leave Rome because they were Jewish. The Emperor Caesar had commanded that all of the Jews to either leave Rome or be killed. Priscilla and Aquila moved to Corinth and set up their business of tentmaking.

It must have been a pretty good business because Priscilla and Aquila were busy enough to hire Paul when he came to town. When you work with someone, you get to know him, and that was the way it was with Paul and the people he worked for making tents. When Paul was not making tents, he was teaching about Jesus in the Jewish synagogue. Many of the Jews in Corinth listened to every word that he said, including Priscilla and Aquila. It was not too long before both Aquila and Priscilla became Christians.

It wasn't easy. Many of the Jews hated what Paul was teaching and they said so. Some of them went so far as to insult Paul and they even tried to hurt him. Paul soon found out that he could no longer live with Priscilla and Aquila for fear that they would be punished because he was working for them and living with them. Paul moved to another house and began to teach to the people who were not Jewish, the Gentiles. He taught them for as long as he could until the Jews became so angry over his teaching that they threatened to kill him. Finally Paul knew that it was time for him to move on to another town. But before he left, he said good-bye to all of the new Christians and urged them to stick together.

When Paul left for the country of Syria, he did not leave alone. As the people were waving good-bye to Paul, they saw another couple standing on the deck with him. That's right, it was Priscilla and Aquila who had given up their business to be missionaries with Paul. When you work with someone you get to know that person. If you like what you learn about the person, he or she becomes your friend for life. That is what happened to Paul and his tentmaking friends, Priscilla and Aquila. They were not only partners in business, but also friends in Christ.

You and I can learn a lot from playing and working together, but the most important thing that we can learn is to be close friends, and to share the Lord Jesus with each other.

Using The Name Of Jesus

Acts 19:13-14

Then some itinerant Jewish exorcists tried to use the name of the Lord Jesus over those who had evil spirits, saying, "I adjure you by Jesus, whom Paul proclaims." Seven sons of a Jewish priest named Sceva were doing this. (vv. 13-14)

Object: none

Good morning, boys and girls. Have you ever heard someone use the name of Jesus when it didn't sound right? (*let them answer*) I think that you know what I mean. People use it when they are angry at someone else or they hurt themselves and they shout the name of Jesus. We know that this is the wrong way to use the name of Jesus. There are other ways to use the name of Jesus. Some of them are right and there are some other ways that are wrong.

Paul had that kind of experience while he was in the town of Ephesus. He had lived there for almost two years when seven men whose father was a priest decided to use the name of Jesus. They were magicians who tried to make people believe in their power to change things as well as people. One thing that they liked to do best was to find someone who suffered from some kind of problem and convince the person with their magic that the problem was over. People were pleased by that kind of magic, and they paid well for it.

The seven sons of Sceva had heard about the way that Paul had healed people of their diseases and how he had prayed to God in the name of Jesus to do this. Now the seven sons of Sceva did not believe in God or Jesus as the Son of God, but they thought it was a powerful name and one that should be added to their list of names. That meant that they would walk around town and when they found someone in trouble they would use the name of Jesus as though it were magic. It made people who heard the preaching of Paul think that the seven sons of Sceva were doing the right things. Paul knew that they did not believe, and others knew that the sons of Sceva were not the kind of people Paul said a Christian would be. It was a real problem that haunted Paul and the other Christians.

One day two of the seven sons of Sceva came to a particular person who was very troubled. They decided that they should use a powerful name to get rid of the evil spirit that was in the man. They shouted, "I adjure you by Jesus, whom Paul preaches, to come out!" That meant that they were commanding the evil spirit to come out of the man in the name of Jesus. You can imagine how surprised they were when the evil spirit answered them by saying, "I know Jesus and I know Paul, but who are you?" With that the man jumped on the two sons of Sceva and gave them a terrible beating so that when they finally got away, they left without their clothes and their bodies were all scraped and bleeding.

The people in Ephesus were amazed. They did not know that the name of Jesus was so important. But they knew now. The name of Jesus was a holy name and you never use it unless you are praising God. The Bible goes on to tell us that many other magicians saw the power of Jesus that Paul preached about and came over and confessed their sins and burned their magic books and became Christians. But it was not only the magicians who learned something about the name of Jesus that day. Everyone in town found out that Jesus was someone very special.

That is something for us to remember today. People still play with Jesus' name as if it were magic rather than holy. They bring children to be baptized in the name of Jesus, but then they never bring the children to church. People are married and confirmed in the name of Jesus, but they never do much more than use his name. That is magic and it means nothing except an insult to Jesus. According to Paul, we are like the sons of Sceva when we use Jesus' name in that way. People should know better than to use it in this way, but they have never seemed to learn. In Ephesus it made a difference. The people there learned their lesson so that the only time they used the name of Jesus was to praise God and to ask or thank him for a blessing.

The next time you hear or use the name of Jesus, you can ask yourself if it is being used in the right way. If it is, then you can be sure that God will bless you or the person using it. But if it is not, then you will remember the story of the seven sons of Sceva.

Making Money On God

Acts 19:25b-26

"Men, you know that we get our wealth from this business. You also see and hear that not only in Ephesus but in almost the whole of Asia this Paul has persuaded and drawn away a considerable number of people by saying that gods made with hands are not gods." (vv. 25b-26)

Object: none

Good morning, boys and girls. Have you ever heard about people who sell religion? (*let them answer*) It is not the kind of thing that people like to talk about, but it is something that is done every day. I am going to tell you a story about two men who were involved in a big struggle over making money on God. The one man is our hero, Paul. Paul was a man who believed in God as Jesus had shown people to believe. God is a spirit, a loving spirit that is more real than anything else.

There was a man by the name of Demetrius who lived in Ephesus and was a silversmith. He was a great artist and a very rich one. He made statues of a false goddess called Diana. There were large temples in Ephesus built for the worshipers of Diana. But people were urged to have many copies of the big statue in their homes and their places of work. People like Demetrius, who were silversmiths, made their living by making these expensive statues of Diana.

There were not very many Christians in Ephesus, and there were a lot of people who followed the worship of Diana, but everyone seemed to be listening to what Paul said. People were not buying as many silver statues, and Demetrius began to worry about his business. He called the other silversmiths to come to a meeting where he told them about the serious situation that Paul was causing with his preaching of a God who was a spirit and not a statue. The other silversmiths listened. Demetrius told them if Paul were allowed to continue to preach, then someday no one would buy statues of Diana and that would mean that there would be no money for the families to buy food and clothing. Something had to be done. Besides, Demetrius said that if there were no statues then there would be no believers.

The town of Ephesus owed a lot to Diana and everyone should remember that she had been a great goddess for their town, Demetrius told them. The more he talked, the more the crowd of men got excited. Some of them did not even know Paul, but they hated him anyway. No one was going to ruin their business and hurt their families. No one was going to destroy their religion of Diana worship.

Before many knew what was happening, the people poured out of the meeting with shouts to kill the Christians. It was a mob that ran down the streets picking up and pulling out anyone who even looked like a Christian. Some of the people they picked up had only listened to Paul, and some of them were disciples of Jesus, but it made no difference to the mob. Paul wanted to go where they were holding his friends, but other Christians would not let him. They knew that he would be killed for sure if he entered the big arena where they were holding his friends. Inside there was nothing but shouting and confusion. "Great is Diana of the Ephesians! Great is Diana of the Ephesians!" they shouted.

It looked like the end for the Christians who were held prisoners. But then something quite unexpected happened. The mayor of Ephesus came to the front and stood on a platform. He told the people that none of the Christians had harmed anyone or that they had not stolen anything from the temple of Diana. If they had done something else that was wrong, they should be brought to court, but nothing should be done while the captors were so angry. The people listened and they thought about what the mayor had said. They agreed that he was right. The Christians were freed and told to go home. It was a very frightening experience and one that no one would soon forget. Paul spoke to his friends that night, and then left for Greece.

It is strange what happens to people when they are afraid that they are going to lose money. It changes them into a different kind of people. It still happens today. People try to make money on God and the things that they think people will buy as a god. We have to be careful today as Christians that we do not make something else our god instead of the real God whom Paul preached about.

The next time you hear or see something that is being sold as a reminder of God, you can think about Demetrius and the way he sold silver statues. Maybe they are not doing anything wrong and then maybe again they are helping people believe in a false god, and not the real God at all.

Sleeping In Church

Acts 20:8-9

There were many lamps in the room upstairs where we were meeting. A young man named Eutychus, who was sitting in the window, began to sink into a deep sleep while Paul talked still longer. Overcome by sleep, he fell to the ground three floors below and was picked up dead. (vv. 8-9)

Object: nodding — have the children practice nodding

Good morning, boys and girls. Have you ever fallen asleep in church while the pastor was preaching? (*let them answer*) I think almost everyone has done this at one time or another. Sometimes you are listening when all of a sudden your eyes just get heavier and heavier, and you fall asleep. Let's all pretend that we are getting sleepy. How does a sleepy person act? (*have the children close their eyes and begin to nod*) It doesn't only happen in church. Some people fall asleep while they are watching television or riding in a car. There is nothing wrong with it, but I suppose that it can be a little embarrassing.

Paul had it happen to one of his listeners. There was a young man by the name of Eutychus who came to a meeting in Troas, Turkey, with his parents.

Do you know anyone named Eutychus? (*let them answer*) No, it's not a common name today. But that's what this young man was named.

Anyway, it was a communion service that evening and Paul was rather new in the community. He began to preach, and the Bible says that he preached on and on. Poor Eutychus was sitting on the window sill and the window was open. Maybe he had crawled up there with the hope that the fresh air would keep him awake. Paul kept preaching, the room got warmer and warmer, and Eutychus' eyes got heavier and heavier. Before he knew what had happened, he fell out of the window and down three stories where he hit the ground so hard that he died! It all happened that fast. Someone must have seen him fall and screamed, but it was too late. Eutychus was dead from falling out of a window where he had fallen asleep listening to Paul preach.

Paul rushed out of the room and down the stairs where he found the dead man. But Paul did not panic. He told the people not to worry, because Eutychus would be all right. How could anyone believe that a dead person would be all right? Paul could, because he believed that God would answer his prayer and breathe new life back into Eutychus. While he was praying, Paul picked the young man up and, sure enough, Eutychus came back to life.

We have no idea how good Paul must have felt. You would think that this would end the service, but it didn't. The people followed Paul back up the stairs where they had the communion, and then Paul began to preach again. He preached the whole night about the wonders of God and his love. The Bible says that he preached all night and until the sun came up. That is quite a sermon. I don't know where Eutychus sat for the rest of the service, but I am pretty sure it was not in an open window.

169

This is a good story for young people who sometimes fall asleep in church. They get bored because they don't understand everything that is said, and sometimes it seems like the service is just for adults. But that is not a bad way for children to feel. Some things are for adults, just as some things are for children. Parents must listen to things that are for children, and children must learn to listen to things that are for adults.

Church can be fun. There are a lot of things that everyone can do. The music is beautiful, the stories in the Bible are exciting to listen to, and there is time to sing and pray out loud. If you fall asleep once in a while when the pastor is preaching a sermon, I know that he or she will not mind. As a matter of fact, the pastor will be glad that you are there and will also know that some day you will grow up and bring your children to church. They, too, will fall asleep while you listen. That is the way it is, and the way it always has been.

The next time you get a little drowsy and feel like you are going to fall asleep, just think about the young man named Eutychus and how he went to sleep in a service at which Paul preached. The important thing to remember is that you should never sit in an open window, but instead find a nice soft place on your father's or mother's lap, and then just gently go to sleep.

Chosen By God

Acts 21:27—22:29

Then he said, "The God of our ancestors has chosen you to know his will, to see the Righteous One and to hear his own voice; for you will be his witness to all the world of what you have seen and heard." (vv. 14-15)

Object: straws of different lengths for drawing straws; have more straws than children

Good morning, boys and girls. Are you ready for a wonderful day with God? (*let them answer*) Great! God is always with you, but we feel especially close to him in his house of prayer. We sing hymns of praise to God, we read his inspired word in the Bible, we have conversations with him in prayer, and we find forgiveness for our sins and blessings to remember. That is exciting. I love to come to church and join you in loving our God.

Today, I want to tell you that God has chosen each of you to be one of his disciples. Let me show you what I mean. I brought along some straws and I want each of you to choose the straw that you want. (*hold out the straws of different lengths and have each child draw one; remark about some of their choices*) That was a good choice. You chose a long straw. Do you like big things? And you drew a short straw. Short straws are kind of neat; they don't get in the way of other straws. Small things are often very important things. Let's see what you drew. Isn't that a nice straw? It is so round and has such a good feeling to it. I like really round straws. Let's look at one more straw. I like your straw; it is very easy to see from one end to the other. The passage is very clear. Keep it open. You made a very good choice.

All of your straws are a little different, but each one of you chose the one that you have. It was your choice, wasn't it? You chose the kind of straw that you wanted.

Did you know that God has chosen you? (*let them answer*) You have been chosen. The Bible teaches us that we are chosen people. God actually chose you (*name each of the children*) to be one of his special people. As a matter of fact, the Bible teaches us that we are to tell others what we have heard about God and what we have seen of God.

God actually chose you. That's why you are here and why it is so important that we learn more about God. When we come to Sunday school we learn about God's commandments. We also learn about forgiving, sharing, and giving. Then God says after you learn about it, you should do it. Go out and find people who do not know about God and teach them how to share, teach them how to forgive, and teach them how to give love. I want you to know that you are not the only people chosen by God. God chose your parents to love you and raise you, your Sunday school teacher to teach you, and your pastor to care for you. All of us were chosen as a family.

Doesn't that make you happy to know that you were chosen? Now you know that you belong and all of your friends in church belong to God. We are brothers and sisters of Jesus and the Holy Spirit lives within us.

The next time you see a straw, remember how you chose this straw to be your friend. I also want you to remember that God chose you and made you part of his family.

171

The Right Side

Acts 24:1-27

When the governor motioned to him to speak, Paul replied: "I cheerfully make my defense, knowing that for many years you have been a judge over this nation." (v. 10)

Object: things with two sides but only one of them is usable, such as a dinner plate, an umbrella, or a coat

Good morning, boys and girls. Have you ever heard that there are two sides to every story? (*let them answer*) A lot of people say this. I remember the time when some people were very unhappy with Paul and they wanted him to be put in jail and kept there. The story is in the Bible. People were upset with Paul because they thought he was teaching about another God. Paul told them he was true to the same God as they were only he had new information. They didn't want any new information, so they began to tell lies about the way Paul acted. They told the governor who was like a judge that Paul was causing problems. They tried to take a story and make a different side of it.

Let me show you what I mean. I brought along a few things that we have all seen. For instance, I brought this plate. How many of you use a plate when you eat? (*let them answer*) Good, everyone uses a plate. When you use your plate, which side do you use? (*let them answer*) Good, that is the same side I use. But the people who wanted to make trouble were the kind of people who used the other side of the plate. (*show them what you mean by turning the plate over and putting some kind of food on the wrong side*) That doesn't work, does it? The food will keep falling off of the plate.

Or how about this? (*show them an umbrella*) Which way do you hold the umbrella when it rains? (*hand it to a child and let them hold up the umbrella*) Very good, but the kind of people who were accusing Paul would hold the umbrella upside down. What would happen if you held the umbrella upside down? (*let them answer*) Very good, the rain would fill up the umbrella and soon you would be very wet.

Let's do one more. I brought along a coat. Which side of the coat would you use? (*let them answer*) Very good! You would wear the coat with the tag inside and not outside. Wearing a coat inside out would look really funny. The people who wanted Paul to be in prison were the kind of people who would wear the coat inside out.

Paul did not cause trouble and he told the truth about Jesus. He taught people about the God of love and joy. Jesus died for our sins. God forgives us and promises us a new life.

But there are people who do not love God and want people like you and me to say ugly things about God. We are talking about the same God only we see it from two different sides.

Remember the right ways to use your dinner plate and your umbrella and to wear your jacket. And remember Paul was right when he taught about Jesus Christ as new information about the same God. We believe in Jesus like Paul did and we want to share the news about Jesus with everyone.

Paul Meets A Celebrity

Acts 25:23

So on the next day, Agrippa and Bernice came with great pomp, and they entered the audience hall with the prominent men of the city. Then Festus gave the order and Paul was brought in. (v. 23)

Object: none

Good morning, boys and girls. Have you ever met a celebrity? (*let them answer*) A celebrity would be someone who is well known because of a talent he has or because he is a government official, or because he is rich. Movie stars, baseball and football players, presidents and kings, and owners of large companies are usually celebrities. When we meet people like this we usually feel different from when we meet other people like ourselves. They seem so powerful or beautiful that we act differently from the way we do with our family or friends. Sometimes we talk differently and we try to impress them with the things that we know about them or things that they are interested in doing. It is easy for us to change into a different person from what we really are.

Paul had a chance to be like a changed person. As you know, there were a lot of people who wanted Paul imprisoned and some who wanted him killed. They did not like the things he taught about Jesus because he was changing people's minds. Many of the men and women who were Jews and many who were Gentiles were beginning to believe in Jesus, and they were being baptized and made Christians. So the people who did not like what Paul said had him arrested and asked for him to be put to death. He was arrested and put in prison.

A few days later he was brought to court and heard by the Roman governor, who was the most powerful person in all of Israel. Now you would think that a person would act a little differently when he met the most powerful person in his land. Not Paul. He spoke right out and told the Roman governor, Festus, how he had become a Christian. He also told Festus why the Jewish authorities were against him. Festus did not understand the arguments between Paul and the Jewish authorities, but he was sure that whatever Paul did was not bad enough to be killed. He did not know what to do, but Paul demanded that he have a chance to speak to the Emperor Caesar who was the most powerful man in the world. Festus agreed that he should have the chance that he asked for.

The next day the Jewish king, Agrippa, who was appointed by Caesar, came to the home of Festus, the Roman governor. Festus told King Agrippa about Paul, and Agrippa said that he wanted to meet and hear Paul. Festus was glad, and he made arrangements for Paul to be brought back to court the next day. When Paul arrived at court and was introduced to King Agrippa by Governor Festus, Paul was delighted. He could hardly wait to tell Agrippa about all that he believed. He preached about Jesus and how Jesus did everything that the prophets had said that the Son of God would do when he was born into the world. It was a wonderful sermon.

Agrippa was overwhelmed. He knew that Paul expected him to believe. He could hardly keep up with Paul's enthusiasm. Finally he broke in and told Paul to stop. Agrippa said, "You want to make me a Christian in a few moments." Paul told him that he wished that everyone could be as happy as he was except for the chains and being a prisoner. Paul felt that Jesus was the answer for everyone. It did not make any difference if you were rich or poor, king or peasant, famous or not famous. That's still true: Jesus is the answer for everyone.

Governor Festus and King Agrippa could not get over Paul and the way that he believed. They did agree that he had done nothing wrong and that he should not be kept in prison. But since Paul had insisted on having his side told to the emperor, and since he was a Roman citizen, there was nothing that they could do but send him to Rome. Paul was glad for the opportunity to speak to Caesar and could hardly wait to go.

Maybe the next time you are asked to stand or be near someone famous, you will remember that Paul did not try to be someone different. He was the same to the governor and the king that he was to the people in the street. Paul was a man of God and a brother to every person.

Paul Shipwrecked

Acts 27:1—28:16

Paul advised them, saying, "Sirs, I can see that the voyage will be with danger and much heavy loss, not only of the cargo and the ship, but also of our lives." (27:9-10)

Object: some broken boards and a torn piece of canvas

Good morning, boys and girls. How many of you like adventure? (*let them answer*) Have any of you had an adventure? (*let them answer*) Some adventures are exciting and others are kind of exciting and scary. Have you ever been on an adventure that is exciting and scary? (*let them answer*)

I want to tell you about an adventure that Paul had as a servant of the Lord. Paul wanted to go to Rome and share his teachings of Jesus with the most powerful people on earth, including the emperor. Paul was a prisoner and sometimes he looked like a prisoner. He had chains around his feet and hands. He was kept in a jail and he ate prison food and slept on a prison bed. But Paul didn't act like he was in prison because he thanked God for every day of his life. He taught his jailers about Jesus and even baptized the jailer's family.

But finally he got his wish to go to Rome. He was going to tell the world about Jesus. But in order to travel that far, he would have to be put on a ship with other prisoners going to Rome. It was a big ship and there were 276 people on the ship. When they got out to sea, the weather turned frightful. First there was wind and then there was rain. The waves were terrible and the sailors were unable to change the direction of the ship. Everyone thought they were going to die. Everyone, except Paul, was afraid.

But Paul heard the voice of God that told him what to do to save the ship. First they had to throw the cargo, all the boxes and packages, into the sea. Then they had to put up the sails and change directions. Soon the ship was going too fast and heading for the rocks. They pulled down the sails and dropped the anchors. Finally, when men were thinking about jumping overboard to save their lives, Paul told the soldiers to make sure that everyone stayed on board or they would die. The soldiers made everyone sit down and wait for God to bring them to a safe place where they could come on shore. But first, before they found safety, the boat crashed into the rocks and came apart. But no one died and everyone found safety. Then God brought them to a place with friendly people and the people shared their food and clothing and everything that they had.

After the ship was repaired, the 276 people boarded it and sailed to Rome. God was with them. It was a great adventure and Paul was a great hero to almost everyone on board the ship. But Paul knew it was not he that made them safe but God, his God of love and courage. Other people learned from Paul and also became believers.

175

Sometimes things look really bad. We think it is going to be a fun adventure but life changes. The only things we are left with are some broken boards and tears. But if we are like Paul, we will always know there is a God who is with us.

You may not be in a shipwreck or airplane crash but you will have some very sad times. God is with you when you have those tears. He will love you and share with you his love and his protection. The next time you hear about a plane crash or something awful, remember God was with those people where they were just like he is with you today.

Goldie Belongs To Me

Romans 1:1-7

Including yourselves who are called to belong to Jesus Christ. (v. 6)

Object: a pet dog, cat, or even a goldfish

Good morning, boys and girls. I brought along a friend with me today to help me tell you a story. I love this friend very much because it is one of the things that belongs to me in this world. (*show the children your pet*) This is "Goldie," my goldfish. She is beautiful, and one of the very best swimmers in the whole world. She would have to be good the way that she can swim around corners and through the little openings in the sea castles that I have put in her bowl.

Do any of you have a pet fish? (*let them answer*) Fish are wonderful pets. Sometimes I sit and watch Goldie and I am amazed at the things that she can do. Have you ever watched your fish? (*let them answer*) Do you see the way that Goldie swims with her eyes open? Can you swim under water with your eyes open? And sometimes she swims standing still. She is an excellent swimmer and she belongs to me. I guess that is the best part of it. Goldie loves belonging to me because I change her water when it is supposed to be changed, I feed her, and I love her as a pet. That is what is called belonging, and Goldie belongs to me.

Now here is why I brought Goldie along to share with you this morning. Goldie is my pet fish and she belongs to me, but I must belong to someone also. I guess I belong to my mother and father and to all of my family. I belong to my friends and neighbors. But I want to belong to someone even more special, and the Bible tells me that I do. The Bible tells me that I belong to Jesus. I want to belong to Jesus, but even more important is the fact that Jesus wants me to belong to him. He tells people how much I belong to him and I am glad. If I love Goldie so much because she belongs to me, then think how Jesus must feel when he says that I belong to him. That is a good feeling.

The same thing is true of you. The Bible teaches us that you belong to Jesus and that he is happy about it. You belong to Jesus and it is very important to him that you do. The next time you see your pet or you think about Goldie, remember how much we love our pets, and then you will think about how much Jesus loves you and how you belong to him.

Target Practice

Romans 3:21-25a, 27-28

Since all have sinned and fall short of the glory of God. (v. 23)

Object: some rubber bands, candy to pass out to the children

Good morning, boys and girls. Today we are going to have some real fun and also find out something about ourselves and why we need Jesus. I brought along some rubber bands that I want to share with you this morning. As a matter of fact, we are going to have target practice, and to the one who hits the target I will give a piece of delicious candy. How many want to try to hit the target? (*let them all volunteer*) I brought along enough rubber bands for everyone to try at least once and maybe more. Our target is the ceiling of the church. Now let me show you how to shoot the rubber bands. (*put the rubber band on your finger and shoot it in some direction other than the ceiling*)

Now, when I count three we will fire at the ceiling. One, two, and three. Fire. Who hit the ceiling? Did anyone hit the ceiling? (*let them answer*) You all fell short of hitting the ceiling. Would you like to try again? Remember, there is some delicious candy waiting for you if you hit the ceiling. (*have everyone armed with a rubber band and when you give the count, let them fire*) Everyone fell short again. Not one of you were able to hit the ceiling with your second try. You all fell short.

But don't feel bad. Let me tell you why we tried this experiment. Shooting rubber bands at the ceiling is like trying to live the perfect life. You can't do it. Everyone sins, and when we sin we do not live a perfect life. Only one person ever lived and did not sin. His name is Jesus. Everyone else has failed and fallen short of the perfect life. If we had to live a perfect life to get to heaven, where we will live with God, then no one would ever make it. The Bible says that we can never make it by ourselves. The only way that we will ever make it to heaven is if God helps us. God forgives our sins and loves us so much that he does it all for us so that we can live here on earth without a lot of worry and fretting. You don't have to worry about being a friend of God if you love him and trust him. God promises all of us who fall short that he will take care of us.

It is like getting the candy even when you are short on your shot. I am going to give you the candy I promised even though you didn't hit the ceiling, so that you will remember that even when we fail to be perfect, God still loves us enough to share his world with everyone who loves and trusts in him. (*pass out the candy*)

The next time you try to shoot a rubber band and you miss the mark, think about how much God loves you. When you think about that, you will remember how he forgives you when you ask for it and how he shares his world with all who believe in him.

Jumping With Help

Romans 4:1-5, 13-17

For if Abraham was justified by works, he has something to boast about, but not before God. (v. 2)

Object: string or rope

Good morning, boys and girls. Today we are going to have a lot of fun and I hope that we are also going to learn something. I brought along a piece of rope and I want to use it to make a line on the floor. This rope is the starting line for a contest. I want to see how far you can jump, starting at this line. (*line the children up so that they can take turns jumping*) The winner of our contest will be the person who can jump the farthest. (*select the winner*)

You can really jump far. We are going to let you brag a little about yourself. Would you like to tell everyone what you do to jump farther than anyone else in the room? (*prompt her or him with a few questions and draw out her bragging so that she thinks you are serious*)

The thing that is so important about this is that our winner did it all by herself. She jumped from here to there without any help. That means a lot, and she is allowed to brag. Now I want to show her something I hope will help her learn something else. She jumped from the line to this place without any help, but let's see how far she can jump with a little bit of help. (*let her line up at a place on the rope and get ready to jump again, only this time count to three and then lift her as she jumps so that she far exceeds her first jump*) What a jump that was! It is a lot farther than she jumped by herself.

That was fun, but it should teach us something. All of us like to brag to one another. But have you ever had someone brag to God? (*let them answer*) Did you ever tell God how good you were when you know that God is a lot better? Have you ever told God how good you made something when you know all of the good things that God has made? I don't think so. You can't brag in front of God.

The other thing is this and I want you to remember it. If you can do something by yourself, then think how good you could do it with God's help. God is always ready to help, and God does a super job of helping people when they let him. You know how much farther you can jump if you have a little help. The same thing is true when you pray to God and ask him to help you with whatever you are doing. God can make you go farther and do better, and he can help us do our things far better than we can do them ourselves.

179

You're Worth A Million

Romans 5:1-11

But God proves his love for us in that while we still were sinners Christ died for us. (v. 8)

Object: a make-believe check for $1,000,000 (be sure to void the check!) and an old rag

Good morning, boys and girls. Today I am going to show you something that you won't believe, but it's true. I have a check here for one million dollars and I am going to spend it in just a few minutes. Do you know how much money one million dollars is? (*let them answer*) What do you think one million dollars would buy? (*let them answer*) A million dollars is more money than I have ever seen.

I want you to look at something else I brought with me today. Do you see this old rag I have in my hand? It isn't very pretty. I guess you wouldn't even dust your house with a rag like this, would you? (*let them answer*) Would anyone wear it for a shirt? (*let them answer*) You wouldn't wear it or use it. It is ready to be burned or thrown away in some garbage can. That means the rag is in pretty bad shape, doesn't it? (*let them answer*)

Guess what? I am going to spend my check for a million dollars to buy this rag. That's right; this is the reason that I brought my check for one million dollars. I want to buy this rag with all the money that I have ever seen. Would you do that? (*let them answer*) You wouldn't do it, would you? You think I am silly, don't you? (*let them answer*) Well, maybe I am, but I want to tell you that I am not the only one that people think is silly.

You think about spending one million dollars for a rag while I tell you something else. Did you know that God spent more than that for something that was worth about as much as my old rag? (*let them answer*) That's right. God gave Jesus to the world for raggedy old sinners. Would you die for a million dollars? If I put a million dollars in your bank account would you die for it? (*let them answer*) Of course you wouldn't. But God took a look at us, and he saw a bunch of raggedy people. Then he thought about how much he loved us and he decided to give the life of Jesus for all of us. He had Jesus die so that we would have all of our sins against him forgiven. Jesus paid for our sins with his life. We were filled with sin, and God forgave all of us for the price of Jesus' life.

That's how much God loves us. More than a million dollars for a rag! That's nothing. Jesus gave something more than a million dollars for us. He gave us his life.

The next time you see a rag or hear about a million dollars, I want you to think about what God spent to forgive you and me for our sins. That was really spending, and it means that you are worth more than a million dollars to God.

The Key Ring That Unites Us

Romans 6:2b-11

For if we have been united with him in a death like his, we shall certainly be united with him in a resurrection like his. (v. 5)

Object: a round key ring with a lot of keys and one large key

Good morning, boys and girls. Today is a wonderful day to share with one another and to thank God for being so good to us. I have been thinking about a lot of things recently and one of them is the idea that we are sharing a promise that was given to Jesus.

Do you remember hearing about when Jesus died? (*let them answer*) I remember that also. You and I will also die. We hope that we will not have to die in the same way that Jesus did, but we know that we must still all die sometime. We stop breathing, we stop running or walking, we stop eating, and all of the other things that we do now, and we die. The same thing happened to Jesus.

But do you also remember that Jesus came back to life again? We call that the Resurrection. When Jesus came back to life, he ate and drank, walked, talked, breathed, and he also did some things that he did not do before he died. God promises that the same thing will happen to all of us. We will also be resurrected in the same way that Jesus was resurrected.

I brought a key ring to help show you what it means to be a Christian and to share in the promise that God makes to us. The Bible talks about being united with Jesus in his death, and in his Resurrection. The key ring is the uniter. The big key is Jesus and all of the rest of us are the other keys. If I put the key ring in my pocket all of the keys go in my pocket. If I take the keys out and lay them down, then all of the keys lay down. If I carry the keys in my hands, then all of the keys are in my hand. The key ring unites us with Jesus and with one another. When we are Christians, we are united with Jesus and with one another.

That is the way that God has planned it. We are sharing our lives with one another, but most of all we are sharing our lives with Jesus. Jesus died and we shall die. But Jesus was also resurrected and had a new life that was even better than the first one, and we shall have the same.

The next time you see a key ring and you think about all of the keys on the ring, I hope you think about the way that they are united and how we are also united with Jesus in death and resurrection.

Missing The Bull's Eye

Romans 7:15-25a

I do not understand my actions. For I do not do what I want, but I do the very thing I hate. (v. 15)

Object: some darts and a dart board

Good morning, boys and girls. I brought along a game today that I played a lot when I was about your age. I always enjoyed the game, but I think that it was one of the hardest things I ever did. (*show them the dart game*) How many of you know what this game is called? (*let them answer*) That's right, darts. Have you ever played it? (*let them answer*) What do you try to do in this game? (*let them answer*) That's right; you try to hit the very center of the board, and that is called the "bull's eye." That's where the big points are, and you need to hit it if you are going to win. But that is also the hard part. As often as you try to hit it, you seem to miss it. I am going to let some of you try to hit the bull's eye to show you what I mean. (*set up the board and let each child throw one dart at the board; make sure that the distance is such that they miss, but not far enough that they cause any damage*) That was a good try, but you can see how hard it is to hit the bull's eye.

The Apostle Paul said something like this when he was talking about the way he acted and talked. Paul wanted to act, think, and speak right all the time. He wanted to be good. He didn't want to be good part of the time, but he wanted to be good all of the time. In other words, Paul did not want to sin. But he did sin. He acted badly, or thought some bad thoughts, or spoke in a rough way when he didn't have to. Paul said that he did not understand why he was like that, but he knew that he was. How many of you want to act, think, and speak right all the time? (*let them answer*) Of course you do. But do you do the things you want to do all the time? Of course not. You and I and everybody sin just like Paul sinned. We miss the bull's eye time after time after time.

That is why it is so important that Jesus died for our sins. If he had not loved us so much, we would have been lost. But thanks to him and to the fact that he hit the bull's eye every time, we have the promise of God that everything will be all right. That's why we love him so much and are so thankful that he came to take care of our misses.

The next time you play darts or see someone play darts and they miss the bull's eye, you can think about your misses, called sins, and then think of how glad you are that Jesus came to save us from our sins.

182

Bill And Bert Bell

Romans 8:1-10

For the law of the Spirit of life in Christ Jesus has set me free from the law of sin and of death. (v. 2)

Object: two bells, only one of them having a clapper

Good morning, boys and girls. I brought along with me today two things that look alike but are as different as they can be. (*display the two bells*) What do we call these two things? (*let them answer*) Bells; we call them bells. And what do you do with bells? (*let them answer*) That's right; we ring them. We ring them when we want to get someone's attention. We ring them in school and at church. It used to be that every church had a big bell and it would ring at certain times to tell people that it was time to come and worship. Some mothers ring a bell so that their children know it is time to come home and eat lunch or dinner. Of course bells only have one note, don't they? (*let them answer*)

Today, I brought two bells. One bell I call Bill and the other bell I call Bert. This is Bill and this is Bert. (*identify the bells*) They both have a special place in my house. I use Bill all of the time. Would you like to hear what Bill sounds like? (*let them answer; then ring Bill Bell*) Pretty sound, isn't it? I really like Bill. Would you like to hear Bert? (*let them answer; then pretend to ring the bell without the clapper several times*) How do you like Bert's sound? (*let them answer*) Not much of a sound, is it? What do you suppose is the trouble with Bert? (*let them answer*) That's right; Bert is missing something pretty important, isn't he? (*let them answer*) The missing part we call a clapper. If a bell is going to ring, it must have a clapper.

People are not all the same either, are they? (*let them answer*) The Bible teaches us that some people seem a lot different than others. I like to think that Christians are people with clappers. And the clapper is Jesus Christ. He makes us ring. He forgives us our sin and teaches us truth and makes us free. Jesus shows us what God is really like and we learn the real kind of love that only God can give to us.

People without Jesus are like bells without clappers. They are missing something important. Sometimes we simply need to share Jesus with them and they change from Bert to Bill. But some people don't want to hear about Jesus. They tell us to go away. They don't know how beautiful life can be when they have Jesus in their heart. They are lonely without God; they do not have the joy that God puts in hearts. They are like a bell without a clapper.

So the next time you look at a bell, you can tell the difference if it plays or it doesn't play because you will find the clapper. If it has a clapper, you will thank God for making you a Christian with all of your joy. If it doesn't have a clapper, then you will think about how hard life is for people without Jesus. For now, I want to tell you to keep on ringing. Share the love of Jesus with everyone and make all of the people you know be like Bill Bell.

Throw Your Worries To The Lord
(Appropriate for use in Lent)

Romans 8:31-39

Who will separate us from the love of Christ? (v. 35a)

Object: some business forms with carbon paper separating each sheet

Good morning, boys and girls. It is time for us to think about some different things. Here we are in church on the first Sunday of a brand new month. Does anyone know what month this is? (*let them answer*) That's right; March, and what does March make you think about? (*let them answer*) I think about the wind and how hard it blows in the month of March. I also think about spring and how soon it will be with us. But today I am thinking about Lent. How many of you know something about Lent? (*let them answer*) This is a time of year when we think about Jesus and how he suffered and died for our sins. How many of you have thought about that today? (*let them answer*)

We have a lot of things to think about, don't we? I think about spring and I think about my friends. I like to think about good things, but sometimes I worry about being sick or having people angry with me for something. When I think about the things that cause me a lot of worry, I seem to forget about Jesus.

How many of you ever forget about Jesus? It seems like when we are worrying or forgetting about Jesus, we feel separated from him. Let me show you what I mean. (*take out your carbon forms*) Let's pretend that this first sheet of paper I have with me is Jesus, and the black piece of paper is one of my worries. Let's say this worry is about a friend who is mad at me. The next sheet of paper is me. (*hold up next set of forms*) Then I have the worry of getting really sick, and then there is me.

Just think of how far I am getting away from Jesus. I am being separated from Jesus. Jesus is way up front and I am getting further and further away because of all my worries. That's really bad. When you get that far away from Jesus, you may be afraid that Jesus will forget you.

But before you worry about Jesus forgetting you, let me show you something. I am going to have Jesus write you a note. Remember I told you that Jesus was the first page. Well, Jesus is writing you a note that says I love you. (*write it out on the page*) Now let's see if Jesus got through your worries. Here is your worry about the friend who is mad at you. We will look under that worry and see what is there. The next page is you. Look at this: the message from Jesus is written on you! Let's look at the next worry. That was our fear of getting really sick. Let's look at you under that worry. Jesus got through that worry also. His message is there. He loves you. Nothing can separate you from the love of Jesus. All your worries are not big enough to keep Jesus from you.

That's something to remember. If you remember that Jesus will always be with you, you can forget about your worries because he cares for you. Will you remember? I hope so.

184

Your Lifetime Teeth

Romans 9:1-5

They are Israelites, and to them belong the adoption, the glory, the covenants, the giving of the law, the worship, and the promises; to them belong the patriarchs, and from them, according to the flesh, is the Messiah, who is over all, God blessed forever. Amen. (vv. 4-5)

Object: a baby tooth or a drawing of a baby tooth

Good morning, boys and girls. How many of you have lost some of your teeth, your baby teeth? (*let them answer*) Almost all of you, and some day every one of you will lose the teeth that you have had since you were babies. Then what happens? (*let them answer*) That's right; you get new teeth with big roots that will last all of your life. Teeth are very important to us because they help us to eat the correct kind of foods that we need to grow. They also make us look good when we smile. We all kid each other when we lose our front baby teeth. Does anyone here this morning have a big space up front when they smile because they are missing their two front teeth? (*look for a good example of missing front teeth and let them show off a big smile*) Some day you will have some beautiful new teeth to take up that empty place in your lovely mouth.

There is a reason why we have talked about your baby teeth and about losing them. I want you to think about something that Paul talked about a long time ago. Many of you will remember that the Israelites were God's chosen people. That meant that God chose the Israelites to be the messengers of his teachings. If God wanted the world to know about what was right or wrong, he told the Israelites and they told the rest of the world. That is how God worked out the teaching of the Ten Commandments. It was a fine system and the Israelites liked being the chosen people.

But then things got mixed up. Instead of listening to what God taught, some of the leaders began to make up their own rules that they thought would be a help to God. Soon they were making more rules than God was making. They stopped listening and before long they lost their place with God. They lost their closeness with God, just like you will lose your baby teeth. Things are really different when you lose your teeth. It is hard to eat corn on the cob and other good food. You must do things differently.

But Paul did not want anyone to think that God had given up on the Israelites. He said that they would come back again because the Israelites belonged to God, for they were especially chosen. Some day things would be the same again with God and the chosen people. That is like knowing that you will have your lifetime teeth some day. Of course the sooner the better, but you just have to wait until that time comes. You can't hurry it.

So the Israelites will be taken care of by God just like you will some day have your new teeth, but only God knows when that time will come. Always remember: Never stop listening to God, and never start making up your own rules and calling them God's rules.

185

Gifts For God

Romans 11:33-36

"Or who has given to him, to receive a gift in return?" (v. 35)

Object: a box of candy, some flowers, a piece of jewelry

Good morning, boys and girls. I thought that since this is Sunday morning and it is such a nice warm day, we should do something for our God who made it this way. I have thought a lot about what we might do for God, and I cannot decide what would be the best kind of gift. Do any of you have some ideas of what we could give God on this Sunday? (*let them answer*) What would you like to have if someone were going to give you a gift today? (*let them answer*) We should have just the right kind of gift if we are giving to God. I did bring a few things along to help us think. I have a box of candy. I always like candy and I thought that maybe God would like the same kind that I like. What do you think about giving candy to God? (*let them answer*)

You don't like that idea? How about some flowers? These are just beautiful at this time of year. We could give God some wonderful flowers, or even a plant if you think he would keep them watered. Do you like the idea of giving flowers? (*let them answer*) You don't think that God would like either as a gift from us?

I have one more thought. I have this beautiful piece of jewelry. It has been in my family for years and people just love to look at it and they always tell me that they wish they had a piece of jewelry that looked like this. Do you think God would wear my old family jewelry? (*let them answer*) The answer is still no. What do you want to give to God that will help him remember you? (*let them answer*) Don't you have any suggestions? You see, if we can give God a gift, then he will owe us a favor. I think it would be pretty nice to know that God owed me something, don't you? (*let them answer*)

I am really trying to trick you. We can't give gifts to God, can we? God doesn't take gifts from us, and he has never owed anything to anyone. God shares his world with us and everything that is in the world belongs to him, including you and me. We belong to God, and we cannot give him candy, flowers, jewelry. All of these things belong to him, and he made them.

But we can give God one thing that is very important to him and to everyone else. The one thing we can give God is our love, and show him how very special our love is to him.

Maybe the next time you hear someone talking about owing money or a favor, you will think about the day we tried to think of something that we could give to God so that he would owe something to us. Then you will remember how impossible it was and how the only thing we had to give was our love. And God thinks that our love is the most important thing there is to give to him. We don't have to worry about giving anything else. What we do and how we act will show our love. God bless you very much.

Every Letter Is Important

Romans 12:1-8

So we, who were many, are one body in Christ, and individually we are members one of another. (v. 5)

Object: a computer keyboard

Good morning, boys and girls. I brought along a very important part of my office to show you this morning and to help teach an important lesson. Sometimes we belong to something that seems very large because there are so many people who are a part of it. Our church is a good example. There are a lot of members in our church. People were asking Paul that question all of the time. How important are they to Christ's church? That is a good question.

I want to show you my computer keyboard because it has all of the letters on different little keys. There are also numbers and signs on these little keys. Each key is important. Not all of them are used a lot and some of them are used in almost every word. But each one of them is important. I don't use the letter *Z* a lot or the letter *Q*. But if I did not have these letters I could not write the word *quick* or the word *zebra*. Every letter on my keyboard is important, very important. Suppose that I wanted to write you a letter and your name was Betty. I wanted to say, "Dear Betty," but my keyboard did not have a capital B. I would have to say, "Dear etty." Now many people would think that this was a strange way to write my friend.

Every letter is important no matter how often it is used. The same thing is true in Christ's church. Every one of us is important to Jesus and to his father in heaven. Every member is like a part of my keyboard. That means that some members are needed to teach Sunday school every Sunday. Some people are needed to sing in the choir, some people are needed to be ushers, and every church needs at least one pastor. But if the church is missing the people to go and tell others about Jesus, or it is missing the ushers to help seat the people, then the church is like a keyboard without some of the keys.

You are a key to our church. Our church needs you to show your love for Jesus in a special way. When you find out what that way is, then you will be like my letter *Z* or letter *A* or number *7*. Whatever you do best, the church of Jesus Christ is counting on you to make it work. I want you to remember, when you see your next keyboard, how important you are to the church of Jesus Christ.

What Taxes Do

Romans 13:1-10

For the same reason you also pay taxes, for the authorities are God's servants, busy with this very thing. (v. 6)

Object: a street sign, some school books, and a fascimile of a food stamp voucher

Good morning, boys and girls. How many of you have ever heard of the word *taxes*? (*let them answer*) What are taxes? (*let them answer*) Taxes are money that your parents pay for things that we use. We like to complain about taxes, and we always think that our taxes are too high and they cost too much, but they are something that we must have to keep our country running.

Let me show you some things that our taxes buy. (*show them a street sign like 55 MPH or No Parking*) How many of you have seen a sign like this when you are riding in the car? We call them street signs, and our taxes pay for these signs. We need these signs to keep the roads that we drive on safe for traffic. Our taxes also pay for the streets and roads that we travel on. Here is something else that our tax dollars buy. (*hold up some school books*) What are these? That's right; books. These are school books and our taxes pay for the books and for the schools that the books are used in. Everything in a school is paid for by taxes. Our taxes also buy help for people who need it because they are too poor or because they have a problem like being blind or deaf or injured so that they cannot work. Here is a food stamp voucher that our government uses to help people who cannot help themselves. People use food stamps instead of money to buy food at the grocery.

Our taxes are very important, and we elect people to choose how our taxes are to be used. The Bible says that people who work for the government and spend our tax money are chosen by God. They are a special kind of person whom the Bible says are like ministers. I wonder if you knew that the people that spend our taxes are called ministers by God? Most people do not know that, but it is true, and very important for us to remember. A minister of God must also remember that he or she was chosen by God to do the very best with the tax money so that the people who need help are getting it. Tax ministers must be sure that people who have special problems, such as a sickness, are cared for with our tax dollars. They must build good roads and fine schools so that we can travel safely and learn more happily about God's world.

The next time you hear someone talk about taxes, remember that God said he had chosen people to be ministers of our taxes and that our taxes should be used for everyone's good.

Really Living!

Romans 14:7-9

If we live, we live to the Lord, and if we die, we die to the Lord; so then, whether we live or whether we die, we are the Lord's. (v. 8)

Object: a beach ball and a grave marker (stone) possibly made out of cardboard and painted gray with a name and dates on it

Good morning, boys and girls. Let me share with you two things that we do not always think go together, but which I hope will really teach you how close God is to you.

The first thing that I have is a beach ball. How many of you have ever played with a beach ball? (*let them answer*) What do you think about when you see a beach ball? (*let them answer*) Swimming, sand, having fun, and going on vacation are some of the things that I think about when I see a beach ball. I had a friend who told me that a beach ball reminded him of really living. He just loved to swim and play and when he was doing both he called it really living.

Now I have a second thing that is a little different. (*bring out the grave marker or stone*) How many of you know what this is or what it stands for? (*let them answer*) That's right, it reminds you of a cemetery or graveyard. It could also remind us of death and dying. How many of us are going to die? (*let them answer*) That's right; all of us are going to die. We don't like to think about dying because we are having so much fun living and we don't want to quit doing what we like so much.

But there is a good reason we have the beach ball and the gravestone together today, because we need to learn something very important. The Bible tells us that we belong to the Lord whether we live or whether we die. It doesn't make any difference to God how we are. It makes a difference to us, we think, but to God it doesn't make any difference, and it would be good if we felt like God. We belong to him when we are really living, out at the beach and having a great time. God is there and he enjoys us while we are swimming and playing in the sand. God made the water and the sand for us to enjoy. But God is also with us when we die and when we are buried in the earth. Not only is God in both places, but he tells us that we belong to him alive or dead. That is wonderful news because God also promises us that even when we die he will make us alive again to enjoy a new world that is even more fun than the one that has beaches and warm water.

So be glad that you belong to God and enjoy him now wherever you are, and also be glad that God will be with you when you die. Only after we die will we find out about the new life that he has made for us to live with him in a new world of love.

The Greatest Secret Ever Told
(Appropriate for Christmas)

Romans 16:25-27

Now to God who is able to strengthen you according to my gospel and the procla-mation of Jesus Christ, according to the revelation of the mystery which was kept secret for long ages. (v. 25)

Object: a famous secret recipe (such as Kentucky Fried Chicken)

Good morning, boys and girls. The time has almost come and we are only a few hours away from the day that you have been waiting for. Just think, it is almost Christmas and you have made it. Is there any other day in the whole year that you wait for so much as for Christmas day? (*let them answer*) I don't think so. Waiting for Christmas is something that people have done even before there was a Christmas. For thousands of years people waited for the promise of God that a Savior would be delivered. Everyone knew there would be a Savior, but the Savior did not come until that night almost 2,000 years ago in the small town of Bethlehem. Jesus was almost like a secret recipe that someone was keeping.

I have with me this morning a piece of chicken that is called Kentucky Fried Chicken. It tastes a little different than any other chicken you can find. It is made with a secret recipe that was invented by a man a number of years ago. Only a very few people in this country know how to make Kentucky Fried Chicken, because the secret is kept in a place where they make the batter to put on the chicken. And the people there want to keep it a secret so that no one else can make it.

God knew the secret of Jesus, and when he was going to send that secret into the world; he told no one of the day that Jesus was coming. It was God's secret to be kept until just the right time. Only then did God tell the rest of the world what he had known for thousands of years. Jesus was saved for just the right moment when everything was according to God's plan.

It isn't easy to keep a secret. How many of you know a secret that no one else knows? (*let them answer*) If you have a secret, you usually want to tell it so that someone can share it with you. But God kept his secret all to himself so that no one would know the time of Jesus' coming until the moment had come.

Keeping secrets is not easy for anyone, but God kept his secret until he knew that every-thing was just right. The next time you see some Kentucky Fried Chicken, or you have a secret to keep to yourself, you will remember the time that God had a secret he had to keep about the coming of Jesus. And he kept it a long time. It was a wonderful secret, and one that we are all glad he kept until the night in Bethlehem. God bless you very much.

Believing In Jesus

1 Corinthians 1:22-25

But we proclaim Christ crucified, a stumbling block to Jews and foolishness to Gentiles. (v. 23)

Object: a carpenter's sawhorse

Good morning, boys and girls. I want to share a problem with you this morning. How many of you like problems? (*let them answer*) We all like problems we can solve, but there are not many of us who like problems that we cannot find answers to in a short period of time. I can't fix my car when it doesn't work, and I don't like that kind of a problem. I have the same kind of problem when my radio or television is broken. I can't make them work. Saint Paul had another word for problems that I like, and I want to share it with you.

The Apostle Paul called problems-without-answers "stumbling blocks." I don't know what a stumbling block looked like to Paul, but it could have been something like this. (*show them the carpenter's sawhorse*) Suppose you were walking in a dark room and you ran into this thing. What do you think would happen? (*let them answer*) That's right; you would probably fall over it. This sawhorse, that's what carpenters call it, would keep you from getting to where you are going. You would fall or trip over this stumbling block.

Paul said that Jesus being crucified was a stumbling block for many of the people he knew. People could not believe that their sins were forgiven because Jesus died on the cross. That was not logical. How could Jesus being crucified help forgive their sins? People like it when they hear that God is love and God is forgiving, but how could Jesus dying like a criminal help them be saved? That was a problem. People whom Paul knew thought that they were saved when they learned all the great teachings of Jesus and knew how to use them. That kind of learning and understanding is called wisdom. People were saved by law or wisdom. That's what they believed. The idea of Jesus being crucified and dying for their sins was impossible to them. Paul said it was a stumbling block. They tripped over the crucifixion and they never went any further.

We know differently today. It was God's plan to have Jesus die for our sins. We all break God's law and we will never know enough about anything to save ourselves. But when we trust in Christ and his dying for our sins, then we are saved to live forever with God in his world.

Believing in Jesus, and Jesus crucified, may be a stumbling block for some but not for us. We thank God for his plan to save us through Jesus.

How Special You Are!

1 Corinthians 6:12-20

Or do you not know that your body is a temple of the Holy Spirit within you, which you have from God, and that you are not your own! For you were bought with a price; therefore glorify God in your body. (vv. 19-20)

Object: a brand-new dress, suit, or some very special piece of clothing

Good morning, boys and girls. Isn't this a wonderful Sunday morning? (*let them answer*) Everything seems to be just right with the world and all of you look so good. I brought along with me some very special things that I have seen in the store and I thought that you would like to look at them with me. I think that they are about the most beautiful clothes that I have ever seen. They are special because they are to be worn to some special place. Maybe they are for a party or a wedding. You can see that you would not wear this kind of a dress to clean the house or go outside and play in it. It's so bright and cheerful looking that you just know that the person who wears a dress like this is going to be beautiful in it. And how about this suit? Not everyone has a suit like this. I suppose you might wear a suit that is this special to a wedding or a very special dance. The person who wears this will also be special to look at when he has this on.

Clothes are important because they tell us something about the importance of the places that we are going to when we wear them. But the Bible tells us that there is something a lot more special than the clothes we wear. Do you know what is more important than clothes? (*let them answer*) All those things are important, but the Bible tells us that our own bodies are more important than any clothes. The Apostle Paul wrote that our bodies are like temples because the Holy Spirit lives in our bodies. Did you know that God the Holy Spirit is alive within you? (*let them answer*) That's right; God lives in you and that makes your body a very special thing to take care of in a very special way. Paul calls your body a temple. Do you know what a temple is? (*let them answer*) A temple is like a church. It is a holy place where people believe they can talk and listen to God. Your body is a place like a temple. You speak to God and listen to God when he talks to you. That means that your body is such a special place that you should take care of it in a very special way. Don't do anything to your body that hurts it. Always do good things for your body because the Holy Spirit of God is living inside of you.

The next time you see some clothes that really seem special, and you would like to wear them to make you feel special, think about how special you already are since your body is a temple and the Holy Spirit lives in you.

Time Is Running Out

1 Corinthians 7:29-31

I mean, brothers and sisters, the appointed time has grown very short. (v. 29a)

Object: a new bar of soap and a very used bar of soap

Good morning, boys and girls. I brought along with me a couple of friends that most of you probably know but you don't talk to very often. How many of you have ever met Billy Big Bar and his older brother Larry Little Bar? Billy and Larry are good friends but Billy worries a lot about Larry. Every day when they wake up, Billy looks at Larry and becomes very sad. Do you know why Billy is sad about Larry? (*let them answer*) That's right; Larry is smaller today than he was yesterday. Do you know why? (*let them answer*) That's right; someone used Larry and there is less of him today than there was yesterday. One day something is going to happen that is going to make Billy very unhappy if he doesn't learn something that he doesn't know right now. Do you know what is going to happen to Larry that could make Billy sad? (*let them answer*) That's right; Larry is going to disappear. He is going to be gone forever. Would that make you sad if you were Larry's big brother? (*let them answer*)

Maybe it would, but it shouldn't. We must remember that this is the way that Larry and Billy were made, and some day the same thing is going to happen to Billy. It is a plan for soap to be used up and someday to be all gone. Billy shouldn't feel bad, but instead he should feel good for Larry because Larry is making the plan come true.

That is the same way for us. When God made the world that we live in, he knew that there was another world and that we would not stay here forever. Our world is like a piece of soap. Someday it is going to be all used up and we will disappear from this world just like Larry Little Bar is going to disappear. But it will be the way that God has planned it and therefore it will be good.

You and I are not going to live forever. Someday we will die according to the plan. Everyone else will die also. They will be used up just like us. The world that we live in will be used up and it will sort of die. But God has a bigger plan and a better plan for all of us and for all of his world. The time is always closer to the end but none of us knows when the end will come. We must trust that God will take good care of us and make us part of his new world when it is finished.

Of Backs And Cracks

1 Corinthians 8:1-13

But take care that this liberty of yours does not somehow become a stumbling block to the weak. (v. 9)

Object: a string that could look like a crack in the sidewalk

Good morning, boys and girls. Today I need your help. I want you to use your imagination. Do you know what I mean when I say imagination? (*let them answer*) That's right; I want you to pretend.

I have a string with me that I am going to lay down on the floor. We are going to pretend that the floor is a sidewalk and the string is a crack in the sidewalk. How many of you have ever seen a sidewalk cracked? (*let them answer*) Does the string look like a crack? (*let them answer*) Good, then this will help you to pretend.

There is an old saying that goes like this, "If you step on the crack, you will break your mother's back." That is an old saying and I don't believe it, do you? (*let them answer*) You can't break your mother's back by stepping on a crack in the sidewalk. But some people believe things like this. They think it is unlucky to step on cracks, and that if they do, something bad will happen to their mother. It won't happen, but they think it will.

You and I could step on cracks all day long and nothing would happen to anyone's mother because we stepped on the crack. But even so, it is important for us to think about. Suppose you were with a friend and he thought that stepping on that crack would hurt his mother. What would you do? (*let them answer*) That's right; you would try to convince him that it just couldn't happen. But he wouldn't believe you. Then, what would you do? Would you step on it a bunch of times and run home to show him that it didn't make any difference? (*let them answer*) I don't think so. That would just make him mad at you, and nothing good would happen. We don't want to make people mad or angry at us. That is not the way that we teach boys and girls about Jesus.

We teach about Jesus by doing good for them and not by trying to prove everything that we think is right and making them angry. The Apostle Paul had things like this happen to him. He told all the Christians to be very concerned about people who did not know Jesus and to help them learn without making them mad.

You and I have to do the same thing. Don't try to always be right about everything when you know it makes others mad. Listen to them and try to understand them and love them a lot and they will come to know the truth by learning.

Thank you for coming this morning and thank you for letting me use your imagination.

The Man Who Brought People To Jesus

1 Corinthians 9:16-23

I have become all things to all people, that I might by all means save some. (v. 22b)

Object: a pocket knife with many parts, such as a Swiss Army knife

Good morning, boys and girls. How many of you have ever seen a pocket knife that looks like this? (*hold up your special pocket knife*) Isn't this something? Let's take a close look at it and see if you can tell me what all of the parts of this knife are used for? (*take out each part and identify it, then put it back*) Just imagine what you could do with a knife like this! You could cut wood, screw screws, take out corks, eat beans out of a can, and I suppose help yourself with a hundred other things. This is quite a knife. It is about the best kind of knife I have ever seen. There isn't anything that you can't do with a knife like this.

The Apostle Paul would have loved this knife. He was always trying to be to people what this knife was to other knives. Some knives can only cut, but this knife can do almost anything that you want it to do. Paul was that kind of a man to other people. He was a great student to other students and a hard worker to people who worked hard. He could speak many languages so that almost everyone could understand him. He knew how to live with the rich and the poor. Paul was quite a man, and he did all the things that he did for one reason. How many of you know why Paul was the kind of person that he was? (*let them answer*) Paul was this kind of a person so that he could tell everyone about Jesus and show them how Jesus helps them. He taught the rich and the poor. He taught the very smart and the very dumb about Jesus. There was not anyone who was too old or too young that Paul did not help to learn about Jesus.

Paul said that he was all things to all people. He would do anything to make Jesus real to all the people in the world.

That's why I think that Paul is like my knife. My knife has many parts and it can do almost anything for me. I don't need another knife when I have this one. It can do anything that I ask of a knife. People didn't need another teacher when Paul was around. If they wanted to make a tent he would make it. If they wanted to speak Greek or Hebrew or any other language, Paul would speak with them. If they needed food or clothes he would get it for them. Paul was a great missionary for Jesus because he was all things to all people.

The next time you see a knife, maybe you will think of mine, and it will help you to remember our friend and great teacher of Jesus, the Apostle Paul.

195

How Refreshing!

1 Corinthians 10:1-5

And all ate the same spiritual food, and all drank the same spiritual drink. For they drank from the spiritual rock that followed them, and the rock was Christ. (vv. 3-4)

Object: a pitcher of lemonade and some glasses

Good morning, boys and girls. Have you ever told a story to someone that had been told to you about something wonderful that happened a long time ago? (*let them answer*) Maybe it was a pioneer story or a story about some children from another land. But the story was exciting, and it made you feel good the first time you heard it, and it made you feel even better when you could tell it to someone else for the first time.

The Apostle Paul was a man who told stories. He had heard stories about people who lived a long time before he did. These stories were often about God and the people who trusted in God. One of the stories was about a group of people who lived in the desert and waited for God to tell them when they could move into a land they could call home. They lived in the desert for years, and sometimes the living was very hard. One time the people were without any food and water. They didn't know if they were going to starve to death or die of thirst. But God knew of their trust and how they waited for his special word, so he made a miracle happen. Out of a rock came water that was so good that the people thought it was a refreshment.

When Paul told that story, he told it with great enthusiasm. He told the people that even though Jesus was born in the world like a small baby, it still was he who gave the hungry and thirsty people new trust.

Paul called Jesus a mighty rock of spiritual refreshment. You know what refreshment is like, don't you? Do you remember when you were outside playing, and you ran and jumped so much that you were just dying of thirst? Your throat was so dry that you thought you had swallowed a whole bunch of cotton. When you came into your mother's kitchen, she saw how hot and tired you were and she poured you a glass of the best tasting lemonade you ever tasted. Do you remember anything like that happening to you? (*let them answer*) Wasn't it wonderful? I know it was, because I remember when it happened to me.

Paul used to love to tell the story about the way that God cared for his people, and I suppose that every time he poured a glass of cool juice on a hot day, he would tell the story of the way that God helped his people in the desert.

The next time you need a cool drink, and you are so thirsty you don't know what to do, I hope that you are like Paul and think about the great care that God gave to his people.

196

Stumbling Blocks

1 Corinthians 10:31—11:1

Give no offense to Jews or to Greeks or to the Church of God. (v. 32)

Object: things that might be on the floor in a typical child's room before it is cleaned: clothes, books, games, and so on, strewn out across the room

Good morning, boys and girls. Take a look at what has happened here. Have you ever seen such a mess? (*spread out all of the things that you can, so that it is representative of one of the worst rooms that you can imagine*) Do you know what this looks like? (*let them answer*) Have you ever seen a room like this at your house? (*let them answer*) Has your room ever looked like this before you and your mother or father cleaned it up? (*let them answer*) It is pretty messy, isn't it? It's also dangerous. Have you ever tried to walk through a room like this in the dark? If you ever did, I bet you stumbled or tripped. It is really dangerous. You can fall and get hurt in a room like this. We could call these things stumbling blocks.

Sometimes people are like stumbling blocks to other people. Paul knew people like this who kept other people from believing in Jesus. He said that there were some Christians who were so careless with the way they lived and talked that they kept other people from believing in Jesus. Paul called this behavior "giving offense" or "being a stumbling block."

Maybe you know some people like this. They call themselves Christians and they may even come to Sunday school and church, but when they go out to play or to school, they are mean or they say bad things. When other people who are trying to be Christians see how they act or behave, they may decide that they don't want to be Christians if that's the way you turn out. Those are stumbling-block Christians. They keep getting in other people's way.

People who are stumbling blocks are like a room with all of the clothes and toys scattered over the floor. We all know that they don't belong there and we know that someone may get hurt, but we are careless. We forget what it is like to trip and get hurt. Some boys and girls forget what it would be like to be without Jesus. They know how good Jesus is to them, but they don't care if someone else knows or not.

When you are playing or in school or wherever you are, I want you to remember that people learn about Jesus through you. They think that Jesus is like you are, and if you are mean or angry, then your Jesus must be mean and angry. That is a stumbling block for them. So, be good to your friends and show them respect. Love them a lot and they will know Jesus as a God of love and respect. Put away the stumbling blocks and make new friends for Jesus.

No Energy Crisis With God

1 Corinthians 12:3-11

Now there are varieties of gifts, but the same Spirit. (v. 4)

Object: a can of oil, a can of gasoline, a plastic hairbrush

Good morning, boys and girls. Today we are going to talk about power, and about the source of power. We are going to talk about energy. These are some pretty important words. Have you heard that someday our world may run out of oil? (*let them answer*) People who study these things say that this world does not have a never-ending supply of oil. Oil is found in the earth and people drill for it, but just when it seems that we need oil the most we find that we are running out of it and we are going to have to find other sources of energy.

Do you know what we make with the oil that we find in the earth? (*let them answer*) That's right; we make gasoline, we heat our homes, and make the fine oil that we use in our cars. We even make things like this plastic handle on the hairbrush out of oil. Oil is a great source of energy. When you have oil you have power, and when you have plenty of oil, you have plenty of power.

This is something like the story of humans and God. People can do lots of things, but the power that they need to do the things that they want to do comes from one source of power or energy called God. God gives people the power to heal like a doctor, teach like a teacher, and preach like a preacher. God gives people the energy to invent airplanes and rockets and write poetry and make a good dinner. God is the source of all our energy and all of our talents. The wonderful thing about God as our source of energy is that he will never run out. There will always be plenty of talent and plenty of energy because God is overflowing with both. We can run out of oil or any other kind of mineral or supply, but we will never run out of the energy and talent that God provides.

That means that all of us get our energy and talent from the same place. There is as much energy and talent as we want to use. If we use what God gives us only a little, then we will only have a little talent or energy. If we use him a lot then we will have a lot. It also means that as different as our talent or energy is, it still comes from the same power supply. The power supply is God. The next time you read a poet's poem or you take some medicine, or one of your parents fixes a wonderful dinner, you can remember that their talents and gifts all come from the same place. They come from God.

Your talents come from God, too. Isn't that great?

Parts Working Smoothly

1 Corinthians 12:12-21, 26-27

Now you are the body of Christ and individually members of it. (v. 27)

Object: automobile parts (an be borrowed from car dealer)

Good morning, boys and girls. How many of you have ever been to a car garage where automobiles are sold or repaired? (*let them answer*) A lot of you. Don't you just love to go and see the new automobiles and then take a deep breath and smell that good smell that goes with the new cars? I like that. In the garage you can watch the mechanics work under the cars that need to be fixed. They have lights hooked on to a part of a frame so that they can see what they are doing. Whenever I go to a garage I am amazed that someone knows all about those parts that it takes to make a car run. Everything can be fine with the car except one little part and the car won't run right until it is fixed.

I brought along some of those parts so that you and I can take a look at them and see what it takes to make a car run. It's fun to look at them when they are brand new and see all the funny shapes of each part that is made so that each one will fit with another part that fits with another part that fits with another part. It seems like each one of the parts needs another part if it is going to work. Maybe someday one of you will be a mechanic and we can bring our cars to you to be fixed.

I told you that each one of the parts of an automobiles is important and that they need each other to make them run right. The same thing is true about the Christian church and the people who belong to it. The church is made up of people. It takes a lot of people working together to make the whole church run right. God gives us the power to run but we must use the power to make sure that all of us are doing the things that we do best if the church is to run like a smooth-running car. The church needs teachers, preachers, evangelists (*people who tell others about Jesus*), and generous givers of money. It needs people who care about our health, people to take care of the lonely and many others. When something happens to the people who do these things and they break down, they need to be fixed, or helped. One person who is not working smoothly means that the rest of us are not going to work smoothly. We have many parts but we are all one church.

Now you know why a garage reminded me of the body of Jesus Christ and how important it is to have it in good condition. Each part of a car is important and so is every member of the Church of Jesus Christ. You remember this and you will be a strong member of Christ's community.

When A Child ...

1 Corinthians 12:27—13:13

When I was a child, I spoke like a child, I thought like a child, I reasoned like a child; when I became an adult, I put an end to childish ways. (v. 11)

Object: a coloring book, a novel, a toy car, a set of car keys

Good morning, boys and girls. How many of you can hardly wait until you are grown up and can do the things that your mom and dad do now? (*let them answer*) That's good. We want you to want to grow up. It would not be any fun always to be a child, even though many adults wish that they could go back to being what you are today.

There are some big differences between being a child and being a mom or dad. I brought along some things that are somewhat alike and still are a lot different. First of all I have a coloring book. How many of you like to color in a book like this with different colored crayons? Almost all of you. This coloring book is a child's book and you should like it. (*hold up the novel*) This is an adult book and adults like this kind of book as much as you like a coloring book. I have something else that many children like to play with. (*hold up the toy car*) How many of you have cars like this? That's good. You should like to play with toys. I also have a set of keys to a real car. (*hold up the car keys*) Most men and women enjoy driving a car. Even if you wished that you could drive a car, you know that you would not be able to do so for some years until you grow up. There are certain things that belong to children, and there are certain things that belong to adults.

There is a good reason why I have shown you the difference between what it is to be an adult and what it is to be a child. The same thing is true about being a Christian now and being a Christian with God after death in the next life. Now we only understand a little bit about how good it is to be a Christian. When we die and start our new life with Christ in God's new world, we will understand much more and we will like it even better. Being a Christian now is wonderful, but the new life with Jesus will be terrific. Now you like to play with little cars, but I know that you will enjoy driving one of your own on the highway even better. Now you know what it is to be a Christian even though you do not understand everything about God and what he is really like. Now we know a little but when we go to live with God forever, we will understand more, much more.

That is why everyone here on earth is like a child to God, and our grown-up days are all after we leave this earth and go to live with God forever.

Treasures You Can Share

1 Corinthians 14:12b-20

Therefore, one who speaks in a tongue should pray for the power to interpret. (v. 13)

Object: a piece of modern art and a piece of traditional art

Good morning, boys and girls. Today we are going to talk about something that you may not have heard a lot about but something that has been a problem in the Christian church for a long time. Have you ever heard about people who speak in tongues? (*let them answer*) That means that they can speak in a foreign language that even they don't understand, but they believe that it is a gift from God. The Apostle Paul knew about it and, as a matter of fact, he could speak in tongues. But Paul said that we must be careful about the way that we use that gift. Sometimes people are more impressed about what they are saying than what actual good they are doing. Paul thought that this was dangerous.

I have an example of what I am talking about. Here is a painting that you and I might call modern art. The colors are beautiful, and they go together very nicely, but what does it mean to us? The artist knows what it means but that does nothing for you and me. We can't tell what the painter is trying to describe. The only way that we could find out is if the painter were here and could tell us what he or she felt when painting the picture. Even then I am sure that the artist would tell you that it could mean something different to each of us. That is one kind of painting. There are many different kinds of art and a favorite for most people is a picture like this one. (*hold up a piece of traditional art*) What does this look like to you? (*let them answer one at a time*) You all agree that the picture tells the same story to each of you.

There is a big difference between the paintings. I want to explain the difference to you. There is nothing wrong with the first painting, and to the painter it may mean much more than the second painting, but it is very hard to share the first one while almost everyone can enjoy and understand the second one.

It is the same way when we talk about the gift of speaking in tongues. To the person who has the gift, it is wonderful, but it is very hard to share with others. If the person has a gift that he can share with everyone, then everyone can enjoy the gift that is sent from God. That is why Paul thought that the gift of tongues was a real treasure, but not as great a treasure as the gifts that could be shared with all.

Lord Of Light And Life
(Appropriate for Easter)

1 Corinthians 15:19-28

For since death came through a human being, the resurrection of the dead has also come through a human being. (v. 21)

Object: two buckets of water

Good morning, boys and girls and a very happy Easter to all of you. What a day this is for all of us who believe that Jesus Christ is risen from the dead! Just think, one day Jesus was dead and lying in a grave, and the next day he was alive again, walking and talking to people he knew and loved. It is a great day and one that we never forget.

One of the things about Jesus coming back to life that is so great is that he came back to life as a human. He didn't come as a ghost or some kind of big smoke, he came back to life as a person. It was a person who committed the first sin that brought death into the world. Do you remember the story in the Bible about Adam and Eve and how they broke their promises to God? (*let them answer*) When they broke their promises they also brought death as a part of life. Let me show you what I mean. (*bring out the buckets filled with water*)

I have a couple of buckets filled with water. One of these buckets I keep filled so that I can kill a fire. When I pour this bucket of water on a fire, the fire dies and is gone. There is no more light or heat. The fire is cold and dead. That happened because of the bucket of water I poured on it.

Here is another bucket of water. I am going to use this bucket of water to help grow some vegetable plants in my garden. I will water the plants very carefully so that they will grow strong in the ground. Some day I will eat the things that are grown on the plants. The water gives the plant life, and makes it strong.

The water is the same. It came from the same place, but one bucket kills and the other gives life. That is what the Bible teaches us is the difference between the person who sinned and brought death to all of us, and Jesus who came and brought life to us. Easter day is the time that we celebrate the life that Jesus gave back to us after human's sin had brought us to death.

That is why we worship Jesus and show him so much love. None of us want death. All of us want life. We want more and more life and that is because God wants us to live forever. Jesus made that happen when he was resurrected and promised us that the same thing would happen to us that happened to him. We shall be like the plants in the garden that live because of the water that was shared so carefully. We shall not ever again be like the fire that was killed when the water was poured on it.

Both buckets have water. Both sin and life came from persons. Only one of the them was Jesus, and he brought life to share with us forever.

202

Saying "Yes" To Jesus

2 Corinthians 1:18-22

For the Son of God, Jesus Christ, whom we proclaimed among you, Silvanus and Timothy and I, was not "Yes and No" but in him it is always "Yes." (v. 19)

Object: a red floor tile, a white floor tile, and a gray floor tile (you may use three of anything that has these colors)

Good morning, boys and girls. Is everyone happy? (*let them answer*) Do you make other people feel good when you are with them? (*let them answer*) That's good! Some people feel good and never show it. Other people feel good and help other people to feel good. I want you to make people feel good by just being near them.

Today, we are going to learn a lesson that is a hard one to learn. How many of you say, "Maybe," or "I don't care." Is there anyone here who says, "It doesn't make any difference"? (*take out your gray tile*) "Maybe" is a gray answer. "I don't care" is a gray answer. "It doesn't make any difference" is a gray answer. We don't like gray answers.

How many of you say, "No," a lot or "Not me," a lot? "No" is a red answer. (*hold up your red tile*) When I ask someone to help me and they say, "No," or "Not me," or "Ask somebody else," I feel bad because I wanted to share something with you.

How many of you say, "Yes," a lot or "Okay, you can count on me"? (*hold up your white tile*) What a difference "Yes" makes when you are trying to do something and you need someone to help. "Yes" makes you feel great.

Saint Paul told the Christians in Corinth about the same things. They were always in the "Maybe" class instead of the "Yes" class. They could say, "No," but most of the time it was just "Maybe." Paul said there was never a time that Jesus did not say, "Yes," to them.

Paul said Jesus said, "Yes," to forgiving them. Jesus said, "Yes," when it was time to die for them. Jesus said, "Yes," when they needed his help in any way. Jesus was the Savior. Jesus said, "Yes, I love you." Jesus said, "Yes, I will heal you." Jesus said, "Yes," when they wanted to share eternal life. Jesus was a "Yes" person.

When it comes to talking with Jesus, "Maybe" is a habit, a bad habit. "No" is a habit, a bad habit. "Yes" is also a habit but it is a good habit when you are serving God. If Jesus says, "Please help me and share your gifts with my people," he doesn't want to hear "Maybe" or "No." Jesus wants us to lift up our hearts and say, "Yes." Yes, I will learn, yes, I will follow, and yes, I will share with God and all of God's friends.

Changing In The Spirit

2 Corinthians 3:12—4:2

And all of us, with unveiled face, seeing the glory of the Lord as though reflected in a mirror, are being transformed into the same image from one degree of glory to another; for this comes from the Lord, the Spirit. (v. 18)

Object: a heating pad

Good morning, boys and girls. How many of you have a heating pad? (*let them answer*) Aren't they great? I think a heating pad when you are sick is one of the best things that I know. As a matter of fact it seems to make you feel better than all of the medicine. Do you remember the last time you had a cold and you felt just terrible? Shivering one minute and so very hot the next that you knew something had to be wrong. After your mother gave you medicine she might have asked you if you would like the heating pad.

The best part of the heating pad is the little switch that comes with it. Sometimes you put the pad on your cold feet and sometimes you like to lay it under you, but you always hold on to the switch. Do you remember what the switch looks like? (*let them answer*) That's right; it usually has colors and one of them is hotter than the rest. You can have it on warm, pretty warm, or hot. You can change it by degrees. Most people start out with "hot" and then change it to pretty warm and then back to nice, plain warm. You keep changing the heat by degrees with that little switch. How many of you remember that switch? (*let them answer*)

Did you know that Jesus is changing you by degrees just like you change the heating pad by degrees? Did you know that his Spirit was changing you everyday so that you will be a little more like him all of the time? That's right. God is working on you through the Spirit to change you a little bit by a little bit so that you are becoming more like him every day. Isn't that great? We are changing by degrees. Do you remember the heating pad and how you would push the switch and you would never know when it got a little cooler or a little hotter but it just all of a sudden was not as hot or not as cold as it was before you moved the switch? That is the way the Spirit of God is working inside of you. Everyday that you learn and practice the things Jesus teaches you, you find that you are becoming more like Jesus. I think that is wonderful, and I am sure that you think so too.

The next time you take a look at your heating pad, look at the switch and see what I mean. Turn it on to warm first, and then move it up. You will not know when it got hot, but pretty soon you will feel the difference. You have changed the heat by degrees. The Spirit of God is changing you and making you more like the Lord Jesus every day. That is one of the ways God works, and I think it is one of the best.

The Treasure Inside

2 Corinthians 4:5-12

But we have this treasure in clay jars, so that it may be made clear that this extraordinary power belongs to God and does not come from us. (v. 7)

Object: a coffee can filled with jewelry and money

Good morning, boys and girls. Today we want to talk a little bit about the way God shares all his wonderful blessings with us. I have always thought that it was pretty nice of God to share his world with me. He could have chosen the animals or the plants to share his story with, but instead he chose people. The Bible talks about it in another way. Let me show you what I mean.

Let's suppose that you and I are really coffee cans. Has anyone ever called you a coffee can? (*let them answer*) I didn't think so. But I want you to pretend that you are an old coffee can. Do you have any old coffee cans at home? (*let them answer*) What do you use them for? (*let them answer*) For junk, right! I keep old screws and nails in one coffee can. In another one there are string, washers, old paint brushes, and a lot of rust and dirt. There is nothing very valuable in a coffee can. Just suppose that you are one of God's coffee cans and he has chosen you to carry something around for him. What do you think God would put in you if you were one of his old coffee cans? (*let them answer*)

Well, the truth of the matter is that God thinks you are a pretty neat coffee can. If we open the coffee can that I have brought and pretend that this is really you, we find that he has put all his jewels inside of you. (*show them the coffee can filled with pretty jewelry and money*) Wow, what a coffee can! Have you ever seen one like this around your house? Look at the jewels and the money. If you are God's old coffee can, you are really something according to God. He has trusted you with the best that he has. Of course God doesn't put jewels and money inside of us, but he does trust us with the best that he has.

Just think; he gave you the story of all of his heroes to remember. He shared with us his law like the Ten Commandments. He gave us the life of Jesus to keep for ourselves and also to share with others. He taught us how to pray and to forgive. He gave us a place in which to live, all his sunshine, food, and everything else that is really important. All these things he put into people like you and me. We may look like old coffee cans, but we are really something to God.

The next time that you see an old coffee can, I hope it reminds you of this one that I have with me today. When you see it you will say, "I am one of God's coffee cans and that makes me someone really special. I have all God's favorite things inside of me and I can share what he has given with all my friends."

Will you do that too? Wonderful!

God's Guarantee

2 Corinthians 5:1-10

He who has prepared us for this very thing is God, who has given us the Spirit as a guarantee. (v. 5)

Object: A *Good Housekeeping* seal, a guarantee

Good morning, boys and girls. How many of you know what the word *guarantee* means? (*let them answer*) The word *guarantee* sounds like a big word but it means that someone is promising someone else that whatever they say is really going to happen.

Let me show you what I mean. There is a magazine called the *Good Housekeeping* magazine and in it there are advertisements. Sometimes *Good Housekeeping* places a special seal with these advertisements. This is their guarantee that whatever is promised in the advertisement will do exactly as it says. The *Good Housekeeping* magazine promises you that this thing will work or they will give you your money back.

God makes guarantees also. Instead of a Good Housekeeping seal, God sends us the Holy Spirit as his guarantee. God promises you and me that whatever he says to us or whatever he does for us will never fail and his spirit teaches us that truth.

God is preparing you and me for a time when we will live with him. We can't do that now. It isn't time for us to live with God in his world, so he shows us how good it will be by sharing his Holy Spirit with us in our world today. When God's spirit is with us it is very much like the way God will make it in the new world. The Holy Spirit makes our lives wonderful, and when you and I share our lives with him, we know that God's promise is true.

When you see the Good Housekeeping seal, you know that the magazine promises you that their advertisements are true and they work. When God's spirit teaches us a truth in the Bible, it is God's guarantee to us that whatever he says is absolutely true.

Remember this: The Holy Spirit is God's guarantee, and you can believe that promise as long as you live.

Share What You Have

2 Corinthians 8:1-9, 13-14

... but it is a question of fair balance between your present abundance and their need, so that their abundance may be for your need, in order that there may be a fair balance. (vv. 13-14)

Object: an ice cube tray with removable dividers and a pitcher of water

Good morning, boys and girls. We live in a wonderful land, don't we? (*let them answer*) We have so many things that sometimes it is hard for us to appreciate all that we have. We have food, clothes, good houses, yards to play in, parks, cars, and all sorts of other wonderful things. We have so much that we sometimes do not know what to do with it all. The Bible says we have an abundance.

Abundance means more than what we need, and that's good. It is better to have more, than to have less, but not everyone has more. Some people do not have any of the things that you or I have. They are hungry, they wear rags, they don't have any yards or parks to play in. They have much less.

It has almost always been like this. Even in the times of Jesus there were people with abundance, and people who had almost nothing. What should we think about a problem where some people have more than they can use and other people don't have any at all? Let me show you what I think is the answer. (*take out the ice cube tray and the pitcher of water*)

I am going to pour some water into this end of the tray and I am not going to pour any water into the other end of the tray. We will say the end of the tray with the water has an abundance. The other end has nothing. Let us see what happens. (*pour the water into the tray and let the children see how each cubicle fills up to the same place*)

What do you think of this, boys and girls? What has happened? (*let them answer*) All of the parts now have the same amount of water. The end with the abundance has shared with the end that has nothing. The Apostle Paul taught us that Christians should learn to share their abundance with others who have nothing. Some day the people who now have nothing will have an abundance and they will want to share what they have with those who may have nothing. It's a good plan and it helps people to know each other and love one another. The next time you see an ice cube tray, maybe you can remember the story of how Christians learn to share their abundance with others.

Look To The Lord

2 Corinthians 12:7-10

But he said to me, "My grace is sufficient for you, for my power is made perfect in weakness." (v. 9a)

Object: two different kinds of medicine and a heavy pan

Good morning, boys and girls. How are you feeling today? (*let them respond*) That's good, because if you weren't, you could probably take some of this medicine here! (*hold up the medicine*) Did you ever see that commercial on television about the woman who has a very sore arm? In that commercial, she tells us that she has arthritis and that it is very hard for her to pick up something like this pan. (*show them the pan*)

Would one of you like to lift this pan? (*let several children try to lift it*) It is pretty heavy but it isn't too heavy for you, is it? Well, in the commercial, the woman with the sore arm just can't lift it. Her arms hurt too much. So guess what she is told to do? Does anyone know? (*let them guess*) A man with several bottles of medicine tells her to try this one special kind. So she tries it. What happens to her after she takes the medicine? (*let them tell you*) Right! She can lift the pan without any trouble at all! It is almost like magic, isn't it, boys and girls? The woman's pain goes away after she takes this particular pill. That must be a pretty wonderful pill, don't you agree? (*let them respond*)

Then there is another commercial about a person who has a terrible cold. She is sitting in bed, coughing and sneezing and blowing her nose. She looks and sounds just terrible! Did you ever have a coughing-sneezing-dripping kind of cold, boys and girls? (*let them respond*) Well, then you know just how this woman looked and sounded. However, she sent her husband to the drug store for something very special. She knew that there was a kind of medicine which would stop her sneezing, take away her sore throat, clear up her head so she could breathe, stop her coughing, and help her to sleep. Did you ever hear of a medicine like that? (*let them respond*) Well, I guess this medicine really worked — at least on television, because after she took it, the woman was able to sleep.

You know, sometimes we read some of the Apostle Paul's letters during our worship service. Paul must have had a special problem — either a bad pain or some other kind of thing that was hard for him to live with. Paul doesn't tell us what it is — but apparently there weren't any special medicines for it like the ones we have today. Paul even talked to the Lord about it, but the Lord said not to worry. God's grace would help him to stand it. Sometimes all the medicines in the world won't help us feel better, will they, boys and girls? Then we have to remember Paul; he just put his trust in the Lord and let the Lord take care of him. That isn't always easy for us to do, is it, boys and girls? That's what trust and faith are all about — putting our hand in the Lord's hand and letting him take care of us. The next time we see one of these commercials about pills and other wonderful medicines, let's remember that sometimes we have to just look to the Lord — especially when everything else fails.

Jesus Rescued Us

Galatians 1:1-10

... who gave himself for our sins to set us free from the present evil age, according to the will of our God and Father. (v. 4)

Object: some rescue equipment like a firefighter's net or a big rope

Good morning, boys and girls. I have a real surprise for you this morning that I know you are going to like. How many of you have ever been to the fire department? (*let them answer*) Some of you have. How many of you have ever watched a show on television in which the building is on fire and someone is trapped on the sixth floor? (*let them answer*) That person has to jump if he is going to be saved. Almost all of you have seen shows like that. What do the people jump into? Is there a big pool of water or a giant sponge? (*let them answer*) You are right, they jump into the net. Let's hold up the net and see what it is really like. (*take out the net and display it*) It still seems dangerous jumping that far, but when you have the choice of either burning up or jumping I think that you would jump. We call that being rescued. If we understand how important it is that someone can rescue us from a fire, then maybe we can also understand how important it was for Jesus to do what he did.

The Bible teaches us that Jesus died for our sins. Sometimes that doesn't make sense to people. What Jesus really did was rescue us from dying. God knew that if we did not know how much he loved us, we would go the way the devil wanted us to go. The devil is tricky and he knows how to make us think that bad things are good and good things are bad. The devil was doing a good job, and people like you and me were following the devil. God had tried everything to show us what was happening, but we didn't listen. Finally God knew that there would have to be one thing done that would rescue and set us free us from the devil. If God was willing to die so that we would know how much he loved us, maybe we would turn around and follow him. That's what he did.

Jesus' dying on the cross is the best rescue that ever happened. He died so that we would see the trickiness of the devil and know that God really does love us as much as he said he does. In other words, Jesus rescued us just as firefighters rescue you with their net. Firefighters rescue you in this life but Jesus rescues you forever.

Will you think about how Jesus rescues us the next time you see a fire truck? Good.

God Can Even Use Garbage

Galatians 1:11-24

They only heard it said, "The one who formerly was persecuting us is now proclaiming the faith he once tried to destroy." (v. 23)

Object: some sacks of garbage and some clip clothespins

Good morning, boys and girls. Today we are going to learn a great lesson, one that we all hope will be the answer for everyone in the world who does not believe in Jesus this very moment.

First of all, I am going to pass out some clothespins to pinch our noses so that we will not smell what I brought with me this morning. (*put a clothespin on every child's nose*) Now, I am going to show you what I brought with me this morning. (*bring out the garbage*) Do you know what this is that I have in the bags? (*let them answer*) That's right, garbage. Have you ever seen sacks of garbage in church before? I haven't either.

But, did you know that there are a lot of people in this country who think that garbage can provide energy for us? One man even ran his car on garbage that he made into a kind of gasoline. Other people think that it can be used to heat our homes. Garbage! Of course, it would not be able to smell like this to run our cars or heat our homes, but wouldn't it be wonderful if we could use all of our garbage for something useful like heat or fuel? Of course it would. Even something as bad as garbage can be made into something good and powerful.

Garbage isn't the only thing that can turn from bad to good. There was a man by the name of Saul who worked and worked to get rid of every Christian. He was worse than garbage. He thought that he was doing God a favor by getting rid of Christians. He would hunt them like hunters hunt animals and, when he caught them, he would find ways to have them beaten or even killed. It was awful.

But one day, while Saul was on his way after some more Christians, Saul saw Jesus in a vision. Jesus spoke to Saul in such a way that Saul never forgot it. It was really quite an experience. For a while Saul was blind, but that soon passed. Saul believed in what happened and in the voice that spoke to him, and he became a Christian like the ones he had been hunting. As a matter of fact, when Saul started over as a Christian, he changed his name to Paul and became a great missionary for Jesus. When Paul went somewhere, the people came out to see how one man could change from such a hunter to such a lover of God.

Paul was almost like garbage that becomes energy. The way he acted as a hunter no one could stand to be around him. But when he was changed into energy, people were thrilled to be around him. Maybe when you see your next sack of garbage, you will think of the way Saul was changed to Paul, and you will also pray to be just like him.

210

Where Is God?

Galatians 2:20

And it is no longer I who live, but it is Christ who lives in me. And the life I now live in the flesh I live by faith in the Son of God, who loved me and gave himself for me. (v. 20)

Object: a walnut or any nut that has an outer shell that comes off easily

Good morning, boys and girls. How many of you think that you know a lot about that which we call Christian faith? There are many important things we should know about God. These are things that he has told us and important and things that he has included in his Holy Word. I know of no one who asks more questions — and important questions — about God than people your age, and it is time that we tried to answer some of them. We want to talk a lot about Jesus and how and why he died and not only that he died but that he lives again, and, in his own words, he lives within us.

Did you know that Jesus lived within you? He does. Let me show you what I mean. You see what I have in my hand? (*hold up a walnut*) What do we call this? (*let them answer*) That's right, a nut. But do you see the nut? (*let them answer*) What do you do with a nut? (*let them answer*) Is there anyone here who would like to eat a nut, this nut? (*see if you can get a volunteer to put the shell in his or her mouth*)

How does that nut taste? Not very good is it? Do you know why? Because, that's the shell and not the nut. Where is the nut? (*let them answer*) That's right; it is inside the shell. You can't see it but you are very sure that it is there. Shall we open it and see if the nut is in there? (*with great mystery you begin to pry open the shell and at first reveal it only to yourself until you notice some little craning necks*) Sure enough, there it is. The nut is inside the shell.

Now why did I tell you this story? A long time ago, the Apostle Paul answered this very same question for a lot of people who were wondering the same thing that you wonder about, "Where is God?" Paul said that Jesus Christ is not far away for the Christian, but that he is very near, so near in fact that many of us miss him when we are looking for him. Paul said that for the man or woman or boy and girl, Christ is not out there or up there, but that he is inside you. That's right; Jesus Christ is living within you and while you look like Sally or Jane or Pete or Mike on the outside, if you are really a Christian, you shall have Christ within you.

That's what Paul means when he said that it is not I who lives but Christ who lives within me.

So where is God for the Christian? He lives within you and what a warm feeling that must be to know that Jesus is so close that he can never be separated from you!

211

A Warm, Steamy Bath

Galatians 3:26-29

For in Christ Jesus you are all children of God through faith. (v. 26)

Object: a big bath towel

Good morning, boys and girls. How many of you took a bath last night? (*let them raise their hands*) Was it hot and steamy? I just love to take a bath and feel the hot water roll over me. I don't know if I always liked to take a bath, but I surely do like it now. How many of you can remember a time when your mother or father put a big bath towel like this one around you after your bath and gave you a big hug? (*take a big bath towel and wrap it around one of the children so that they can associate the feeling*) That really feels good, doesn't it? It makes you feel like you really belong, or that you are completely safe, doesn't it?

That is the way that we should feel after we have been baptized and made Christians. It is like being wrapped in a big towel by your mother or father. You really know that you belong, because Jesus gives you his name and makes you one of his own. That is the wonderful part about being baptized. You become part of Jesus' family. It is great to know that Jesus is your brother and God is your Father. That is one of the promises that comes with baptism.

Everybody doesn't have that privilege. Your mother or father wraps the big towel around you to show that she or he loves you and really cares about you.

Jesus is that way with baptism. When you are baptized, it is something very special and it is a great gift. Perhaps you will remember how much Jesus cares the next time that you take a bath and your mother or father puts a big towel around you. And when you think about how much Jesus cares, you can also think about your baptism and how you became a member of God's family. That is something to know and be very happy about.

Is It Time Yet?

Galatians 4:4-7

But when the fullness of time had come, God sent his Son, born of woman, born under the law. (v. 4)

Object: an egg timer

Good morning, boys and girls. Today we are going to talk about Mary, the mother of Jesus. All of us know that Mary was the mother of Jesus, but, except for Christmas and maybe a few other times, we never talk much about her. God chose Mary to be the mother of Jesus for his own special reasons. We don't know why he chose her instead of some other woman, except that she was related to King David who had died a long time before Jesus or Mary were born. But God had his special reasons, and we think he chose the perfect mother for Jesus.

I suppose that Mary would have been loved by many and a good friend to a lot of people, even if she had never been chosen to be the mother of Jesus. But the thing that really made her special was the fact that she listened to God when he spoke, and she obeyed what he told her, and she became the mother of Jesus. God wanted his Son Jesus to be like other people. He did not want to just plop Jesus down on earth as a grown-up man and pretend that he had grown up as other people. He did not want to have a man called his Son who did not know what it was like to be loved by a mother who cared for him when he was a child. He wanted his Son to be as much like the other people as he could be and still be the Son of God. Then God chose just the right time in our history to send his Son into the world.

It is almost the same way that your mother or father cooks an egg. Have you ever watched one of them soft-boil an egg? Your mom or dad times it so it doesn't cook too long or too short. The time must be just right. The reason a lot of cooks use a timer is so that they will know just the right time to cook the eggs. That is why your eggs taste so good. A good cook knows just the right amount of time to cook the eggs.

Now that is the way God works. God has a schedule, a time schedule, and he knew just when he wanted his Son born into the world. He chose Mary to be the mother and by doing it that way made her the most famous mother in all of history. But Mary was a good mother — the best — because she trusted everything to God. She knew that God was right, that he would not make a mistake, and that her son would be his Son.

Maybe the next time you see your mom or dad time an egg, you will remember how God timed his Son, and when it was just the right time, he chose Mary to be the mother of Jesus.

213

Getting Untwisted

Galatians 5:1, 13-25

For freedom Christ has set us free. Stand firm, therefore, and do not submit again to a yoke of slavery. (v. 1)

Object: a necklace or chain or some string that easily twists and untwists

Good morning, boys and girls. How many of you have ever played with a chain or a necklace like this and watched it get all twisted up, and then untwist itself? (*let them answer*) Oh, that's good, a lot of you have done this. That means that you will understand what I am talking about in our little experiment. It is important that you watch the chain when it is unwinding, or otherwise it will wind right back up the other way. Now if you want your chain to be straight, then you must let it unwind to just a certain point and then make it stop.

Some people are like chains that get twisted or untwisted, and I want to tell you about the difference. The Apostle Paul tells us about how Jesus frees us from all of our problems and sins, and how wonderful that feeling is. But then some people, after being free, forget and go back to being the same way they once were, all twisted up.

Let's think about that for a minute. Suppose you have done something terrible and you are really sorry about the thing you did. You know that you should not have done it, but you did it anyway. You are sorry and you ask Jesus for help. The next thing you know, he has helped you, and you are very happy that you are forgiven and free from that awful sin.

Some people are like the chain. They never stop. They just keep right on winding until the next thing they know they are in trouble again. A long time ago people were like that about the laws people made. They were so mixed up about the law of eating the right kind of food or working the job in just the right way that they forgot what food was for or why they were working. Jesus set them free from that kind of worry and they were glad. But the next thing you know they were so free from the worry about a certain food or work that they were in trouble about something else.

Jesus makes us free from our twists, but we need to remember that we need Jesus to *keep* us that way and not forget him. Jesus is that answer to getting untwisted, and he is also the answer to keeping us that way.

Don't Ignore The Signs

Galatians 6:1-10, 14-17

Do not be deceived; God is not mocked, for you reap whatever you sow. (v. 7)

Object: some signs, such as "Stop," "Keep Off The Grass," or "Beware Of Dog"

Good morning, boys and girls. How many of you know what the word *ignore* means? It is a very good word, but I wonder how many of you know what it means? (*let them answer*) Very good, it means that you are not paying attention to someone or something. I have a friend who does not pay attention to signs. He ignores them. When he rides his bike in the street, he ignores this sign. (*hold up "Stop" sign*) Do you know what happens? (*let them answer*) That's right; he wrecks his bike. Sometimes he goes through a stranger's yard and he ignores these signs. (*hold up "Keep Off The Grass" and "Beware Of Dog" signs*) Now, what do you think happens? The owner yells at him and the dog bites him! It doesn't pay to ignore signs.

Some people ignore God, which is sometimes called "mocking" God. They know that he is around and is very important to other people, but they forget that God is important for them also. When you forget God, it costs you. The Bible teaches us that we have just the kind of lives in the future that we plan for right now. If you forget all about God and his life and forgiveness, then you will be missing God's love and forgiveness. God has certain rules such as the Ten Commandments, and you must keep those rules and never ignore them. If you do ignore them, then you will have the punishment that God says goes with ignoring the rules.

The Bible teaches us that we should not ignore or mock God. That makes sense just as the signs make sense. The stop sign is there for our protection. If you stop, then no one gets hurt and everyone is happy. If you don't stop, or just ignore the sign, then someone may get hurt.

Listening to God and paying attention makes happy people. When you are paying attention you are finding new ways to love and share with other people. It is is a good thing to remember, for everyone who wants to be happy. Never ignore God and the teachings of God, and you will know love and happiness.

215

Safe With The Spirit

Ephesians 1:3-14

In him you also, who have heard the word of truth, the gospel of your salvation, and have believed in him, were marked with the seal of the promised Holy Spirit. (v. 13)

Object: a large manila envelope

Good morning, boys and girls. How many of you have ever used an envelope? (*let them answer; then show them a big manila envelope*) Have you ever written a letter or sent something to a friend through the mail and you needed an envelope? It's fun to write letters and even more fun to get them, isn't it?

You can't just send the letter without an envelope. The envelope is important because whatever you put inside is kept together. If I just sent the letter without an envelope, there would be no address, the pages would come apart, or the stamp would cover part of what was said. I couldn't send a check or money without putting it in an envelope because no one would know who it was for and it would simply be lost or taken. An envelope is really a very important part of any letter that you send.

The Holy Spirit is like an envelope. A Christian has many parts and all of the parts are important. A Christian learns from other Christians and from the Bible. A Christian believes many things about God and the way God loves him. A Christian shares many of the things that he has, such as money, food, clothes, and all kinds of things. But the Holy Spirit brings all of those things together and keeps them together so that none of them are lost. That's why we say the Holy Spirit is like an envelope. The Holy Spirit not only keeps them together for you but also keeps you for God. The Holy Spirit promises God the Father that what you learn and what you believe and what you share will be kept forever, and the Holy Spirit doesn't do that just for you but for everyone who believes in, learns about, and shares God.

If you have ever seen a post office or if you have looked into a mail carrier's mailbag, you will see all kinds of envelopes. The Holy Spirit shares himself with everyone. There are many hundreds, thousands, and millions of people who have learned and shared and believed in God. The Holy Spirit keeps every one of them safely for God the Father. That's his promise and he keeps it.

Made For Something Good

Ephesians 2:4-10

For we are what he has made us, created in Christ Jesus for good works, which God prepared beforehand to be our way of life. (v. 10)

Object: something handcrafted, like a dress, a piece of woodworking, or some pottery

Good morning, boys and girls. How many of you like to work with your hands and make things to use at home or in school? (*let them answer*) Some boys and girls used to make pencil holders for me so that I would have a place to keep my pencils on my desk. There are other things that people make that take a lot of work, but they really feel good when they are finished with them. I brought a dress with me that one of the women in our congregation made on her sewing machine. I also have a small stool that one of the men made in his workshop. These are not things that were bought in a store, but things that people made with their own hands at home. It makes you feel good to make something that you can use or wear.

Those are some of the things we can make. Did you ever think of some of the things that God has made that are for the good of everyone? Tell me something that you think God made. (*let them answer*) You are so right. He did make the trees, the grass, the sky, and the oceans.

Did you know that he also made you and me and all of the other people in the world? He did. Do you know why he made us? (*let them answer*) Those are good reasons. Let me tell you one other reason why God made us. He made us to do good things for each other. That's right. When God made us, he made us so that we could help each other and do good things for everything that lives on his earth.

That is why God made us. He made us in such a way that we can help each other have fun. He made us so that we can help each other when one of us is sad or hurt. He made us so that we can help each other build places to live, schools where we can learn, and churches where we can worship.

God made us do good things. We can make things like dresses, stools, and vases. That is important and it makes us feel good to do them. God made us the same way that we make things. We make things to do good, and God made us to do good. It is a wonderful plan and one that we should remember always. The next time you make something with your hands, maybe you will think about the way God made you to do good for others as well as yourself.

Growing In Love

Ephesians 4:1-7, 11-16

But speaking the truth in love, we must grow up in every way into him who is the head, into Christ. (v. 15)

Object: a measuring tape

Good morning, boys and girls. Do you know how tall you are? (*speak to one child at a time*) How tall are you? Sometimes we know how tall we are and sometimes we just guess. But I brought with me this morning a measuring tape so I can tell you just how tall you are. Let me measure a couple of you now and after the service is over, if you would like for me to, I will measure every one of you. (*proceed to measure several of the children and tell each one how tall he/she is*) Have you always been that tall? Were you this big when you were born? How did you get to be as tall as you are? (*let them answer*) You grew. How much have you grown in the last year, would you say? (*let them answer*)

Growing up is really fun. Someday you are going to be as tall or taller than your mom and dad. You may weigh as much or even more. You will be big enough to drive a car and wear clothes as big as your dad's suit or your mom's dress. You may even be tall enough to dunk a basketball. That's what happens when our bodies grow and we get big.

But there are other ways to grow besides just getting big in our bodies. When we learn in school, our minds grow. We can spell bigger words and do harder math problems. Our voices grow also. They get bigger, deeper, or higher, and they will become more beautiful if we practice with them.

There is still another way to grow, and that is to grow in love so that our love is more like Jesus' love. Jesus was filled with God's love. He loved everyone, even those who hated him. Jesus had a love so big that he could forgive even the people that crucified him.

Growing in love will let you share the things you like the most with other people. You can share your time in love. You can share your money in love. You can share your games and your friends in love. You can even share your mother and dad with other people when you are growing in love. That is a grown-up kind of love, when you can share it with others. Growing up is so much fun when it is filled with love. It allows you to be free and do what God wants you to do.

We can use a measuring tape to find out how big we are getting. But growing up in love cannot always be seen so easily, even though it is a much more important kind of growing than just getting taller.

One of the first things that Jesus taught all of his disciples was to grow in love. And one of the things that you and I who want to be followers of Jesus must do is to grow in love.

The next time we see someone trying to find out how tall they are, see if you can think about how you could measure someone growing in love. If you can see someone else grow in love, that means that you are growing in love as well. Try it; you'll like it.

Sing A Song To Each Other

Ephesians 5:15-20

... as you sing psalms and hymns and spiritual songs among yourselves, singing and making melody to the Lord in your hearts.... (v. 19)

Object: some sentences with which you greet the children, reading them to a melody which you make up as you go along

(The following is a sample of what you might use after the children are seated, and before you address them in song) "Good morning, children of St. Mark Church, and may God bless you on such a beautiful day. I thank the Lord for your joy and love which he gave you to share with your mothers and fathers and all of your friends. I praise God for our beautiful place to worship and for all of his gifts of food and energy and sunlight and rain. I pray to Jesus that we will have a wonderful time together this morning and that the Spirit of God will go with you all this day so that your happiness will be a blessing to all that meet you wherever you walk and wherever you play."

I like to do that, and I wish I would do it more often. How do you like being greeted with a song? *(let them answer)* It seems a little strange, doesn't it? *(let them answer)* The Apostle Paul suggested to the people in the church at Ephesus that they should always say hello to one another in this way. I don't know if they did it all the time, but it is sure a beautiful way to start the day, isn't it? When you sing songs, your heart is happy and light, and when you are happy and light, it makes the people you meet happy and light. Of course, the main reason that Paul told the people to greet each other this way was so that they could praise God and thank God for his love and the wonderful friendships that God made for people in the Church.

Some of the best friends you will have will be people that you meet in church. By thanking God and saying hello to one another at the same time, we are reminded of how important God is to us and to our friendship. Of course, we don't have to make every greeting quite so long as I did this morning. You could just say, "Good morning, Mark. God bless you." *(sing to one of your children or several in this way)* I think it is kind of fun, and it certainly does what Paul wanted it to, doesn't it? It makes us think of God, and it is a wonderful way to say hello to a friend.

The next time you come to Sunday school, or maybe when you see a friend today, you can try it and see how good it makes both of you feel. *(close by singing)* "Now thank you for coming and sharing this part of worship with me. May God bless you today in whatever you do."

Jesus Is The Head And We Are The Body

Ephesians 5:21-31

For the husband is the head of the wife just as Christ is the head of the church, the body of which he is the Savior. (v. 23)

Object: a nail, a golf club, and a match

Good morning, boys and girls. I brought some things along with me this morning that I hope you will learn a lesson from. (*take out the golf club, the match, and the nail*) I have a riddle for you. What is the same about this match, this nail, and this golf club? (*let them answer*) All of them have something that we call the same name. (*give them some hints*) Do you give up? (*let them answer*) This is a pretty tough riddle so let me give you the answer. All three things, the match, the nail, and the golf club, have heads. (*point out where the head is on each one*) That may sound funny to you, but we call each of these things heads, just like we call your head a head. We strike the head of a match and make fire. We pound he head of a nail, and we hit the golf ball with the head of the club. Your head has a lot of things to do such as think, see, hear, smell, taste, and many others. The head is where the business is done or where the important part of the work begins.

Jesus is also the head. The Bible calls Jesus the head of something that all of us love. Do you know what Jesus is the head of? (*let them answer*) Jesus is the head of the Church. The Apostle Paul calls Jesus the head of the Church. Who do you think is the body if Jesus is the head of it? (*let them answer*) That's right, we are the body of the Church. Jesus Christ is the head of the Church and we are the body of the Church. We go together. Jesus is the head because he is the leader and gives the body direction. We are the body because we follow where Jesus leads us. Jesus taught, and still teaches us, and we learn and do what he says. That is the reason that the Bible calls Jesus the head of the Church. We are the arms, legs, chest, and back of the Church.

The next time you see a nail or a match or a golf club or even when you look at one another, and you look at the heads of one another, I hope you will think about how the Bible teaches that Jesus is the head of the Church, and how we are the body of the Church, and how we work together.

The Armor Of God

Ephesians 6:10-20

Put on the whole armor of God, so that you may be able to stand against the wiles of the devil. (v. 11)

Object: a football uniform with all the equipment

Good morning, boys and girls. How many of you go to your school's football games with your parents or friends? Do any of you play football? (*let them answer*) Some of you go to the games, and some of you even play football. It's a pretty rough game, isn't it? (*let them answer*) Do you ever get hurt playing? (*let them answer*) When I watch the games at the stadium or on television, I always think about what a rough game football is, and how easy it would be to get hurt. Of course, I know that the uniform that each football player wears helps to protect him, and also helps him to be a better player.

Have you ever seen all the parts of a football player's uniform? (*let them answer*) I brought one along with me this morning so that you could see all the parts. (*show each pad and tell them where it goes in the uniform*) You can see how many different parts it takes to protect the body against injury. There is something for the knee, the hip, the thigh, the ribs, the shoulder, and the head. When you are wearing all these pads, it means that you can hit harder and you can take harder hits from other football players.

Christians are a little bit like football players. We have to play in a pretty rough world sometimes with people who are not so nice. Some people we know like to lie and do mean things. Others play unfair and cheat while some will do anything to hurt someone else. If you are a Christian, you can't do the same things that they do. We don't want you to lie or steal from someone else and hurt them because you were hurt. A Christian cannot do those kinds of things. That is why the Apostle Paul tells us to help ourselves with a different kind of equipment. Pretend that these shoulder pads are called "forgiveness" and that this helmet is called "truth." We can name the knee pads the "love" that God has for you and the hip pads, "honesty." When you put on all the good things that God has to give you to protect you in this world, then you are safe. I know that some people are going to try and hurt you, and sometimes you will wonder if it is worth being a Christian. But I know that it is, and you will know that it is also when you know how you feel after telling the truth, or after forgiving someone who has tried to hurt you.

Jesus has a special place for the people who wear his kind of protection, and I know that you will want to share what he has for you. The next time you see a football player, remember the kind of pads that God is asking you to wear, and you will know how much he cares for you in this world. God bless you.

A Great Partnership

Philippians 1:3-11

... because of your sharing in the gospel from the first day until now. (v. 5)

Object: salt and pepper shakers

Good morning, boys and girls. Today we are going to talk about some really good friends. They have been partners for a long time. I am sure that many of you have seen them together, as a matter of fact, you have probably never seen one without the other. In case you have not met them, I want to be the first to introduce the great partnership of salt and pepper. Day after day they do a job on my food. In the morning I eat eggs, and the first thing I do is put a little salt and some pepper on them. At noon I like to eat a salad, and I immediately reach for the partners — salt and pepper. Then at night when it is time for dinner, and I sit down to my vegetables and potatoes, I have, of course, the all-time favorite, salt and pepper. They work so well together. You can always count on them to add a little spice to your life. Salt and pepper, a great partnership and one that I would not be without.

There are lots of partnerships, some just as good as salt and pepper and some not so good. One of the best partnerships that I heard about was between the Apostle Paul and the people at Philippi. The people of Philippi were always helpful to Paul when he carried his message of Jesus to the world. They supported him with gifts and prayers, and they welcomed him to their city when he was in the area. They loved Paul because of his ministry and the way that he shared his knowledge of Jesus. He could sit there for hours and tell them the Good News that Jesus brought to them, and how Jesus loved them so much that he even died for them. They also were glad to take Jesus' teachings and share them with other people in other cities. It was a wonderful partnership that Paul had with the people of Philippi. Once, when the Romans put Paul in prison for teaching about Jesus as God, the people of Philippi came to defend him and support him. They knew that Paul had not done anything wrong, and they were willing to stand by him with their love. It was as Paul said, a great partnership, and I know that you would have been just as glad to have friends like the Philippians as Paul was.

The next time you hear of a partnership, you can think of Paul and the people in Philippi. Perhaps you will think of him this noon when you eat lunch and you look at the table and see that great partnership of salt and pepper. If you do see it, think about the time that Paul's partners, the Philippians, stood by him when he was in trouble. Will you do that? That's wonderful.

The Secret Of Wally Wheelbarrow

Philippians 2:5-11

But emptied himself, taking the form of a slave, being born in human likeness. (v. 7)

Object: a wheelbarrow

Good morning, boys and girls. I brought along one of our friends today that I thought you would enjoy seeing. His name is Wally Wheelbarrow. Wally is a fine fellow. How many of you have ever worked with something like Wally? (*let them answer*) What do you do with Wally? (*let them answer*) You haul dirt in Wally. Some of you picked up rocks and a few of you have even carried some wood in something like Wally. Wally Wheelbarrow has been a lot of places and has done a lot of things. A lot of people don't take care of Wally and they let him sit outside when it rains and he fills up with water and gets rusty. Wally doesn't like to be rusty but there isn't much he can do about it. Some other people I know let Wally sit for days with a load of dirt or rocks and they forget to empty him. That hurts Wally because Wally can't work when he is full of water, dirt, or rocks. Wally has to be empty before he can be used. That's the secret with Wally. You keep emptying Wally and he will keep working for you, but if you let him stand full of something he can't do a thing. The best part of Wally is that he likes to be used.

Did you know that Wally and Jesus were a lot alike in this way? Jesus was the Son of God and because he was the Son of God, he was filled with all kinds of things. Jesus knew everything there was to know. Jesus was filled with power and there wasn't anything that he could not do. But because Jesus was coming to save us from our sins, he had to be one of us. He could not be a superman, he had to be like you and me. Jesus could not be God while he was here on earth so he emptied himself and became our servant. That's why I said that Jesus was a lot like Wally Wheelbarrow. Wally can't serve us when he is full of things, and Jesus cannot be our servant when he is filled with power. Both of them have to be empty if they are to be our servants.

That is what the Bible teaches us and it is something for us to remember. We wonder why Jesus let soldiers kill him on a cross when we know he had such great power. We wonder why he let people make him suffer when he could have stopped it in a minute. But Jesus emptied himself of all God's powers so that he could be like one of us and know what it is like to be a man or a woman, a boy or a girl. Jesus was helpless when he was empty, and he was hurt because of it. But he was glad to be empty so that he could be our servant and die for our sins.

The next time you see a friend like Wally, I hope that he is empty and if he is, then you can think about why Jesus emptied himself so that he could be our Savior.

Jesus Clears The Clutter

Philippians 3:8-14

For his sake I have suffered the loss of all things, and I regard them as rubbish, in order that I may gain Christ.... (v. 8)

Object: a lot of clutter: some books, puzzles, toys, balls and bat, a radio, and the funny pages

Good morning, boys and girls. Today we have a common problem. The problem is called "clutter." I hear many parents complaining about this clutter problem their children. How many times have you heard your mother or father complain about your clutter and say, "Please pick it up and put it away." (*let them answer*) I also hear the youngsters saying, "What can I do? I don't have anything to do." How many of you have said that? (*let them answer*) Almost everyone. You can't find anything to do, but you are living in the middle of games, toys, newspapers, radios, balls, and books. Everywhere you look there is something. The only way to really enjoy something is to have only one thing at a time.

Let us suppose that you put everything away except one thing and then worked or played with that one thing. You would have fun with it or you would get it done. As long as you have a lot of things, it is hard to finish or play with any one of them.

That is what Paul found out about Jesus. He put everything else out of his mind and thought only about Jesus. He put away the idea of being rich, and he put away the idea of having a fast chariot with beautiful horses, and everything else that people wanted in his lifetime. He tried only to understand and love Jesus. It worked. Paul was happy. His life was not all cluttered up. He knew Jesus and why he suffered and died for us, and Paul was happy with that. He was so thrilled at his uncluttered life that he taught other people to live the same way. It was glorious. He even hopes that people like you and me will try it. Put Jesus first. When you love Jesus and worship him then your life is rich and full. You are never bored. I know boys and girls who are always looking for things to do and no matter how much they have it is not enough. These are boys and girls who need Jesus so that they can get rid of the clutter in their lives.

I hope that you will remember this, and if it ever happens to you and you wish that things could be different, maybe you can have your mother or father read you a story about Jesus. Then you will know how important God should be in your life.

A Lesson From Lettuce

Philippians 3:17—4:1

For many live as enemies of the cross of Christ; I have often told you of them, and now I tell you even with tears. (v. 18)

Object: a good head of lettuce and a spoiled head of lettuce (or some other produce)

Good morning, boys and girls. Today we are going to talk about being able to make choices, good choices. It is easy to be fooled about things and it is easy to be fooled about people unless we know what we are looking for when we are choosing.

Have you ever gone to the store with one of your parents shopping for lettuce? (*let them answer*) I have watched how carefully customers in the store choose a head of lettuce to buy. I have watched them pick up each head of lettuce until they find just the right one — the best one. They seem to know by feeling whether or not the lettuce is good. Some of the heads of lettuce feel firm and solid like this one that I have with me. Others feel mushy or like there is not much inside of what you can see through the wrapper. I am going to let you feel this lettuce so you will know what I mean. (*pass the lettuce around*) It takes some experience and some time to shop like this, but that is the way to do it if you want good food.

We must do this with people also, even people who call themselves Christians. I don't mean that you should pick them up and pinch them, but I mean that you must know what Christians are and what they believe in if you are going to follow their example. Some people look like Christians on the outside, but when you listen to them talk or find out how they live, then you are surprised to find that they are different on the inside. Just calling yourself a Christian doesn't mean that you are a Christian. I know some people who say they don't want to be a Christian because they know people who call themselves Christians who talk bad or live bad.

Well, just because someone calls himself a Christian doesn't mean that he or she is Christian. Not every head of lettuce is good to eat, and not every person with the title of Christian can be followed. When you make your choice of which Christian you want to follow, I hope that you do more than look at the clothes they wear or the car they drive. I hope you will listen to them talk and see how they care for the poor, the sick, and the lonely. If they are kind and generous and helpful to people and love others, and call themselves Christians, then you can follow their example and be sure that they are disciples of Jesus.

225

Make A List For God

Philippians 4:4-7

Do not worry about anything, but in everything by prayer and supplication with thanksgiving let your requests be made known to God. (v. 6)

Object: a shopping list

Good morning, boys and girls. Have you ever gone to the store needing to buy several things? How do you remember them all? (*let them answer*) That's right — a shopping list. Lists are a great way to help us remember.

God likes lists also. Did you know that God likes for you to make out lists for him? (*let them answer*) That's true. As a matter of fact, when the Apostle Paul was talking to the people of Philippi, he told them that they should keep lists of things that they wanted to ask or share with God, and then tell God about them when they prayed. That's a good idea. We could all keep lists of the things that we want to talk over with God. Paul said that some of the things could be requests — that means things that we need from God. There are a lot of things that only God can give, and we should let him know about them.

Suppose that we were going to make a list today of the things that we wanted to ask God. I wonder what they would be. I probably would not ask God for a bicycle, but I think that I would ask him for some extra-special love to share with the mean old man who lives across the street from me. I know I don't have enough love by myself and only God could give me enough love to love that mean man. If I loved him really good, then maybe he would not be so mean to anyone anymore.

What would you ask from God if you could write out a list? (*let them answer*) Those are some pretty good things to ask God for, and I hope that you will think about them not only today, but every day. Lists for shopping are great, but you can only look for those things when you go to the store. When you make out lists to ask God, you can ask him every day. That's pretty great. I think so and so do all Christians that love him and share him with each other.

God Is Like A One-A-Day

Philippians 4:10-13, 19-20

I can do all things in him who strengthens me. (v. 13)

Object: some vitamins

Good morning, boys and girls. Did you smell fresh air this morning when you got up? Did it feel good to take a deep breath and smell the fall season? Look at the trees, the fall flowers, and the wonderful colors in clothing that people are wearing. This is a special time of the year for all of us. (*adapt wording for whatever season it is*)

I like fall because it always reminds me that God is really close to us and helping us. Everyone knows that we could not make such a beautiful world, and this all belongs to God. But we also know that God expects us to take care of it and to share it with one another. It takes a lot of strength to work in God's world. We have so many things to do that many of us are busy from morning to night. That means that we must be strong. Of course there are different kinds of strength.

For instance, when we want to make our boys and girls strong so that they can grow, we make sure that they take a small pill each day. Do you know what you can take every day to make you grow strong and healthy? (*let them answer*) That's right; vitamins. How many of you take vitamins? (*let them answer*) That's wonderful, and don't you feel good? What do your vitamins taste like? (*let them answer*) I like the kind that taste like oranges.

God is like a vitamin. Sometimes I have problems that need more than muscles. I need to know how to help someone whom I love very much who has done something wrong. I need an answer to make them see the right way and to get away from something they are drinking or eating that is making them sick. I need help from somewhere else than from my own brain, and so I call on God and he gives me new strength and answers. Sometimes I want to do something I know I should not do, like tell a lie because I don't want people to know the truth about me. I am ashamed of what I have done. Now I can tell a lie or I can ask God for help to tell the truth. When I ask God, he gives me strength and I can tell the truth and I feel great.

That is why I like to think about God sometimes as my vitamins, because he gives me power that I would not have without him.

The next time you take your vitamins, maybe you will think about God and how he makes all of us strong — in a different way than vitamins but in a way that all of us need very much.

Things Change

Colossians 1:1-14

... You have heard of this hope before in the word of the truth, the gospel that has come to you. Just as it is bearing fruit among yourselves from the day you heard it and truly comprehended the grace of God. (vv. 5-6)

Object: a series of school pictures of the same child (or children) showing the change in their face(s) from year to year

Good morning, boys and girls. How many of you feel that you have changed since you were born? (*let them answer*) Are you the same as you were when you were born, or when you were two years old? (*let them answer*) No, you don't look the same as you did when you were a baby, do you? As a matter of fact, I want to show you how much a person changes in just a couple of years. I brought along some pictures of _____. We all know _____, don't we? (*let them answer*) Here is a picture of _____ in the first grade and one of him/her in the second grade, and another in the third grade. Can you see a change? (*let them answer*) Good! But take a look at his/her picture in the seventh grade! He/she has really changed, hasn't he/she?

I guess almost everything changes, doesn't it? (*let them answer*) Most of the time we like change because it is good for us. We can also change our lives in another way. God teaches us that reading and listening to his ways and his teachings will change us and make us better people. The Apostle Paul called these teachings the Good News, and he was sure that wherever the Good News was preached and taught, people had their lives changed and they were made into better people.

It happens all of the time. Here in the church you hear the Good News, and if you listen carefully, your life is changed and made better. The Good News is about Jesus, and what he did for us. But it isn't just happening to you. It is happening everywhere. People are listening to the Good News in Egypt, Russia, Switzerland, Brazil, and everywhere you can think of. The wonderful part about it is that it is not just another story, but instead it is changing you and making you better.

The next time you have your picture taken, I would like for you to compare it with one that was taken about a year ago and see how much you have changed. When you see the change that has happened to you, then you may also think about the changes God is making in you with the Good News about Jesus.

228

Jesus Our Parachute

Colossians 1:13-20

He has rescued us from the power of darkness and transferred us into the kingdom of his beloved Son. (v. 13)

Object: a parachute (tie some strings to a handkerchief and attach a weight)

Good morning, boys and girls. How many of you have ever been rescued? (*let them answer*) Some of you have had some very close calls. When I think of being rescued, I think of firefighters, police officers, or people who are extra brave and help others even where there is great danger.

Sometimes there are things that rescue us as people do. I have something here that has rescued a lot of people who fly. It is a pretty small one, but I am sure you will know what I am talking about when I show you this little piece of cloth with some strings attached to it. What do you call this? (*let them answer*) That's right; a parachute. People who fly planes have parachutes, and if something is wrong with the plane and it is going to crash, then they use the parachute. It isn't a toy — it is a big help if we need to be rescued.

Well, that is kind of the way that Jesus is for all of us. He is like our parachute. We were all headed for a big crash when he came along. Without Jesus, the Bible tells us, we would all end up with the devil, but because Jesus came we are now going to live safely with God. Isn't that wonderful? Here we are going along like we are sure to crash when all of a sudden we are given some help. And instead of ending up in a wreck, we are all floating to safety in the hands of Jesus. Jesus is our parachute.

I hope that you remember this the next time you see a movie or read a book where someone using a parachute is saved. You can think to yourself how glad you are to have Jesus just as the flyer has his parachute. With Jesus we are safe and sound, but without him we are bound to have an awful crash. You can't do anything about a plane that is crashing. You can't get out or run away. You must just sit there and wait for it to happen. That is, unless you have a parachute and you know how to use it. Then you will float safely to the ground.

The same is true about Jesus. Without Jesus we were all going to the devil and there was nothing that we could do. Then God sent Jesus to us and he brought us safely to his world. That's why we love Jesus so much and why we are so grateful for his saving us.

Will you remember that Jesus is like our parachute? (*let them answer*) That's good.

The Sealed Secret

Colossians 1:21-28

I became its servant according to God's commission that was given to me for you, to make the word of God fully known, the mystery that was hidden throughout the ages.... (vv. 25-26)

Object: a large envelope with a wax seal

Good morning, boys and girls. How many of you can keep a secret? (*let them answer*) I want to know if you can keep a secret for a long time. It isn't so hard to keep a secret for a little while, but to keep a secret for a long time like a week or a month is almost impossible. I know how hard it is for some people to keep secrets about birthdays or Christmas gifts and things like that, so you can imagine how hard it must be to keep a secret as wonderful as the secret that God had for people in the world.

Suppose that you were the Apostle Paul, and you had a secret that most of the people in the world knew nothing about, but you were chosen to be the one to tell it. Doesn't that sound like fun? I have the secret in this envelope that has been sealed and kept sealed for hundreds, maybe thousands of years. (*hold up the envelope*) I know that no one has seen the secret because after it was put in this envelope, some candle wax was dripped over it, and the wax has not been broken. I know that as soon as it is opened and the message is read, it will mean that it will no longer be a secret, but instead it will be known to all. Shall I open it? Will all of you promise to help me share the secret with all the people in the world who have not heard about it? (*let them told up their hands*)

If you all promise to help me as Paul's friends helped him, then I will open it in front of you. (*open the envelope very carefully*) Remember now before I read this that you have all promised me that you would share this secret with all who have not heard it. (*read the message that tells that God's plan for salvation is for the Gentiles and that Jesus died to make sure that all people who believed would share God's eternal community*)

What wonderful news. Just think, people who have not heard this message thought that when they died life was all over. Now when you share the secret of what Jesus died for with all of your friends, they will be glad and so very happy. Jesus is the secret plan of God, and what a wonderful secret he is for all the world. Now don't forget your promise to me that you would help me share this news with all the people in the world. Will you be sure to do this?

Your Roots

Colossians 2:6-15

... rooted and built up in him and established in the faith.... (v. 7a)

Object: several plants at various stages of growth with their roots exposed

Good morning, boys and girls. Today we are going to make a little discovery which will help us learn something about the way we can grow with God. How many of you have ever raised a plant like a tomato plant or a flower? (*let them answer*) Almost all of you have done this, haven't you? Can you tell me what you do when you try to grow something like a flower or tomato? (*let them answer*) That's very good. What are some of the important parts of a plant? (*let them answer*) Very good. We have leaves, flowers, stems, and roots.

Today I want to talk to you about the roots. Take a look at the plants I brought with me. Do you see that the bigger plant is, the bigger the whole system of roots is? The roots are where the plant gets the food from the ground. A good root means that the parts of the plant you see, like the stem, leaves, flower, or fruit, are strong.

It is the same way for us, only your root is your mind. If your mind is planted in good things, then the rest of you is going to be good. That is why the Apostle Paul was very concerned that people knew about Jesus and that they had their minds filled with all of his teachings. Fill your mind with love, peace, and joy and you are going to be a very healthy person. Jesus is the best food for your mind that there is, and anyone who knows Jesus and knows him well is filled with good life. People who have their roots in Jesus are not only healthly themselves, but are also so healthy that they can share it with others.

A good root makes a healthy plant. A good mind filled with the love of God and the teachings of Jesus is a healthy mind. The next time that you take a look at a strong and healthy plant, I want you to think about the root system and how strong it must be under the ground. When you think about the root system, then you are going to think about your mind and why it should be filled with the good things that come from Jesus.

The Sponge
(Appropriate for Easter)

Colossians 3:1-4

For you have died, and your life is hidden with Christ in God. (v. 3)

Object: a large sponge, some water, a couple of drops of food coloring, and a flat pan

Good morning, boys and girls. Today we're going to talk about a special day called "Easter." Isn't Easter wonderful? It is one of the happiest days of the year. Jesus Christ came back from the dead on this day and promised that the same thing can happen to all of us. Easter is the happiest day of the year because we think about the promise of Jesus all day long and it helps us to remember it all year long. Just think, some day we will live with God forever. We will be a real part of God's real world. That sounds great doesn't it?

I want to help you think about Easter and what it means. Did you know that the Bible teaches us that when we die our lives will be hidden with Jesus in God? You and I know that Jesus came back from being dead and that he lives with God. We know that, don't we? (*let them answer*) It's true. I know that it is true. But where is Jesus? He came back to earth and we know that he went to live with God in his real world, but where did he go? That is the question.

Let me show you how I understand it. I have some water here that all of you can see. I am going to pretend that this is our world. The world that you and I live in has trees, flowers, buildings, cars, and all of those things. It also has people. The people are going to be these little drops of color that I am going to put into the water of our world. Those people are like you and me. We get all mixed up in the world. People, trees, buildings, cars, and all of those things are in the world. It looks kind of neat in this glass, doesn't it? (*let them answer*) But what happens when we die? It is like being spilled out of the glass when we die. (*pour the water into the pan*) That doesn't look like much fun, does it?

But God has a plan. God is this big sponge that I have in my hand. God comes to us when we die and kind of hides us in him. He takes us up from being dead and makes us come alive again. (*take the sponge and squeeze it out into another glass*)

Did you see how we were hidden in God? (*let them answer*) We are all together with God, and Christ is there with us also. That is the story of Easter. We do not just get spilled out of our world when we die. We are not left out. We are hidden with God as the water was hidden in the sponge. We are there with Jesus, and we stay there until God has his new world ready for us to live in in peace and happiness.

That is why Easter is such a happy day. It is the best, because we know that when we die, we will be hidden with Jesus in God, where we can someday live in the best world ever.

232

The Certificate And The Gift

1 Thessalonians 1:1-5a

... because our message of the gospel came to you not in word only, but also in power and in the Holy Spirit and with full conviction.... (v. 5)

Object: a gift certificate and an actual present

Good morning, boys and girls. What was the best thing that happened to you this week? (*let several of them answer*) Those are some pretty wonderful things. No wonder you are so happy. Today we are going to share some things that I hope will help you understand what a wonderful God we love and worship.

Sometimes people think that religion is just words. We sing words, we pray words, and we preach words. Coming to church is just a bunch of words. But I don't think that is true, and I want you to know that it isn't true. Loving God and sharing God's world is more than words. The Apostle Paul told some people one day that the Good News about Jesus Christ came not only in words, but also in power.

Let me show you what I mean. Suppose I wanted to give you a gift, and so I went to the store and looked around and found the perfect gift for you. I came home and wrote you a note and told you that I had paid the money for your special gift and all you had to do was go and pick it up. We call that a gift certificate. (*show them the gift certificate*) I give you the note and now you know that I have given you a gift. You don't have the gift, but you have the words that tell you that you have a gift. Now when you go to the store you can show the words that I have written to the store clerk and he will go and get the present for you. (*show them the wrapped package*) Now you have the gift. It is yours and it belongs to you.

There is a lot of difference between the gift certificate and the gift. There is a lot of difference between words and faith. Anyone can say nice words about God, but when you have a faith in God, it is more then words. It means sharing your life with other people, helping them when they need help, and celebrating with them when they have good news to share. Being a Christian is more than singing — just like a gift is more than words on a paper. You want the real thing when you are given a present, and you want the real thing when you have religion. Some people think that religion is only words because all they ever do is talk about it. Many people know that God is a lot more to them than words because they share their lives with God and people every day.

The next time you receive a gift on your birthday or at Christmas or any other time, think about believing in God and how the real thing is like having the gift in your hands. Religion is more than words; it is power.

Piggyback Riders

1 Thessalonians 2:8-13

You remember our labor and toil, brothers and sisters; we worked night and day, so that we might not burden any of you while we proclaimed to you the gospel of God. (v. 9)

Object: have children choose partners to give each other piggyback rides; sweeper, dust rags, cleaning supplies

Good morning, boys and girls. Today is a super day. Here we are in church on a wonderful Sunday morning, and we are sharing our love with one another. That means that almost everything is right in the world. Today I want each of you to pick up a partner, and we will learn something about sharing. (*have them take partners*)

Now that you all have a partner, I want you to choose which one of you is going to give the other a piggyback ride. I know that all of you have ridden piggyback, but now we want you to share your back or the ride with someone else. And while you are giving or taking a piggyback ride, I also want you to help me clean up the front of the church. I brought along some dust rags, a sweeper, and the things that you need to clean. The person who is riding, of course, will not have to work, but only the person who is giving the ride will be working. (*let them do this for a couple of minutes until the point is made*) That isn't sharing, is it? One person is doing all of the work and the other person is just going along for the ride. Sharing would be if we took turns or if the other person didn't ride at all, but instead helped with the cleaning.

As Christians we are supposed to share not only the joys of being Christians, but also the work of being Christians. Some Christians think that they are only supposed to share the joy. They love to sing the hymns, go to church, and talk with their Christian friends. But there is a lot more to Christianity than those things. If you are a Christian, you must also visit the sick and teach others what you know about Jesus. Sometimes people don't want to listen, or they don't like the things that you do as a Christian. They make life very hard for us. But Christians share the work just like they share the joy.

If you had to give someone a ride all of the time on your back and still do all of the work, you would get pretty tired of helping your friend. You want your friends to share the work just like they share the joy. That is the way that God wants it also. He wants you to have a good time being a Christian, and you can have a good time working, but he wants you to share the work.

The next time you get or give a piggyback ride, I hope that you will remember how we are to share the joy and the work of being Christians.

How To Be A Christian

1 Thessalonians 3:9-13

Night and day we pray most earnestly that we may see you face to face and restore whatever is lacking in your faith. (v. 10)

Object: some boards, nails and hammers, and screws and screwdrivers

Good morning, boys and girls. How many of you have ever started to do a job, but when you were ready to start, you found that you were missing something? (*let them answer*) Let me show you what I mean. Let's pretend that we want to put these nails in the board. You have the nails and you have the board, now put the nails in it. (*hold back the hammer*) Who wants to put the nails in? (*ask for a volunteer but do not give him a hammer*) What's the problem? Can't you put the nails into the board? Do you need something else? (*let them answer*) That's right; you need a hammer. You can't do the job unless you have a hammer, can you?

The same thing would be true if I gave you a board and some screws. If you did not have a screwdriver, you could not put the screws into the board. You need all of the proper tools to do a job right. The Apostle Paul knew the same thing was true about Christians. He wrote to some of his friends and told them how much he was praying for them and how happy he was for them to be Christians. But he did not stop there. Paul knew that it took a lot of parts to make a whole Christian, and he wanted to see his friends so he could teach them all he knew about being a Christian.

Sometimes we have that same problem. We call ourselves Christians, but we have not learned all the parts about being a Christian. We need to learn to love and forgive as well as to worship and share. We cannot be jealous or cheat, steal, lie, or any of the other things that aren't Christian. When we do commit our sins we must go to God and ask for his forgiveness.

Paul wanted to tell his friends how to be a whole Christian and show them how real Christians live. You and I want to do the same thing with our friends. We want them to be Christians, and full Christians. We want to share the things that we do well, and we want them to share with us the things that they do well. It is a good plan and everybody should support it.

You can't drive nails into a board without a hammer, and you can't be a full Christian without prayer or love or sharing your riches. That is what Paul shared with his friends and it is the same thing that he shares with us today.

Share what you have and what you know with your friends, and both of you will be stronger Christians tomorrow.

What It's Like

1 Thessalonians 4:13-14 (15-18)

But we would not have you uninformed, brothers and sisters, about those who have died, so that you may not grieve as others do who have no hope. (v. 13)

Object: a fluffy bed pillow

Good morning, boys and girls. We need to talk about something that people do not like to talk about. It is a very big part of living. It is a big experience, but people do not like to talk about it. Do you know what I want to share with you this morning? (*let them answer*) That's right; I want to talk to you about dying and death. People don't like to talk about it, because they don't like to think about it. Dying means that they will not share the things they are doing now with other people. Death means being separated or gone. You don't live in the same place, eat at the same table, ride in the same car, or work in the same place. Death happens to everyone, usually when we are old, but not always. You can die in a lot of ways. You can get sick, have a bad accident, or just wear out. We watch other things die — flowers, trees, our pets — and it makes us sad, but we know it is going to happen. Now I want to talk about people dying. That, we never expect. We never expect that we will die. Even if other people do, we think it will not happen to us. But it will. It happens to all of us.

What is dying like, or what it is like to be dead? I don't know. It has never happened to me, but I have some good ideas about it because the Bible talks about it. One of the ways the Bible talks about death is to tell us that it is like going to sleep. Our verse from the Bible refers to people who "have died," but another translation of this verse says they "are asleep."

I brought my big fluffy pillow with me to show you this morning that the Bible tells us that when we die, it is like being in bed asleep with our moms and dads downstairs, only instead of mom and dad, it is like having Jesus downstairs. We would be pretty scared if we had to go to bed in our house and there was no one downstairs. But when we go to sleep at night we know that we are safe because our mom and dad are there and keeping us safe. We just put our heads down on our fluffy pillows, shut our eyes, and have wonderful dreams about what we are going to do the next day.

The same thing is true when we die. We can close our eyes, we know that Jesus is there to keep us safe, and we can dream about the new adventures in the world to come.

So the next time you think about dying, don't worry or be afraid, but imagine putting your head down on a fluffy pillow with Jesus downstairs and plan a wonderful dream. That helps a lot, doesn't it? I know that it helps me.

236

Standing Ovation

1 Thessalonians 5:1-11

Therefore encourage one another and build up each other, as indeed you are doing. (v. 11)

Object: a standing round of applause (use a sign that reads "Give a standing round of applause" and show it to the congregation after the child performs)

Good morning, boys and girls. How are you today? Do you feel really good? (*let them answer*) I am going to make you feel better than you do right now. I am going to make you feel super! Do you think I can do it? Do you want me to try? (*let them answer*)

All right, I need some volunteers. (*select one boy and one girl*) You are my volunteers and I am going to make you feel really good. What I want you to do is to tell me a story or repeat a poem or sing a song that you know. It can be a short story, short poem, or a short song. Do you think you can do this for me? (*let them answer*) Okay, who wants to go first? (*select one of the children who has volunteered; then after he/she has performed, hold up the sign to the congregation and lead the applause; repeat with each performer*)

That was great! Do you feel good? (*let them answer*) Do you feel better than you did before? (*let them answer*) Wonderful. Do you think that all of the people in our church are encouraging you? Do they want you to feel better? (*let them answer*)

The Apostle Paul knew how important it was for Christians to feel good about one another. Sometimes things are hard to accomplish and we don't get a lot of thanks for doing things that need to be done. How many of you have ever received a standing ovation for forgiving someone or sharing something that you have that someone else really needs? If you give one of your toys to someone who doesn't have any toys, or if you take care of someone who is hurting, does a crowd of people stand up and applaud you for doing it? (*let them answer*) Probably not! But having someone say thanks to you sometimes is almost better than applause. When I made a phone call to a shut-in recently she said, "Thank you for calling me and ending my lonely day." I'll be sure to call or write to her again because now I know my call made a difference to her.

We can't always have standing ovations for our work. But we can encourage people who do nice things by saying, "Thanks a lot!" We can help people feel better about the good things they do by telling them how much we love them and appreciate them. We can thank our teachers for teaching us, our doctors for keeping us healthy, our firefighters and police officers for making us safe, and our parents for taking care of us every day of our lives.

Let's stand and applaud our choir for singing so beautifully. (*lead the children in standing and applauding each of the people you name*) Let's thank the organist and the ushers. Let's ask our Sunday school teachers to stand so we can thank them. And then let's thank our parents for giving us such a great life at home. Remember what the Bible says, "Encourage one another and build each other up as you are doing."

People Who Are Like Popcorn

2 Thessalonians 1:1-5

We most always give thanks to God for you, brothers and sisters, as is right, because your faith is growing abundantly, and the love of everyone of you for one another is increasing. (v. 3)

Object: a bowl or bag of popcorn

Good morning, boys and girls. I brought along with me one of my very favorite snacks today. How many of you like popcorn? (*let them answer*) Don't you love to sit down at night and munch on some hot popcorn while you are watching television or working a puzzle? (*let them answer*) Popcorn is one of my all-time favorites.

I also like to watch popcorn pop. You put the kernels of corn in a popper, turn it on, and watch them explode and fill the popper. It doesn't take long for them to grow and increase from a few tiny seeds to a full dish of something delicious.

The Apostle Paul knew some people in a town called Thessalonica who were like popcorn. He used to tell people all over the world about the way these people grew in their love for one another. That meant that being a Christian was a very important thing to them and, because they trusted God, they also loved each other more and more. They were like popcorn.

They were not made any different from other people. They looked like you and me. They wore clothes and ate food and slept when they were tired and worked and went to school. They were people like you and me. But they trusted God. Paul promised them that if they trusted God more and more to help them live, they would find more love for each other. The people believed what Paul said, and they began to trust God a little more each day. They trusted God for their food, for their homes, and for their clothes. They trusted God to help them raise their children and to give them the right answers. They began to give some of their money that they had worked hard for to help other people who were sick or could not work. They did what God told them to do, and they trusted him with their whole lives. This really worked. Pretty soon they found other things to do for each other, and instead of fighting or arguing with people, they were loving each other more and more. It was a good place to live. Christians grew like popcorn and their love grew even faster.

That is the way God wants you and me to be. He wants us to live with trust in him and in love for one another. You could grow in love toward God like popcorn if you tried. I hope you trust God to help you to live your life and to love everyone that you know. That will be wonderful.

The next time you see some popcorn, remember the people in Thessalonica and how they grew when they trusted God and loved one another.

Be A Good Thermometer

2 Thessalonians 1:9-12

... so that the name of our Lord Jesus may be glorified in you.... (v. 12a)

Object: a thermometer

Good morning, boys and girls. How are you feeling today? (*let them answer*) Everybody feels fine. That's good. But suppose you didn't feel so good, and your body ached, and your ear hurt, and everything seemed to be going around in a circle. Then what would you tell someone if he asked you how you felt? (*let them answer*) That's right; sick. Now if you were really sick, and I sure hope that you don't get sick, your mother or father would take you to the doctor. At the doctor's office a nurse would say hello to you and then, before you could hardly answer, the nurse would put something in your mouth or in your ear. Do you know what would be put in your mouth or ear? (*let them answer*) Right, a thermometer. What does that do? It tells the doctor what your body temperature is, and it helps the doctor to decide what kind of medicine to give you. A thermometer tells the doctor what kind of an infection you have and how your body is fighting the infection. The doctor can tell from the thermometer on the outside what is going on in the inside. A thermometer is very important to a tell about your illness.

In a way we are thermometers for Christianity. People can tell a lot about our church and what our church thinks of Jesus by watching us. If we are full of love, kindness, and enthusiasm about Jesus, then people will think a lot about Jesus and the things that he teaches. If we are rather cool and uninterested toward Jesus, then they will know that we don't think that he is very important. When we are filled with Jesus, we are always looking for ways to help others and share the good things that we have with them. When we are empty of Jesus, we are then very greedy and unhappy.

That is the way people can tell if we have Jesus in us or not. We are like a thermometer, and whatever that thermometer says on the outside is what we are like on the inside. There are a lot of people who have found Jesus as the Savior because they liked what they saw in other Christians they knew. I suppose there are some people who have never known about the love of Jesus because they felt that some of the people who called themselves Christians are not any different than they were.

Be a good thermometer and show everyone how much you are for Jesus and how you have plenty of his love to share with them, just as he shared his love with you.

He Makes The Bad Good

1 Timothy 1:12-17

But for that very reason I received mercy, so that in me, as the foremost, Jesus Christ might display the utmost patience, making me an example to those who would come to believe in him for eternal life. (v. 16)

Object: a good example, such as a picture that shows a person before and after he has lost weight or before and after he has added muscle

Good morning, boys and girls. How many of you have ever looked through a magazine or a newspaper? (*let them answer*) Almost all of you. Have you ever seen something like this? (*show them the ads*) What does it mean when you see a picture of a very fat person in one picture, and a not-so-fat person in the next picture? (*let them answer*) That's right; it means that the person has lost weight. How about this one that shows a very skinny person in one picture and then a very strong-looking person with lots of muscles in the other. Do you know what that means? That's right. It means that the person has built his/her body with exercise and great effort.

These are what we call examples, good examples. The people who have accomplished what is shown in these pictures feel good because they know that they look better now than they did before. Not only that, but they believe that they are good examples for other people and that others will feel better if they work hard at being like them.

The Apostle Paul felt that he was an example. It was a lot different from the pictures that I have shown you. Paul was not an example of how a man looked with new muscles or how a person would feel if he lost a lot of weight. Paul thought that God had chosen him as an example of how, by coming to know Jesus, a bad man could be made into a good man. Paul told everyone how he had tried to hurt the church and the Christians who followed Jesus. He was a bad man. But God wanted Paul to work for him. In spite of all the bad things Paul did, God forgave him for his sins and asked Paul to work for him.

Just think about how God can make a bad man into a good man. It is a good example for all of us. Some people feel that they are not good enough to work for God and to be near God. But Paul said he is a good example of how God will care for the worst sinner and bring him into the church.

Maybe the next time you see one of these pictures in the paper you will think about Paul and how God used this bad man and made him a good man to tell everyone about the love of Jesus.

Is Jesus Like A Stapler?

1 Timothy 2:1-8

For there is one of God; there is also one mediator between God and humankind, Christ Jesus, himself human, who gave himself a ransom for all.... (vv. 5-6)

Object: a stapler and some pieces of paper

Good morning, boys and girls. How many of you have ever thought that Jesus is like a stapler? You know what a stapler is, don't you? It looks like this. (*hold up the stapler*) Now, how do you think that Jesus could be compared to a stapler? (*let them answer*)

Those are some pretty good ideas, but I would like to try a different one on you. Let's suppose that one of these pieces of paper is God and the other piece of paper is all of the people in the world. I am going to mark one piece of paper "God," and the other piece I am going to mark "people." God is holy and perfect. People are sinners and not holy. God wants people to be with him. God loves us, but there is such a difference in his world and our world that there doesn't seem to be any way that we can get together. I could try to put the God paper and the people paper together, but I don't think they will stay. (*hold the two pieces of paper together and then let them fall*) They just will not work together.

Then of course we have the stapler which we are going to call "Jesus." You know, of course, what will happen when I use the stapler on the two pieces of paper. That's right; they become tied together and they will stay together forever. That is exactly what Jesus did for God and for people. Jesus came from God and he was perfect and holy. Here on earth he lived as a human and took all of the people's sin and was killed. Now God is holy and people can be without their sin because of what Jesus did. God and people can live together. That is why I think that we can talk of Jesus being like a stapler. It is Jesus who brought us together.

Maybe the next time that you see a stapler you will think a little bit about how I explained to you that a stapler is something like Jesus, and that we are a little bit like pieces of paper. It would be wonderful if you could remember the plan of God and how he sent Jesus to bring us together. That is the reason he came and died for us. Will you try hard to remember? Wonderful.

New Leaves

1 Timothy 6:11-16

Which he will bring about at the right time — he who is the blessed and only Sovereign, the King of kings and Lord of lords. (v. 15)

Object: a leaf or leaves of color that depict the changing of seasons

Good morning, boys and girls. I brought something with me this morning that all of us see, but we seldom think about. I hope that when I tell you a little about this object it will help to answer one of the questions that people will ask you as a Christian all of your life.

What do you call this? (*hold up a leaf*) That's right; a leaf. But it is no ordinary leaf. Do you know what is special about this leaf? (*let them answer*) I didn't find this leaf on a tree. I found it on the ground in my front yard. It had been on a tree, and it grew there all summer, but I found it on the ground. Do you know what has happened? (*let them answer*) That's right; the wind blew it off the tree, but only after a certain time had come. The wind blew this leaf all summer and it never fell, but when the season of fall came and a change of the weather occurred, this leaf changed color and finally fell to the earth. It was time for it to come down. Next year there will be a new season called spring and when it comes, there will be new leaves on the tree. There are seasons — spring, summer, fall, and winter — and every one of them is different. The best part of seasons is that all of them are different and they make different things happen.

Now what is the question that you are going to be asked all of your life as a Christian? It's this: People are going to ask you when Jesus is going to come back to earth as he promised he would. People want to know the answer to that because it means that God's kingdom is working as God planned it. The Bible promises us that God has a plan and a certain time for everything to happen. There is going to be a special time for Jesus to come back to earth and begin a whole new plan of God for all of his followers. Do we know when that time is? No, we don't, and there is no way for us to know until it happens.

Could you tell me the day when there are going to be new leaves on the tree? No, you can't. You know that it will be next spring, but you don't know the day. Could you have told me when this leaf was going to fall off the tree? You could not. You knew that it would be in the fall, but you did not know the day. The same thing is true about when Jesus is coming back. I do know that he is coming because God promised it would happen, but only God knows the day and the time of the day. We are going to wait as all of the other people are waiting and be glad when he comes. There is a season for everything, and there is even a time for Jesus to come back to earth. Only God knows when.

Fizz!

2 Timothy 1:3-14

Do not be ashamed, then, of the testimony about our Lord or of me his prisoner, but join with me in suffering for the gospel, relying on the power of God.... (v. 8)

Object: an Alka-Seltzer tablet and a glass of water

Good morning, boys and girls. Did you know that sometimes God is like medicine? I would like to show you how I mean this. I wonder if you have ever felt like telling someone about Jesus, but you just could not get the words out of your mouth. I know what you think because it has happened to me. You want to say something but you are afraid of what others will think about you.

That has happened to a lot of people and it must have happened to Paul, because he wrote one of his best friends about it and told him what to do when this happened. He said a lot of people have this problem, and they need to stir themselves up. There is the Spirit of God in us telling us what we should do, but God's Spirit and our spirit don't seem to mix. We need to not be ashamed, Paul says, or as one translation puts it, "stir up this inner power," so that we can act.

This is where I believe God is like a medicine. Let's pretend that this is my spirit. (*hold up glass of water*) It is a spirit that looks like all other spirits. It just lies there. It doesn't do anything but sit. I want to show you what happens when I mix God's Spirit up with mine. Pretend that this is God's Spirit. (*hold up the Alka-Seltzer*) When I mix God's Spirit with my spirit, and stir them up together, I get some real action. (*stir the two together*) That glass of water has come alive, and you know if you drink something like this when you need it you are going to get action.

That is the way it should be when we want to tell our friends the right way to live. We know what we should say, but we don't say it. Take courage and read and think about the teachings of God, and a little bit of this will go a long way. You will be a new person. You will have great courage and you will be able to stand up for what you believe is right.

Paul knew what it was like and he told his friend Timothy. I am sure that Timothy used it because he was one of God's early heroes. I hope the next time you want to do the right thing, or say the right thing to a friend and you don't feel that you have the courage, you will remember when God is like a medicine. Then remember what he says and get stirred up. It will work. I promise you.

It's Mine!

2 Timothy 2:8-13

Remember Jesus Christ, raised from the dead, a descendant of David — that is my gospel. (v. 8)

Object: your watch, your billfold, your comb, a handkerchief with your initial on it

Good morning, boys and girls. How many of you have something that you think belongs to you? It must be something about which you can say, "This is mine." (*let them answer*) You have a lot of things that belong to you.

I brought along some of the things that I have in my pocket that I can say are mine. I have my billfold. (*show them the billfold*) I have my watch. (*show them the watch*) I also have my comb and my handkerchief. (*show them each of these things*) Things that I have like this, I call mine, and they are important to me. I may share them with a lot of people, but they belong to me. I am glad that I have them, and I would be lost without them.

The reason I have shared with you some things that are mine is that I have something else that is even more important to me and that is *also* something I call mine. It is a word that you have heard me use a lot of times, but I am not sure if you know what it means. I have my *Gospel*. Do you know what the word *Gospel* means? (*let them answer*)

The word *Gospel* means "Good News." I have Good News about Jesus Christ. As a matter of fact, Jesus Christ *is* the Good News. But it is my Good News because I use it, read it, and share it with others when I talk about it. And often I listen to it. You also have the Gospel and you can call it your own if you want to. But you have to *use* it to have it. If you use it, you will share it, and soon someone else will be able to say that the Gospel is theirs also.

The Gospel is more important than a watch, a billfold filled with money, a comb, a handkerchief, or anything else that you can think of that belongs to you or to me. The Gospel, the Good News about Jesus Christ, is the news that Jesus was born, lived, died, and lives again forever. It is the news that he shared his life and died for us and that he promises us that he will share a new life with us when we use up the one that we already have.

The Gospel is mine and I hope that it is yours. If you know it, then you will see how important it is for you and how important it is that everyone else knows about it.

A Real Champion

2 Timothy 4:6-8, 16-18

I have fought the good fight, I have finished the race, I have kept the faith. (v. 7)

Object: a big piece of cardboard with the words "Round 15" on it and some boxing gloves

Good morning, boys and girls. I have a piece of cardboard with a word and a number on it, and I want you to guess what you think it means. (*hold up the card*) How many of you have ever heard of "Round 15"? Here is another hint that will help you guess what the word and number mean. (*show them the boxing gloves*) That's right, a boxing match. But not just any boxing match. When you go fifteen rounds that means you are a champion boxer or you are fighting for the championship.

The Apostle Paul was a champion, and he talked a lot about fighting. Of course, Paul did not use his fists. Paul fought against all people who worked against Jesus. Paul was a champion of Jesus, and wherever he went he taught everyone who would listen about the good things that Jesus did for them. Sometimes it meant going to prison or being chased out of a town. Sometimes people threw rocks at him or beat him with a whip. But never once did Paul give up. It had not been an easy life, and Paul had many scars. When we listen to the lesson he wrote to his young friend, Timothy, we learn that he is now ready to retire and rest. Paul is going to quit fighting, but he is not giving up. It is the fifteenth round, and the fight is over for Paul. He is ready to die and glad that soon he will be with God in heaven.

There are others like Timothy, who must now fight the battle. They, too, must fight with love, patience, kindness, and all the things that Paul fought with, but they must never give up until the end, or the fifteenth round. God looks for champions like Paul and Timothy, people who are ready to stay with him all the way.

There are many different kinds of champions, but none of them is as rewarded as the champion of God. Imagine how Paul must have felt as he prepared to die and go to heaven. It was all worth it, and he was glad that he had served Jesus. You, too, can be a champion for God. Think how good you will feel when you see the fifteenth round. That will mean that you have been a champion, a real champion, and that you will have shared the teachings of Jesus with other people in the world.

In Training

Titus 2:11-14

Training us to renounce impiety and worldly passion, and in the present age, to live lives that are self-controlled, upright, and godly. (v. 12)

Object: a whistle and a leash

Good morning, boys and girls. The people who wrote the Bible, after listening to what God told them to write, remembered what God had done for them. Whenever they had a chance, they told the people who read their letters what a wonderful plan God had for making us Christians.

There was a man by the name of Titus whom Paul loved very much, and who received a letter from Paul about Jesus. Paul told Titus that he should stay in training to be a Christian. Do you know how to train? (*let them answer*)

Have you ever trained a dog? (*let them answer*) I brought some things that you might use to train a dog. I have a whistle and a leash. If I want to train my dog to come when I whistle, I must use a whistle to train him. I use the leash to teach him where to walk, how fast to walk, how to sit and when to sit, and things like that. That is what you call training a dog. How many of you have ever trained a dog with a whistle or leash? (*let them answer*)

If it is important to train a dog, then think how important it is to train ourselves. Paul said that a Christian should train himself or herself to be a Christian. It isn't something that just happens. Training can be hard work. You can't tell a dog to sit once and then expect him always to sit whenever you want him to. You must train him over and over. The same thing is true with being a Christian. You need to practice prayer by doing it over and over. You need to practice forgiving over and over. You need to practice living good lives that share your good things with others over and over. That is what is called training to be a Christian, and you must be willing to work at it every day. That's what Paul told Titus and that is what he tells us. We must train everyday to be good examples of what Christ wants us to be.

Fresh Starts

Titus 3:4-7

He saved us, not because of any works of righteousness that we have done, but according to his mercy, through the water of rebirth and renewal by the Holy Spirit. (v. 5)

Object: a check with your name written on it and a gift that you received from someone who loves you

Good morning, boys and girls. This morning I want to tell you a little bit about the way God feels toward you and me. Do you like to know how other people feel about you? I do, especially when I think that they like me. I am not so sure that I want to hear from the people who don't like me. Well, God likes you. As a matter of fact, he loves you, and I want to tell you a little bit about that love.

I suppose most of you know that I get paid for working. That's right, at the end of each month the treasurer comes up to me and gives me my paycheck and says, "Here is your paycheck, Pastor. You earned it." Now there is a very important word in what the treasurer said. The word is "earned." Do you know what that means? (*wait for response*) When you earn something it means that you worked for it. Your dad earns his paycheck. He worked hard to get what someone paid him. Your mom earns her paycheck. She, too, works hard to get it.

Now I have something else with me this morning that I am sure you all recognize. (*hold up some things that you received as gifts*) Can you tell me what this is? (*let them identify each object*) Do you think that I earned this? (*wait for answers*) I could have earned it, but I didn't. I never worked the first minute for this. Do you know why? Someone gave it to me as a gift. But not just any someone. No, sir, this is a very special gift because my daughter gave it to me. This is a gift of love.

This is the way that God cares for us. This is the way he makes us a part of his world. While we live on earth, he loves us, and after we leave the earth, he loves us, and he gives us the gift of life with love. We don't earn our life with him. He doesn't pay us off with life, but rather he gives it to us with love. It is a free gift just like this gift of love that I received from my daughter. She gave it to me with love, and expected nothing in return. That is the way God loves us. He would love us if we did nothing for him just because he cares so much for us.

Life Is Like A Seed

Titus 3:4-7

This Spirit he poured out on us richly through Jesus Christ our Savior, so that, having been justified by his grace, we might become heirs according to the hope of eternal life. (vv. 6-7)

Object: some seeds, preferably vegetable or flower

Good morning, boys and girls. Do you remember when we celebrated the new year? What was new about it? Did the world put on new clothes like a brighter sun or a bluer sky? (*let them answer*) No? Well, then what was new about it? You don't know! I'll tell you what is new: we all started over! That's right; the new year means we can begin all over so you can forget your mistakes and your broken promises and begin again.

I have something with me this morning that I saved so that it could begin again. It grew once and is now dead, but what I have will begin all over. Does that sound like a riddle? What could I have that once was part of something that lived, is now dead, but will live again?

Do you remember that God promised us that if we believe in him he will take us after we die and make us live again? How many of you remember God saying something like that? (*let them answer*)

Last summer I had some tomatoes that I grew in my backyard. How many of you know what a tomato plant looks like? It has a long stem, kind of looks like a fuzzy piece of celery and has leaves that are rough and kind of pointed in places, but the best part is the round red ball that we call a tomato. Well, inside of that red ball called a tomato are seeds. Now my plants got brown and finally gray after they died and they no longer stood up but just fell on the ground. Finally, we had to cut them up and burn them. But I kept some of the seeds and people tell me that if I plant them and water them and take care of them inside my house, those seeds that came from those dead plants will live again. God promised that it will happen, too.

How many of you would like some of my seeds? Wonderful! Now you have to take good care of them just like God takes care of you. Will you take care of them? You will, that's fine.

Someday even after we die we shall live again just like those seeds. God promised. God bless you.

Special

Philemon 7-17

No longer as a slave but more than a slave, a beloved brother — especially to me but how much more to you, both in the flesh and in the Lord. (v. 16)

Object: some ordinary coins and some collector's coins

Good morning, boys and girls. How many of you know what the word *special* means? (*let them answer*) That is very good. Very few things are special, and when we have something that is special it means a lot to us. The funny part of this is that we do not always know or understand the special things. For instance, I have with me some coins. You all like money, don't you? I want to show you some money and tell you a little bit about it.

Here is a penny. It is worth one cent. That's all you can buy with this penny, something worth one cent. Here is another coin that is also a penny, but it is worth _____ (*use a value associated with a rare penny*). It looks like a penny, and if you went down to the store and gave it to a clerk at the store she might think that it was an ordinary penny and use it that way. But just think what you missed by not knowing that this coin was special.

That is the way it is with Jesus. A lot of people know who Jesus is, but they do not know how special he is. They have heard about him as a great storyteller, a good doctor, and a wonderful teacher, but they do not know him as the Savior. That means that they do not know how special he is for them. It is true that he told terrific stories and made lots of sick people well, and when it came to teaching there was no one better. But when it comes to the special part, they have forgotten, or have never known what it is that makes him special. Jesus is the Savior, and that means that he is able to forgive your sins. Jesus died for you so that you can live forever. Jesus is your brother, and that means that he is very close to you and to your heavenly Father. That is the special part about Jesus.

The next time you see a special coin, perhaps you will remember that Jesus is your brother, your special brother. That is really wonderful, and worth more than all of the money in the world. It is really important to you and to me that we know how special Jesus is and that once we know it, we share it with all of our friends.

I don't want to forget to tell you that you are also very special to your brother Jesus, and that he loves you and all who know him very much.

Friends And Favors

Philemon 8-10

For this reason, though I am bold enough in Christ to command you to do your duty, yet I would rather appeal to you on the basis of love — and I, Paul, do this as an old man; and now also as a prisoner of Christ Jesus. (vv. 8-10)

Object: none

Good morning, boys and girls. One of the very best things about having a friend is being able to ask favors. Favors are the kinds of things that you would like to have happen to you, but which you would only ask a friend to do. You wouldn't ask just anyone to share his or her candy bar with you, or to carry your books home from school while you go somewhere else for the afternoon. That kind of a person is a friend, and a friend likes to do favors.

Paul had a friend like that whose name was Philemon. Paul was in jail for preaching and teaching about Jesus. In those days it was against the law to teach and preach about your God in places where there was another god. The teachings of Jesus were new, and priests were afraid that when the Good News of Jesus was shared, the people would begin believing in what he taught rather than in the old teachings about idols and laws. For those reasons, Paul was often put in jail. Paul did not like jail, but he always took the time to teach other prisoners and the jailers about Jesus, and many of them came to believe.

One of the men who had been jailed was named Onesimus. He was a runaway slave. He belonged to a man named Philemon, the friend of Paul. Onesimus hated slavery and the idea that his master owned him, just like a cow or a chair or a piece of clothing. He hated it so badly that he ran away and tried to hide from his master. In those days it was all right by law to have slaves, and people who had the money could buy them and keep them as long as they wanted to.

Onesimus was caught and put in prison, the same prison that kept Paul. While they were there, Paul taught Onesimus everything that he could about Jesus and the Christian life. Soon Onesimus began to think of how good it was to love rather than hate, and he wanted to make things right with everyone. He had not only run away, but he had stolen some things from Philemon that he felt bad about.

Paul understood how Onesimus felt. He wrote a letter to Philemon telling him about the way Onesimus' life has changed. Because of Paul's preaching, Philemon had become a Christian, a very wealthy one. Paul told him about the way that Onesimus had become a Christian also and what good care Onesimus had given Paul in prison. The name Onesimus means "useful," and Paul told Philemon that while this slave had not been very useful to Philemon before, he was of great use to Paul now. Paul would have liked Onesimus to stay with him and care for him while he was in prison, but that would not be fair, although Paul felt that Philemon owed him anything that he would ask.

Instead Paul said he was going to ask a favor. He was sending Onesimus back to Philemon as soon as he could be released, with the hope that Onesimus would not be treated like a slave, but instead like a Christian brother. Then if Philemon was satisfied with what Paul had given him — Jesus Christ — he could return Onesimus to Paul as that special favor. Paul felt that Onesimus would make a great missionary for Jesus and a wonderful help to him personally. That was a real favor to ask of a friend. We don't know what the final answer was, but we have a real feeling that Philemon would have had a hard time refusing the Apostle Paul who had shared Jesus with him.

Maybe the next time you ask a favor of a friend or you do one for a friend of yours, you will remember the time that Paul needed a favor from Philemon. He asked for a slave Onesimus to be made a brother in Christ.

Jesus Was A Pioneer

Hebrews 2:9-11 (12-18)

It was fitting that God, for whom and through whom all things exist, in bringing many children to glory, should make the pioneer of their salvation perfect through suffering. (v. 10)

Object: an antique that would be representative of the pioneer period of our country, such as a butter churn, a coonskin cap, a musket or any other item that is easily obtained

Good morning, boys and girls. How many of you like to see movies about old days? (*let them answer*) What do you think about when I say the word *pioneer*? (*let them answer*) You think of people like Daniel Boone and Davy Crockett. Do you think about hunting in the woods and living in log cabins? (*let them answer*) The people had to make all their own clothes. They wore caps that were made out of animal skins. We call a hat like this a coonskin cap because it was made out of the skin of a raccoon. They had to make their own butter by churning it for many hours in something that looked like this. (*show them a butter churn*) They had to hunt all of their meat in the woods. To do that, they had to carry these very heavy guns that were called muskets. It was a hard life, but they must have enjoyed living in the wilds and being free to do whatever they wanted to do.

Jesus was a pioneer. The Bible even calls him a pioneer. Jesus lived a life that was different from anyone else's life because he went in new directions that God sent him. Jesus came to do something that had never been done before. He came to save people from their sins. He had to teach new things and show people how life was supposed to be lived with God rather than against God. That wasn't easy. People don't like to change. People often think that they know best. God wanted people to live free from sin, and so he sent Jesus. God told him to go in a different direction than the way people were living. Many times Jesus had to do something all by himself. There was no one else to help him or share it with him. It was a hard life to live, but one that Jesus felt right about. Finally, Jesus was the true pioneer, because he died for our sins. Just like the pioneers made our country safe for us to live in, Jesus, by dying for our sins, made life safe for us after death. That is why the Bible calls Jesus a pioneer. Jesus died for our sins so that we would never have to worry about dying again, if we believe in his teachings and the love that God wants to share with us.

The next time you see something that makes you think about pioneers, I hope that you will think about Jesus and the way that he was a pioneer for all of us, and how he died for our sins so that we could live forever in safety with God.

We Are The Church

Hebrews 3:1-6

We are his house if we hold firm the confidence and the pride that belongs to hope. (v. 6b)

Object: some bricks, wood, a miniature tent

Good morning, boys and girls. I have some very strange things with me today. (*show them the bricks, the wood, and the tent*) Why do you suppose I brought these bricks and this wood with me to church? (*let them guess*) Well, today we are going to talk about houses. What is your house made of, do you know? (*let them tell you*) Your house probably has a lot of wood in it. Maybe it is also made out of brick. Houses are made out of very strong materials so that when the storms and winds come, they won't blow over or get damaged.

A long time ago people lived in houses that looked very different from ours. What did the Indians make their houses out of? (*let them tell you*) Some had houses that looked like tents. Others had houses that were made of mud and straw and even animal skins. If you had been an Indian, you wouldn't have had a very big house, would you? It would have been like living in a tent. (*hold up the tent*) There was only one big room and that's where everyone slept and ate and lived. Do you think that you would have liked being an Indian? (*let them answer*)

What kinds of houses do you suppose the people of Jesus' day lived in? (*let them guess*) Some of their houses were built right into the side of a hill. It would be like living in a cave. The houses of Jesus' day probably weren't very big, either, and they didn't have all the nice things that we have — like garbage disposals and running water and showers and dishwashers and carpet on the floor.

Today's scripture lesson talks about a very special kind of house — the house of God, the church. This house is very special because it is where we all come together to worship God our Father. This is where we sing his praises and learn more about him each Sunday. Most churches are nice big buildings where all the people can come together. But you know, boys and girls, our scripture tells us something very unusual about the church. It says that the church isn't really made of brick or stone or wood. Can you guess what the church is really made out of? (*let them guess*) The church is made of people! You and I and your moms and dads and brothers and sisters and aunts and uncles and neighbors — all of us are the church. That means that even if this building weren't here, we would still have a church. The church isn't made up of things — it is made up of people who follow Jesus. You and I are really God's house.

That is a very wonderful thought, isn't it, boys and girls? That means that we have to be the very best kind of house we can be — a house that is better than all of the lovely churches all over the world. Today as we worship God in this building, let's remember the special message of our scripture lesson: We are all God's people — God's house — the church!

God Sees Right Through

Hebrews 4:9-16

And before him no creature is hidden, but all are naked and laid bare to the eyes of the one to whom we must render an account. (v. 13)

Object: a big piece of clear plastic used to cover many or all of the children

Good morning, boys and girls. Today we are going to find something out about God and something about ourselves. Have you ever done something that you were really ashamed of? (*let them answer*) You don't have to tell me what it was, but I want you to think about it. When you have thought about his awful thing that you did or the stupid thing that you did that makes you ashamed, then just raise your hand. (*wait for a few hands to be put up before moving to the next part*) When you feel ashamed or embarrassed for something you have done, you feel like hiding, don't you? (*let them answer*) Of course you do. You wish that no one could see you. If there was any place to hide, you would like to hide.

I guess that is the way we should feel when we commit any sin. Some people stay away from coming to worship services when they have done some sin that they think is really awful. They try to hide from God.

Let's pretend that all of us have done some pretty awful things, and we want to hide from our parents. I am going to help you hide so that no one here today will see you. I brought along a big covering that I will put over the top of all of you. You stay under it and be pretty quiet and no one will know that you are here. (*take out the plastic covering*) Now think about the stupid thing that you did or that pretty awful thing that you don't want anyone to know about while I am covering you. (*put the plastic covering over them*)

Is everyone covered? (*let them answer*) Do you feel better now that you are hidden? Are you glad that no one can see how embarrassed or sorry you feel? (*let them answer*) I don't think anyone here can see you, do you? (*let them answer*) That's right. Of course, they can see you. Everyone here can see right through the plastic covering that I put over you.

That's the same way it is with God. People try to hide their sins from God, and they think that they are doing a pretty good job of it. But they are only kidding themselves. You can't hide from God in his world no matter where you are. God sees and knows everything about us.

Suffering ... A Good Teacher

Hebrews 5:7-9

Although he was a Son, he learned obedience through what he suffered. (v. 8)

Object: a speeding ticket

Good morning, boys and girls. (*hold up the speeding ticket*) Have you ever seen one of these? (*let them answer*) This is a speeding ticket. A police officer gave me one of these because he said I was driving too fast in the city. I sure didn't like the way he told me that I had to slow down while driving in the city. Of course, the thing that I didn't like the most was the idea that it is going to cost me a lot of money when I go to court. Then the judge will give me a big talk, and I will have to listen and promise him that I won't drive the way I was driving in the city. Even after the talk the judge gives me, I will still have to pay the fine. That kind of driving sure does make me suffer and suffer a lot. How do you think you would feel if you were arrested by a police officer, made to go to court, and then pay a big fine for driving a little bit too fast? Pretty bad, that's how you would feel. But you learn a lot when you suffer. I don't drive as fast in the city as I used to drive.

We all learn to obey by suffering. Sometimes our moms and dads make us suffer to teach us to obey. The police officer made me suffer and now I obey the speed laws. Suffering may hurt for a little while but if it teaches us to obey, then it is worthwhile. Maybe the next time you think you are suffering too much, you will remember how Jesus suffered for us, and then you will be thankful for his obeying the Father.

A Bolt, A Nut, And A Washer

Hebrews 7:23-28

Consequently he is able for all time to save those who approach God through him, since he always lives to make intercession for them. (v. 25)

Object: a nut, a bolt, and a washer

Good morning, boys and girls. Today, we are talking about a very big word, and also a very important one. The word is *intercession*. What do you think the word *intercession* might mean? (*let them answer*) Those were all good tries, but they are not the answers. I said it was a big word and not one that we use very often. I think that I can help you learn what it means in just a minute. First of all, I want to tell you that Jesus is our intercession. That will help us to learn more about what the word means.

I brought with me a bolt that you might use when you are building a table, or chair, or almost anything. Sometimes when you are building something, it is necessary to drill a hole and use a bolt. But when you use a bolt, you must also use a nut. The nut just twists right on the bolt and helps to hold something together. There is one thing missing if you want to keep the bolt and nut from pulling right through the wood. You need a washer, something to come between the bolt and the nut.

Now here is where you must pretend. Let's say that the bolt is God; and we are the nut. God wants you and me to be close together but because we are not always good and right, we have some problems with God. Our problems are called sins. We just don't belong in the same place with a very holy God. God wants us and we want God, but because God is pure and holy we don't belong together. Jesus is the washer. Jesus comes between God and us just like the washer is in between the bolt and the nut. Jesus makes us fit good with God because Jesus takes all our sins and gets rid of them. Jesus listens to God the Father just like he listens to us, and he brings us together. We fit better because of Jesus, just like the bolt and nut fit together because of the washer.

The washer comes between and is called the intercessor or intercession. He listens and works for both sides.

That is why Jesus is so important to you and to me. He speaks for us and acts for us with God the Father. Jesus also speaks for God the Father and acts for God the Father. He is the intercession. We pray to God the Father through the name of Jesus, and God gives us forgiveness through his Son Jesus Christ.

Intercession is a big word and a very important one to all of us. When you pray, you use the name of Jesus who speaks to the Father for us. A bolt, a nut, and a washer help us to understand the way that God works with us through Jesus.

A Time For Giving
(Appropriate for Christmas)

Hebrews 10:5-10

And it is by God's will that we have been sanctified through the offering of the body of Jesus Christ once for all. (v. 10)

Object: a very pretty package, wrapped like a Christmas package

Good morning, boys and girls. Today I have a very special problem that I need to share with you. I have heard about children your age all over the world who will have a very different Christmas than the kind that you are going to have. These children are called refugees. Does anyone know what the word refugee means? (*let them answer*) That's right; a refugee is someone who no longer has a home. Most of the time a refugee doesn't have many clothes, much food, and perhaps not even parents or relatives. Most of the time, people become refugees as the result of war.

There are millions of refugees in the world today, and while we are getting ready for one of the best Christmases we have ever had, the refugees will try to stay alive for another day. We are going to have all kinds of presents, food, and new clothes given to us on Christmas Day. I was wondering if any of us would be willing to make a sacrifice in the name of Jesus' birthday and give something that we have gotten for Christ's birthday to a refugee child? I think that it would be a wonderful time for us to consider making a sacrifice.

The scripture lesson today talks about the coming of Christ and how he is born into our world as a sacrifice for us. Jesus came to save us from our sins, and he was born to die for us. That was the most important sacrifice the world has ever known. He died to be a sacrifice once and for all for everyone's sins. He taught us how important it was to sacrifice ourselves for one another. Jesus gave his life for us.

There are millions of people who have no help. They have little food, and so they have no strength to work and no place to work. They live out in the field, a field, with maybe a tent over their head. The only clothes they have are the rags that they escaped with and those will not last long. Christmas is a wonderful time for us, but it is also a time when we might learn how important the sacrifice of Jesus was by making a small sacrifice ourselves.

When you go home today, you may want to talk to your parents about making a sacrifice this Christmas so that another child just like you some place else in the world will also be reminded of the gift Jesus gave with his life.

Plan For Heaven

Hebrews 11:1-3, 8-16

By faith he stayed for a time in the land he had been promised, as in a foreign land, living in tents, as did Isaac and Jacob, who were heirs with him of the same promise. (v. 9)

Object: a pup tent

Good morning, boys and girls. Today I want to take a moment to set up our object so that all of you know what I am talking about. (*set up the pup tent*) How many of you have ever been camping in a park or somewhere far away from home? (*let them answer*) It is a lot of fun, isn't it? First you set up your tent, find a safe place to put the food where the raccoons and bears can't get it, and then lay out your sleeping bags. Sometimes you have to walk a long way to find your water and bring it back to camp, but no matter what kind of work you do, it still seems like fun.

But it isn't home, is it? Do you remember how good it felt to get home and sleep in your own bed, and walk over to the sink to get a drink of water, or sit in a soft chair? That's home. It is good to have a home.

God thinks of heaven as our *real* home and of being here on earth as like camping. This is not where we are going to live forever. The longest time is going to be spent with God in heaven.

A long time ago God had a very loyal follower by the name of Abraham, and wherever God told him to go, Abraham went, and he stayed as long as God told him to stay. He lived in a tent because he knew that God was going to use him in a lot of ways and in a lot of places. He could move his tent wherever God wanted him to go, but he couldn't move a house. Abraham wanted to be able to go on a moment's notice.

That is the way it should be with us. We don't want to spend all of our time working and building something here on earth that will only last for a short time. Most of our lives will be spent with God, so we should spend most of our time preparing to live with him. Some people spend all of their time working and planning for the things here on earth such as their houses, their yards, their boats, their cars, or other possessions. They have little time to listen to God as Abraham did. But God thinks that it is better to plan for heaven and be ready to live with him than it is to spend all of our time thinking and planning about earth. Maybe you can take part of your time today to think about God and plan for heaven. Will you do that? Good. That will make God happy.

Jesus Helps Us See Better

Hebrews 12:18-24

But you have come to Mount Zion and to the city of the living God, the heavenly Jerusalem, and to innumerable angels in festal gathering. (v. 22)

Object: a pair of eyeglasses

Good morning, boys and girls. How many of you wear glasses? (*let them answer*) Some of you do. Did you know that about 100,000,000 people in the U.S. wear some kind of glasses to help them see better? That is almost half of the people in this country. Tell me how glasses help people see better? (*let them answer*) Some people get headaches if they do not wear their glasses. Some people can read better if they wear glasses. Some people can see far away and some people can see close up if they wear their eyeglasses, but they cannot see things far or close without them. Glasses really make a difference. If you wear glasses, you know what I mean and you are really grateful for them.

I want to tell you about something else that really makes a difference. I want to tell you about the differences that Jesus Christ makes to us. The writer of the book of Hebrews, which is a very beautiful book in the New Testament, tells us how good it is to have Jesus make a difference in our lives. Let me tell you about it!

This writer remembered how people knew God before Jesus came. People knew God as someone of whom they were afraid because of his terrible power. They used to think about the way that God would punish them for the things they did and how he caused them great trouble. That's the way the people of the Old Testament thought about their God. He was a God who was great, but he was also to be feared.

Now the writer of Hebrews says Jesus really made a difference. People came to know God a lot better, and they understood that God is filled with love, and that he is always ready to forgive them instead of punish them.

Jesus helped people to see God better, just like eyeglasses help people to see other things better. Jesus makes a difference. Perhaps the next time you put on your glasses, or you see someone else put on their glasses, you will think to yourselves how glad you are that there are glasses to wear. But at the same time, you can also think about how Jesus and glasses are a lot alike. They both help us to see better. Of course we are really grateful for Jesus because he has helped us to see that our God is more than a terrible judge. God is a loving Father.

Anger Doesn't Work!

James 1:17-27

For your anger does not produce God's righteousness. (v. 20)

Object: a pitcher of water, a strainer, and an empty bucket

Good morning, boys and girls. Today I have a small experiment for you, and I hope that by doing it, we will learn something about the ways of God and the ways of people. I brought along with me this pitcher of water and an empty bucket. I need to get the water from this place where the pitcher is, to the empty bucket, without moving either the pitcher or the bucket. I also brought along this thing that we call a strainer to help me get the water out of the pitcher and over to the bucket. Do you think it will work? (*let them answer*) You don't think it will work? Why not? (*let them answer*) You think it won't work because the strainer has holes in it! Do you want me to try? (*let them answer*) Some of you want me to try and others don't want me to try. I am going to try it. (*begin to pour some of the water into the strainer and run as fast as you can over to the bucket; let as much as possible fall onto a tray or some object that will take the overflow*) It didn't work that time, but I am going to try it again. Maybe if I run a little faster. (*try it again*) It didn't work that time either so now I am going to try and pour it a little faster. (*try it once more*) It just doesn't work. Using a strainer to carry water from a pitcher to a bucket just does not work. Our experiment has failed.

But doing that experiment has taught me something about God and people, and let me tell you what it is. Have you ever heard someone trying to tell someone else about God in an angry voice? Suppose I told you (*say this in a very angry and loud voice*), "God wants you to worship him every Sunday in this church." Do you hear God speaking, and have you learned something that you will always remember? I could try another one. (*again in a very loud and angry voice*) "Love your father and mother!" How did you like that? Have you learned how loving your heavenly Father is? Of course not. Some people think that they can teach about their loving God in a very angry way. People don't learn what is right for them according to God through their anger. That is like trying to carry water in a strainer. It just doesn't work.

The next time that you hear someone trying to teach about God in an angry way, you can think about the time I tried to carry water in a strainer. It just doesn't work. If you want someone to know about our God and his love, teach it in a quiet and joyful way. Then people are sure to listen, and when they listen and are not afraid, they will learn. That's what the Apostle Paul said, and I believe that he is right. I hope you do too. God bless you.

Faith Needs Work

James 2:1-5, 8-10, 14-18

So faith by itself, if it has no works, is dead. (v. 17)

Object: a calculator

Good morning, boys and girls. Today we are going to talk about something that all of us need to learn and understand as soon as possible. We are going to talk about faith, and how to make our faith work. How many of you have heard about the word "faith"? (*let them answer*) Faith is something that all of us should have and use. Our faith means that if we believe in something enough, something surely will happen. If I believe that God will heal me when I am hurt, then I have faith in God as a healer. If I believe that God will make enough sunshine and rain so that the corn will grow then I have faith that God is a grower. That is faith.

Some people think that they have so much faith that they do not have to do anything because God will do it all. They don't have to worry about anything since God will do everything. A man by the name of James listened carefully to God and gave us some answers about what people are supposed to do as partners with God. He called it working with God.

Let me show you what I mean. I have a calculator. The answer to almost any problem that I can think of that has to do with numbers is in this calculator. If I want to know how much 16 times 16 is I know that the answer is in this calculator. I have faith that the calculator has the answer. Do you think the calculator has the answer? (*let them answer*) You think the answer is in there also. Do you think that the answer is right? (*let them answer*) You think that the right answer is in the calculator. How are we going to get the right answer out of the calculator? (*let them answer*) That's right; we have to push the buttons. If I push 16 and the button for times and then another 16, I will get the answer of 256. That is the correct answer. My faith that the calculator had the right answer in there is good. I can do it again by asking how big is a room 25-feet long and 15-feet wide. The answer is 375 square feet. Again, I have done some work to push the buttons, but my faith that the calculator would give the right answer is correct.

I believe that God wants everyone to be happy, healthy, and have a warm place to live. That is what my faith tells me. But as a Christian, I also know that God has given me land to grow food, love to make other people happy, and hands to help build warm houses. I can help people to know my God and his love by sharing my life with them. I must do good things, or work to help others know the God that I believe in. Having faith in God is not enough if we don't share our lives and our work to help others know God as well.

When you see a calculator you have faith that the right answers are inside of it. But you must use the buttons, do the work, to get the answers to your problems.

We must believe that God will answer our problems, but we must also do things that let God help us and all our friends.

Try For A Good Life

James 3:16—4:6

And the harvest of righteousness is sown in peace by those who make peace. (v. 18)

Object: bricks and raisins

Good morning, boys and girls. I brought along with me some things that I found to help me tell you something that I learned from the Bible.

The first thing I have with me is a brick. How many of you know what a brick is used for? (*let them answer*) That's right; it is used to build houses. When you build a house with bricks, do you have a wood house? (*let them answer*) Of course not. You build a house of bricks, and you have a brick house. Bricks don't change to wood shingles or boards. A house built with brick is a brick house.

I also brought some raisins. I like raisin bread. If the baker uses raisins in his dough and bakes it, then what kind of bread will the baker have when it is finished? (*let them answer*) Right, raisin bread. He won't have rye bread or whole wheat bread or just plain white bread when he finishes; he will have raisin bread. That means that whatever he puts into the bread is the kind of bread that he will have when it is baked.

The Bible tells us that the goodness of our lives and the world we live in is a little bit like the bricklayer making a house and the baker making bread. Your life will be just as good as the good things you put in it, or just as bad as the bad things that you put in it. Our world will be as good or as bad as the people are that live in it. If you want peace in the world, then you must have peace in your heart. If you want happy and joyful people in the world, then you must be happy and joyful. If you want people who are filled with love and like to share, then you must have love and be ready to share the things that are yours. Our world is made up of people like you and me, and the kind of world we get is the same as what we put into it.

You can't have raisin bread unless you put the raisins in the dough. You can't have a brick house unless you make it with bricks. You can have a good life if you are good. God made his world this way, and it is the best kind of world that I can think of.

You make our world a better world by loving, sharing, forgiving, and being joyful. You will also help other people in the world be good and joyful, too.

Share Your Life

James 4:7-12 (13—5:6)

Humble yourselves before the Lord, and he will exalt you. (v. 10)

Object: two buckets of water, some powdered household cleaner like Spic And Span, and some dirty boards

Good morning, boys and girls. Today we are going to meet a friend of your mother's, and see why she likes it so much. How many of you ever help your parents clean house? (*let them answer*) That is a hard job and one that has to be done over and over. I think parents are really great the way that they keep our houses clean. Suppose that your mother or father did not clean your house for a month or maybe a year. What do you think your house would look like? You wouldn't be able to find a thing. It would be buried in newspapers, and in mud off your shoes, if you could find your shoes. All of the dishes would be lost in the garbage of your kitchen, if you could find the kitchen, and your bedroom would be filled with dust, paper, and dirty clothes.

But because we have parents who care, our homes are different. I brought along a very humble friend. You noticed that I said humble. This friend is cleaning soap. It comes in a powder and can only be used when it gives up its life to become something else.

Let me show you what I mean. I brought along some dirty boards and a couple of buckets of water. I am going to try and clean one of the boards with this plain bucket of water. (*wash the board*) Not bad, but the board is still dirty. All the dirt did not come off. Now I am going to take a little bit of this powder and put it in the other bucket. If you watch very carefully you will see the powder give itself up and disappear in the water. It is something special now. The water has become very powerful and can do things that the other bucket of water could not do. (*wash another board with the second bucket*) Look at the difference. The very humble soap and friend has given up being just a powder and become something very different. It can now clean the dirtiest boards and make them look like new again.

You can be like this also only in a different way. The Bible teaches us that when we give up our selfish ways, share our lives with others, and become workers for God, we can become very powerful people who can do many good things. We are like the soap. When we try to stay to ourselves and be selfish, we are not worth very much. But when we give ourselves up to God and get mixed up with all his goodness, then we become very powerful people.

The next time that you see your parents cleaning the house, ask if they are using some very humble soap that becomes very powerful when it is mixed with water. Then thank them for making your house such a wonderful clean place to live.

Straight A's — Forever!

1 Peter 1:3-9

For you are receiving the outcome of your faith, the salvation of your souls. (v. 9)

Object: a grade card or grade printout with all *A*'s

Good morning, boys and girls. Have you ever wanted something so much that you would do almost anything to get it? (*let them answer*) What would you like right now that you do not have? (*let them answer*) We want a lot of things, don't we? I suppose that it is good that we can't have everything that we want or otherwise we would stop trying.

Some things are more important than other things for all of us. For instance, you would all like to have good grades in school. Good grades do not come easy, do they? (*let them answer*) Let's suppose that you worked very hard in school and did all your homework. If you did all of this, you would have a grade card that looked like this grade card looks. (*show them a grade card with straight A's*) That very good grade card is the outcome of your hard work, your special effort.

Let's think of something else that all of us want. How would you like to live forever with joy in your heart? (*let them answer*) All of us would like to live forever in joy. The Bible tells us that it will happen to everyone who has faith. The outcome of our faith is living forever with God in joy. What is faith? We talk a lot about faith and we tell each other that we must have it, but what is it? Faith is doing what we say that we believe. A lot of people believe that Jesus is the Son of God, but they don't act like Jesus is the Son of God. They believe, but they don't have faith. When you obey the things that you believe, then you have faith.

God promises us life with joy. We believe that God gives life when we are born. We also believe that God will give us new life when we die. Now we must live in faith just like we must work in school. If we work in school and do the things that we say we want to do, then we will have good grades. If we have faith in God, and that is doing the things that we say we believe in, then we will have a new life of joy after we die. That is the promise of God — and God keeps all of his promises.

First we must believe that God gives us life. It is a free gift. We must do what we say we believe, and that is faith. The outcome of faith is living forever with God in peace and joy.

God's Stamp Of Approval

1 Peter 2:19-25

For it is a credit to you if, being aware of God, you endure pain while suffering unjustly. (v. 19)

Object: a rubber stamp that reads "Paid"

Good morning, boys and girls. How many of you have ever had to suffer? (*let them answer*) Suffering is not much fun, is it? I don't know anyone who likes to suffer. There is usually a lot of pain connected with suffering. If you have ever broken a leg or had a lie told about you that other people believed, then you know what it is like to suffer in pain. God knows that we have pain and he tried to show us how to get along and use the pain to become better and stronger people. Christians have to use pain often to help them learn to love more and hate less.

Work is hard and most people would like to work less, if they could. But if they want certain things such as a house to live in, a car to ride in, clothes to wear, and food to eat, then they have to work. If they want to take a vacation, then they work a little harder so they can have some free time without any work. All of the things that we like so well must be paid for with our work. When you pay for a house, a car, food, or a vacation, the person you buy them from stamps the bill with a big word that says, "Paid." These things are all yours after that word is stamped on your sales slip. You must work very hard to get something stamped "Paid." You may even suffer a little to have a lot. But when you get the big stamp that says, "Paid," it all seems worth it.

It is something like suffering for God's sake. God doesn't cause you to suffer, but you want to stick up for what God says is right. Being a Christian means teaching Christian ways, and a lot of people in this world think that there are other ways. They like to cheat, lie, steal, and have whatever they want, when they want it. You would not want to get things this way and you may have to tell others to stop doing it. That could make you suffer. They may lie about you or try to hurt you. It may be painful being a Christian at a time like this, but you have to do it. You must suffer the pain. You could pretend that you didn't see or hear it when people do things that are wrong. You could even help people do what is wrong, pretending that you did not have any choice. But that would be wrong, and it would not be doing what is Christian.

Sometimes Christians must suffer pain. They must even suffer a long time for what is right. But when they suffer for doing right, then God approves them. God does the same thing for the person who suffers while doing right that the clerk does when he or she marks "Paid" on something that you have worked very hard to get. Life is not always easy and fun. Sometimes you must suffer a lot to be someone that you will like. God knows this and approves the Christian who sticks with it. He will not mark you with a stamp, but you will know when God smiles on you for doing what is right, even though you had to suffer through it.

Troubled Carrie And Clear Connie

1 Peter 3:15-18

Keep your conscience clear, so that, when you are maligned, those who abuse you for your good conduct in Christ may be put to shame. (v. 16b)

Object: two jars of water, one clear and one filled with particles

Good morning, boys and girls. How many of you have a conscience? (*let them answer*) Do you know what your conscience is? (*let them answer*) It's part of you that tells you what is right or what is wrong. If you do something wrong and you try to hide it or lie about it, your conscience will bother you. The Bible teaches us that we should have a clear conscience. Do you know what that means? (*let them answer*) I brought along some friends of mine that will help you learn what I am speaking about.

My first friend's name is Carrie. Carrie Conscience is all mixed up. (*hold up the jar with the particles in it; then shake the jar so that the particles are swirling about*) Do you see all of the things that Carrie has floating around in her? (*let them answer*) Those things are a lot of troubles. It is hard for Carrie to be a Christian with her problems. One of the things that is bothering her is a story she told about her friend. Her friend had shared a big problem with her and had asked Carrie to keep it to herself, but Carrie ran out and told someone else. Then there is the lie that she told her mother about some broken glass. She told her mother that she didn't know how the glass got broken. She also broke a promise to her sister when she did not make the bed this morning. I could go on and on about all of the things that are bothering Carrie Conscience, but I think you understand. The worst part is that she doesn't feel that she is a good example for anyone else. She can't help other people, because her own conscience is all messed up.

I have another jar with me that is my friend Connie Conscience. (*shake it up to show them how clear it is*) Connie is not perfect, but she has a clear conscience. When Connie does something wrong, and she has done many wrong things, she takes care of it right away. Connie doesn't lie to her mother, but she tells her if she broke the glass. If she makes a bad mistake, she goes to the person and tells them what she did wrong right away. This is the way that she keeps her conscience clear, and it is a wonderful feeling.

Because of Connie's clear conscience, she is a good example of the Christian life. She can teach others about the love of God and how he helps you when your life is filled with trouble.

A clear conscience is a wonderful thing to have and everyone can have it if they trust in God, admit their mistakes, and share Jesus Christ with all of their friends. Be like Connie and get rid of Carrie, and you will love life.

Do The Dishes?

1 Peter 4:13-19

But rejoice insofar as you share Christ's sufferings, so that you may also be glad and shout for joy when his glory is revealed. (v. 13)

Object: dirty dishes

Good morning, boys and girls. I want to talk to you about a very popular subject: doing the dishes. How many of you like to do the dishes? (*let them answer*) Not one of you likes to do the dishes? That's hard to believe. Isn't there one of you that would like to do the dishes? Think about sticking your hands down in the hot, greasy water. Don't you like to scrape the plates and fill up the garbage bags? Or what about the way you get to wipe each knife, fork, and spoon with your damp towel? Doesn't that sound like fun? And don't forget the fun of working together with your brother or sister and how much they enjoy working with you. All of that fun, and not one of you likes doing the dishes! That's hard to believe. But it's so and I know it.

Washing dishes is like suffering. All boys and girls suffer a lot when it comes time to do the dishes. The worst part is that they have to be done every day. Doing the dishes is suffering; it is filled with pain, and I don't know anyone who thinks it is fun. But it has to be done. You would not want to eat off of dirty plates, and you cannot afford to eat in a restaurant every meal. Even paper plates for every meal is expensive, and you must still do the pots and pans.

Washing dishes is suffering. But there is one thing that almost makes it worth it. How many times have you felt good when you have heard your mom and dad tell you how much they appreciate it when you help? That is a good feeling, isn't it? (*let them answer*) Sure it is. You are glad that there is something that you can do to help. When a parent praises you for your work, you feel good.

Christians find that loving and serving Christ can also mean sharing some of the problems that Jesus has in the world. Not everyone loves Jesus — and some people even hate him. The people who do wrong against Jesus often also do wrong to you. They hate you, hurt you, and tell lies about you because you love Jesus. That isn't any fun. You may even wonder sometimes if you want to be a Christian.

But Jesus tells us that when we share in his suffering, then we also will share in the praise and the glory. That means that there will be a time when Jesus will share with us all of the wonderful things that can only happen to God.

You may not like to do the dishes, and you may not always want to be a Christian, but stay with it because just like your parents share their love and praise with you, so will God share his love with you. It isn't always fun or easy to be a Christian, but it's worth it.

It Really Happened Once Upon A Time

2 Peter 1:16-19

For we did not follow cleverly devised myths when we made known to you the power and coming of our Lord Jesus Christ, but we had been eyewitnesses of his majesty. (v. 16)

Object: a story book

Good morning, boys and girls. I have a book that I want to show you so that you can help me with a story that I want to share with you. How many of you read story books or listen to your parents read them. Do you know how a good story almost always starts? (*let them answer*) That's right, it begins, "Once upon a time ..." and it usually always ends, "They lived happily ever after." We all like stories about once upon a time, and we especially like stories with happy endings. That is the best part of good stories.

Peter knew some good stories and he liked to share them with people. But his stories were not make-believe. He told about things that happened to him while he lived and traveled with Jesus. Some of the stories were a little hard to believe because nothing happened to others like they happened to Jesus. Peter remembered the time when he was on a mountain with Jesus and the two brothers James and John, and Jesus was turned from looking like any other man into someone who was so bright that he actually shone. While he was still shining white, there came two men by the name of Moses and Elijah who had died a long time before Jesus, Peter, John, and James lived. These two men began to talk to Jesus. If that was not enough, they also heard a voice come right out of heaven that said, "Jesus is my Son and I am very happy with him and the things that he says and does." When they heard that voice, they knew that it was the voice of God — and Peter, James, and John fell right on the ground and covered their faces because they were so afraid. Afraid but full of wonder. That was quite a day.

If you told someone about a day like this, they would tell you that you were making it up. They would think it was a story that should start, "Once upon a time ..." But Peter was there and he saw Jesus do some other things that no one else could do. He saw things happen when Jesus was around that never happened before. That is why Peter wanted all of us to know that what happened that day on the mountain was not a big story, but the truth, and one that we should never forget.

I hope the next time that you are reading a story that begins, "Once upon a time ..." you will remember that it is make believe, but that the story you heard about Jesus on the mountain this morning, happened exactly the way I told it.

A Daze Of Days
(Appropriate for Advent)

2 Peter 3:8-14

But do not ignore this one fact, beloved, that with the Lord one day is like a thousand years and a thousand years are like one day. (v. 8)

Object: a box of salt

Good morning, boys and girls. Do you know that today begins a new year in church? (*let them answer*) Everything starts over with the first day, the first week, and even the first month. It all seems fresh to us as we wait for Jesus to come into our hearts all over again. Have you ever wondered how many times Christians have done this? (*let them answer*) I wonder why God doesn't send Jesus so that we can be done with all of our waiting. Most of us are ready, aren't we? (*let them answer*) Doesn't everyone know about Jesus and love him as their Savior? (*let them answer*) The reason that God doesn't send Jesus is that he wants everyone to have a chance to receive Jesus as their Savior. That's what the Bible says. But you may think it is taking too long for Jesus to come.

I brought with me some salt this morning to help us learn something about our waiting for Jesus. There is a lot of salt in this one box, but we are going to pretend that every one of these pieces of salt is a day. Now the Bible says that one day is like a thousand years to God. A thousand years is a long time to us since none of us will ever live that long. But one day doesn't seem like a very long time since we have already lived many days. But the Bible says God has lived so long that time doesn't make much difference to him. If one of these pieces is a day and you would have to count out 365 of the pieces of salt for one year, then you would have to have 365,000 grains to make a thousand years. But if we counted out 365,000 of them we would not have all of the pieces of salt in this one box. And if you think of all the boxes of salt in one grocery store and then think of all of the grocery stores, then you see how little that one piece of salt is compared to all of the salt in the world.

One piece of salt in a box (*put the piece back into the box*) is not much, but it is important to that box just like one day is important to you. We may get tired of waiting, but God knows just the right time to send Jesus back to us so that everyone will have an opportunity to know Jesus as Savior. We must be patient and trust God since only he knows when it is just the right time.

The next time you put some salt on your food, you can think of what the Bible means when it says: one day is like a thousand years. Will you do that? God bless you.

Let God's Light Shine

1 John 1:1—2:2

If we say we have no sin, we deceive ourselves, and the truth is not in us. (v. 8)

Object: a light bulb, washable black paint, a small paintbrush, and a bucket of water to wash off the paint

Good morning, boys and girls. It is getting warmer every day and soon it will be summer. How many of you remember the cold days of winter? (*let them answer*) It's fun to be outside without our coats and hats, isn't it? (*let them answer*) I love to walk in the sunshine. It seems so good. I like these days much better than the dark and cloudy ones. God must like sunshine also. The Bible speaks of God as if he were a bright light. It also talks about sin as being dark shadows.

I brought along an object today to help us understand how we can be close to God. All of us sin. Do you remember the last time that you sinned? (*let them answer*) When we sin it makes us dark and cloudy. We always hide our sin. We don't want other people to know that we are sinning so we try to hide it from them also. (*take your light bulb and begin to paint it black*) I want you to pretend that this light bulb is God and we are sinning. Do you see how we are clouding over God? The light is getting harder and harder to see. Pretty soon we will almost shut God out all together. That's the way that we feel when we sin. We are hiding from God and from his light. We don't want God to know what we are doing. We are getting further and further away from him. (*finish painting the light bulb black*) Now that God is gone from us we feel terrible. We are in darkness. What can we do? (*let them answer*)

The Bible tells us that we should confess our sins. We should talk about them to God and to each other. If I have done something to you that is wrong, I should tell you. I should also tell you how sorry I am. When I do this, something happens. (*begin to wash off part of the paint*) A little bit of light shows where we have confessed our sin. God is peeking through. There is some light coming back into our life. We feel good about this and we confess all our sins. We tell other people of the mean things that we did to them and then we confess to God about the way that we have forgotten him. Pretty soon our hearts feel different. (*wash off all the black paint*) The darkness of our sin is gone and the light of God is back. How much better we feel to be able to walk with God in the light.

That is what the Bible teaches us to do. We should confess our sins to God and to one another. When we do, we share our lives with him in light and we never have to live in the dark. Maybe you have something that you feel sorry about and you want to get rid of it. Tell that person you hurt and see if you don't feel the light of God all around you. I just know that you will.

270

Heaven Will Wait

1 John 3:1-2

Beloved, we are God's children now; what we will be has not yet been revealed. What we do know is this: when he is revealed, we will be like him, for we will see him as he is. (v. 2)

Object: two exact kinds of packages that do not have the picture of the product on the outside but do have some descriptive material of what is inside (an example would be some dishwashing product or some packages of nails or screws)

Good morning, boys and girls. We are going to work on a problem today. How many of you like to solve problems? (*let them answer*) That's good, because I like to solve problems too. It makes me feel like a good detective when I have found the answer to a big problem.

I brought along with me this morning a couple of packages. You may have seen these packages in the store, or one of your parents may have brought them home to use in your house. What do you notice about the packages? (*let them answer*) They are both packages of soap used for washing dishes. The packages are the same size and have the same name. They are both the same colors. I wonder if it says the same thing on both packages. Let's read what it says. (*begin to read from one package then read the same sentence from the other box*) It sounds the same on both. (*read on from the one package and then do the same with the other package*) Both packages seem to be the same thing.

If you went into the store and bought two packages that looked exactly alike, would you expect them to have the same thing on the inside? (*let them answer*) You think that they would be exactly alike. I would too. Do you know what the things on the inside look like? (*let them answer*) I don't know because I have never seen them. But if I opened one box I could be very sure that the same thing was in the other box and they would look the same, right? (*let them answer*) You are very good detectives. Now here is another problem. See if you can give me the answer. What will we be like in heaven? How will we look? What will we wear? How old will we be? Will we live together? These questions and a lot of other questions are the ones that we have about heaven. We don't know the answers. But the Bible tells us something that we can be sure about. God made us a promise that we will be like Jesus when he comes back. We will look like him, talk like him, act like him, be like him. We know some things about heaven, but we do not know much about how we will be except that we will be like God's Son when he comes back.

We are not ready for heaven yet. When it is time for us to live with God, then Jesus will come, and when he comes, we will know what he is like and then we will be very sure of what we will be like. That's the way God planned it and that's the way it will be.

God Is Love

1 John 4:1-11

Whoever does not love does not know God, for God is love. (v. 8)

Object: some ice and some rubber balls

Good morning, boys and girls. How many of you remember my telling you that love is doing things for one another? (*let them answer*) You can't just tell people that you love them, you must show them that you love them. Love is shared. When you have something that is good, you want to share it with others. Love is good, so it should be shared.

Today we are going to find out where love comes from. But before we do that, I must show you some things that will help me show you where love comes from. First, I have something that you might use every day. You put it in a glass with water or with cola or tea. Take a very good look at what I am talking about and tell me what it is. (*let them look at some ice cubes*) What do we call these things? (*let them answer*) That's right, ice. What do we know about ice? (*let them answer*) That's right; it is cold. All ice is cold. The one thing that we know about ice is that it is cold. We even call other things that are very cold, "ice" cold.

The next thing that I brought with me bounces; it is played with in games where you use a bat and glove or a basket. What do we call these things? (*let them answer*) Yes, we call them balls. What do we know about balls that bounce? (*let them answer*) Very good, they are round. Ice is cold and balls are round. Ice is not warm and balls are not square.

Now where does love come from? That was our question. I know that I can always find love if I look to God. God is love just like balls are round and ice is cold. The words go together. Love comes from God just like roundness comes from balls and cold comes from ice.

The Bible tells us that God is love. The Bible teaches us that God is love in the same way that a science book might tell you that ice is cold and a game book would tell you that balls are round.

God is love. The big secret that I want to share with you today is that your love comes from God. God is love and when he shares himself with you then you are filled with love. When you share your love with a friend, then you are sharing God. If I give you some ice, I am giving you something cold. If you take the ice and give it to someone else, then you are sharing the cold ice.

God is love. That is where love comes from and if you want a lot of love you must receive it from God.

Doing What God Wants

1 John 5:1-6

For the love of God is this, that we obey his commandments. And his commandments are not burdensome.... (v. 3)

Object: a list of chores, like doing the dishes, setting the table, caring for the pets, cleaning a room, mowing the grass, and so on

Good morning, boys and girls. Today we are going to talk a little bit about belonging to the family of God. This is really something important, but we don't talk very much about it. We talk a lot about the things that God does for us, and we should because he has done and continues to do everything for us. But we want to talk about what it is like to belong to the family of God, and about some of the things that we should do.

Let me explain. If you live in a family, you do certain things. Your father works, maybe your mother works, so that you have money to buy the things you need such as clothes, food, and a house. There are a lot of other things that your parents do for their family. They make the meals that we eat and repair the things that break and help us with our problems.

But you have things to do also. I have a list of chores, or jobs, that maybe you do around the house. When you do them, the family is happy. I suppose you know how it is when you forget to do them. My list has things like doing the dishes and taking care of the pets. I also think that a lot of children take care of their rooms, set the table, help mow the grass, take out the trash, and a lot of other things. Do any of you do things like this? (*let them answer*) Good. A lot of you do chores or jobs. Do you ever forget to do them? (*let them answer*) Does anyone get unhappy when you do forget to do them? (*let them answer*) I know that kind of unhappiness. But I also know how happy the home is when everyone is doing what they are supposed to do. It makes a good place to live.

The Bible teaches us that the same thing is true about the family of God. We all know what God has done for us. That is great. But we also know that there are some commandments that God gave us to keep. It is very important that we keep doing the things that God told us to do, like loving our God and loving our neighbor. We should do things that make others happy or help them when they need help. We should worship God every day of our lives and come together at least one day a week to worship as a big group. We should visit the lonely and help people who have done wrong to try again to do right. There are a lot of things that we should do to make the family of God a very happy family. When we forget that there are others, then we also forget that we are a family.

So, remember the commandments of God, just like you should remember to do the things that are asked of you at home, and we will all have wonderful families and God will bless us with great love.

273

Walking The Walk

2 John 6

And this is love, that we walk according to his commandments; this is the commandment just as you have heard it from the beginning — you must walk in it. (v. 6)

Object: some exercise equipment like a jump rope or a barbell

Good morning, boys and girls. How are you today? Do you feel good and ready to go? (*let them answer*) How many of you watch your mom or dad do exercises? (*let them answer*) Are they pretty good? (*let them answer*) Can you show me an exercise that you have seen someone like your mom or dad do? (*encourage a couple of children to do an exercise*) Those are very good! I can see your mother or dad doing exactly what you just showed us.

Have you ever heard someone say, "If you talk the talk, you must walk the walk"?

Do you know what that means? (*let them answer*) Let me see if I can explain. A lot of people talk about exercising but they only do it a few times and then they give up. That is called "talk the talk." They talk about it but they don't do it. It is like being on a diet and still eating cake and chocolate candy bars. It is like making a promise and then not keeping it.

But when you talk the talk and walk the walk then you are doing what you said you were going to do. A person who walks the walk exercises everyday. A person, who says they are going to diet, stays on the diet.

This is not something new. In the Bible, John told his friends that they must walk in the commandments of God. They must walk the walk with loving and forgiving and trusting and sharing and all of the other things that we promise God we will do.

If you promise God you will forgive your brother or sister then you must forgive. If you promise God you will love your enemy then you must walk the walk and love your enemy. If you promise your mom or dad that you will not tell a lie, then you must walk the walk and tell the truth.

Pretty cool, this Bible, isn't it? John says that we should walk according to the commandments. Don't talk the talk but walk the walk.

The next time you see the jump rope just hanging up somewhere or see the weights just lying around say to yourself, "Are we talking the talk or are we walking the walk?" And the next time you don't keep your promises to God about loving and forgiving and sharing and all of those good things then ask yourself the same question. Do I walk the walk as well as I talk the talk?

Be A Believer

2 John 9

Everyone who does not abide in the teaching of Christ, but goes beyond it, does not have God; whoever abides in the teaching has both the Father and the Son. (v. 9)

Object: a pitcher of water, some cups, and some cooking oil

Good morning, boys and girls. Today is a very special day for all people who believe in Jesus Christ and are gathered together in worship. Look at the faces of the people who are here today. God calls them saints and we call them saints. These are believers. Did you know that (*name of a church member*) is a believer? (*let them answer*) Did you know that (*name of a church member*) is a believer? (*let them answer*)

Let me show you what I mean. I brought along some small cups and I would like to pour something out of this pitcher. (*begin to fill the cups with water*) When you have your cup filled you may drink it. Now tell me what you drank. (*let them answer*) That's right; water. It is good water and it is good for us. I want you to pretend that what you drank is the faith that your mother and father, your pastor, your Sunday school teacher, and all of your friends who are Christians have shared with you. Your faith is filled with love, forgiveness, hope, joy, and all of the other good things that God gives to us. Can you imagine that you just received something like I just described? (*let them answer*)

One Christian gives to another Christian the love of Jesus. Isn't that wonderful? (*let them answer*) I think so. All of the people here this morning are sharing the love of Jesus with one another and they are going to take it home. They are going to take it to school and they are going to take it to work. Isn't that wonderful? (*let them answer*)

Of course, it doesn't always work out that way. The writer of the book in the Bible called Second John says that some people don't think the words of the Father and Jesus are enough. They want to add something to it. They want to add their own rules or tell people like you and me that they should not only believe what God teaches but something extra. Maybe they want you to let a poisonous snake bite you so that you can prove you are a better Christian. Sometimes they want you to eat a special food or not eat certain kinds of food because they think it will make you a better Christian.

Let me show you what I mean. Let me add a little something to my pitcher of water. (*pour in the clear oil*) Now, I would like to fill your cup again and ask you to taste my new drink. (*let them try it; many will not and that is all right*) Do you like the taste? (*let them answer*) Some of you didn't taste it and that is all right because what I added makes the water taste different. It is something added and the water doesn't need it.

That is the way it is with God. We can't improve what he taught us and when we try it makes it bad. Be a believer. Trust Jesus. Learn from the Bible and you will have what God promised.

The Welcome Mat

3 John 5

Beloved, you do faithfully whatever you do for the friends, even though they are strangers to you.... (v. 5)

Object: a welcome mat

Good morning, boys and girls. Today we have a wonderful lesson that our Bible writer teaches us. It is called hospitality. How many of you know what it means to show hospitality? (*let them answer*) It is a big word but it means being friendly to people who share our faith and love in Jesus.

How many of you talk to strangers? (*let them answer*) Good, none of us talk to strangers. What does your mom or dad teach you about strangers who want to talk to you? (*let them answer*) Very good! Stay away from strangers. Don't get in their cars and don't follow them. Just walk or run away toward home and try to stay with your friends. Do not get separated from your mom or dad when you are in stores or malls. Those are good rules.

However, how many of you know everyone in church this morning? (*let them answer*) Does your mom or dad invite people from your church over to your house? (*let them answer*) When they come to your house, do they see a big welcome mat outside and a very friendly smile from you when they come inside? (*let them answer*)

Christians should be friends with Christians and share the gifts that God has blessed them with. Do you have friends in Sunday school? (*let them answer*) Do you invite them over to your house to play? (*let them answer*) Christians should make friends with other Christians and support them with prayers and gifts. We want to make every boy and girl in our church and Sunday school our best friend. We want them to know how much we love them. When they are sick or hungry, we will help them with prayers and food. When they are lonely, we will visit with them and invite them over to our house. When they are sad we shall listen to them. We are their friends and the Bible says we should make them feel welcome.

Do you have a welcome mat at your house? (*let them answer*) Do you make people feel welcome when they come to see you? I hope so because the Bible teaches us friendship. The Bible teaches us love. The Bible wants us to know that we should be best friends with everyone in our church.

So the next time I see you I hope you are like a welcome mat. There you are with a big smile and maybe hug and a promise to invite me into your home and then we'll enjoy each other. Did you ever think you wanted to be a welcome mat? (*let them answer*) Maybe you didn't before but you will from now on. Make really good friends with Christian friends and show them the love God gave you to share.

Imitating The Good

3 John 11

Beloved, do not imitate what is evil but imitate what is good. Whoever does good is from God; whoever does evil has not seen God. (v. 11)

Object: two drums and two drum sticks

Good morning, boys and girls. How many of you would like to be like your mom or dad when you grow up? (*let them answer*) How many of you would like to be as good of a basketball player as Michael Jordan? (*let them answer*) How many of you would like to be like me? (*let them answer*) Well, two out of three isn't bad, is it? All of us have heroes or people that we would like to be like. Some of us want to be like a favorite uncle or a grandmother or a Sunday school teacher. That's good. Heroes or good people remind us of our goals of trying to be better people.

I brought along a couple of drums and some drum sticks. I need two volunteers but they must be able to follow directions. Do I have two volunteers? (*select two children and send one to one side of the nave and the other to the other side*) Now, we want to see how clearly one of you can imitate the other. Do you know what imitate means? (*let them answer*) Imitate means to do the same thing or be the same way that someone else is being. For instance, if I ask the first drummer to drum three times on his drum then I want the other to drum exactly the same way. Let's try it. (*have the first drummer follow your directions and then see if the other drummer can follow; then reverse it and have the second drummer be the lead person*) Pretty good. Each of you did a good job of imitating the other drummer.

The Bible teaches us to imitate God. How can we imitate God? (*let them answer*) God loves so we should also love. God shares so we should share. God forgives so we should forgive. God cares so we should care.

Does the devil love? Does the devil share? Does the devil forgive? Does the devil care? I don't think so. But what happens when we are hateful, selfish, unforgiving, and not caring? Are we imitating God? (*let them answer*) I don't think so. When we hate, we are imitating the devil. When we are selfish, we are imitating the devil. When we are loving, then we are imitating whom? (*let them answer*)

Very good! If you are in the band and playing the drum, we hope that you both play together. We don't want this drummer to drum five times when the other drummer is only drumming once.

When we are Christians and we want to be like God, then we must do the same as God does. The Bible teaches us to be imitators of God. How many of you want to be like God? (*let them answer*) Wonderful, 100 percent want to be like God.

The next time you see a band or some drummers, see how they imitate one another. The next time you hear about God and the good things he does for us, try to imitate God.

Good Guys And Bad Guys

Jude 4

For certain intruders have stolen in among you, people who long ago were designated for this condemnation as ungodly, who pervert the grace of our God into licentiousness and deny our only Master and Lord, Jesus Christ. (v. 4)

Object: a bandana to tie around your neck and face

Good morning, boys and girls. Today I brought along with me a big handkerchief; some people call it a bandana. How many of you have ever seen something like this? (*let them answer*) What would you use something like this for if you had one? (*let them answer*) Good answers! Cowboys wear bandanas. They fold it like this and tie a knot with the two ends and they wear it around their neck. Then if they get into a bad windstorm where the dirt is really flying, they raise it up and wear it around their face covering their nose so they can breathe better. Have you ever seen a cowboy wear a bandana? (*let them answer*) Very good!

Who else wears bandanas over their nose? (*let them answer*) That's right, crooks or thieves. They wear them so that people will not know who they are. It is a disguise. When they are committing a crime, they wear the bandana up, covering part of their face. When they are trying to pretend that they are honest people they wear the bandana around their necks like honest people. It is hard to describe the thief who wears a bandana because we don't really know what he or she looks like.

The Bible talks about people who disguise themselves and try to become part of a Christian community like our church. They look like everyone else, but they teach strange things. They seem like good people. They dress the way we dress, eat the same kind of foods, work in the same kind of places, but they do not like the teachings of Christ.

For instance, they would teach that we should hate some people. They also teach that you should be very careful who you share your gifts with instead of sharing with everyone. They teach you that it is all right to call some people names or disobey your parents some of the times. They might also teach you that drugs are all right certain times and things like that. They are very sneaky, but they don't really believe in the Bible or that Jesus is our Lord.

The Bible calls them intruders and false teachers. They want you to make them part of your Christian faith even if they don't believe in it. They just want you to think they are nice guys who think a little differently about God. They don't pray, they don't read the Bible, and they don't like for you to go to worship on Sunday.

The Bible teaches us to stay away from those people and don't invite them in because they are trying any way they can to separate us from God and the Lord Jesus.

The next time you see someone wearing a bandana, you need to check and see if he is a good guy or a bad guy. Maybe while you are thinking about that you will also be reminded of the intruders or false teachers who are trying to work their way into our churches. Be strong and be careful, but love God and all of his people.

Never Divided

Jude 19

It is these worldly people, devoid of the Spirit, who are causing divisions. (v. 19)

Object: a piece of fence

Good morning, boys and girls. Today we are going to talk about something that we see all of the time. Some houses have a lot of it and others only a small piece. Some people use them to grow vines or to keep their dog out of trouble, while other people use them to cause trouble. Do you know what I am talking about? (*let them answer*) That's right; it is a fence. How many of you have a fence at your house? (*let them answer*) A lot of you have a fence. What do you use your fence for? (*let them answer*) Good, you have a fence to keep your dog safe and close to home. Some of you have fences around your gardens to keep the rabbits out of the vegetables. And some of you let vines grow on your fence so that you can have pretty flowers. Those are good fences.

Some people build fences so that they can pretend that they don't have neighbors. They use the fence to divide themselves from other people because they like to fight. Those kinds of fences are not good fences.

We need neighbors and we need to make them our friends. When we are filled with the Spirit of God, we look for ways to help our neighbors. We share our firewood, care for each other when we are sick, have picnics together, and make a wonderful neighborhood.

But some people have an argument and instead of saying they are sorry they go out and build a fence, a big fence. The fence is so big you cannot see over it or under it or around it. It turns the people next door into enemies instead of friends. They are so far away that we never know if they are in trouble or if they need us. All we know is that the people who live on the other side of the fence are not our friends.

Fences can be good or they can be bad. You have good fences. They are meant to help keep our pets safe, grow beautiful flowers that we can share with our neighbors, and protect the vegetables from those pesky rabbits. You also have the Spirit of God. You must always encourage the Spirit and grow up by finding ways to help your neighbors be your best friends.

When you see a bad fence, remember that bad fences do not allow the Spirit of God into our hearts. When you put up a bad fence, you are asking God to leave you alone. So look around your neighborhood and see how many good fences there are and how many bad fences. If you see a bad fence, try to tell the people how much God loves them and wants them to live in peace and be friends with their neighbors.

Good fences, bad fences. Be sure to thank God for giving us good fences.

I Am The Beginning And The End

Revelation 1:4b-8

"I am the Alpha and the Omega," says the Lord God, who is and who was and who is to come, the Almighty. (v. 8)

Object: a stepladder

Good morning, boys and girls. Today, we have some verses from the book of Revelation where Jesus, the Christ, says that he is the beginning and the end of everything. He is the first and the last, or the *A* and the *Z* of the alphabet. In other words, there is nothing before Jesus and there will not be anything after him.

Let me show you what I mean. I brought along with me a stepladder. You are able to do a lot of things with a stepladder. You can wash walls, paint houses, clean cupboards, change light bulbs, and lots of other things. It has steps. It has a first step and a last step. There are no steps before the first step and there are no steps after the last step. If you have to reach above the last step, you are going to do what? (*let them answer*) That's right; you are going to fall. If you wanted to step before the first step, there is what? (*let them answer*) That's right; nothing. The ladder has a first step and it has a last step. There is the beginning and the end of the ladder.

So that is the way it is with Jesus. He wanted everyone to know that he was there before the world was made. He was there when the Father created the heavens and the earth, the land and the sea. He was there when the Father created people. He was with all of the great heroes like Abraham and David, and he has been with all of the heroes and their people ever since. Now Jesus is telling us he is going to be with us to the very end, to the last. There is nothing beyond the Christ.

The next time you see a ladder and you look at the steps and you see that there is a first step and there is a last step, maybe you will think about Jesus and how he has always been with us and always will be with us. Jesus said, "I am the beginning and the end."

Important Keys

Revelation 1:9-19

But he placed his right hand on me, saying, "Do not be afraid, I am the first and the last, and the living one. I was dead and see, I am alive forever and ever, and I have the keys of Death and of Hades." (vv. 17b-18)

Object: a large keyring with two keys

Good morning, boys and girls. How many of you have ever had a key that worked in a lock? (*let them answer*) What kind of a key do you have or what can you lock or unlock with your key? (*let them answer*) A key is something very important. If you have a key, then you are in charge of whatever that key unlocks or locks. For instance, I have two keys with me this morning that are very important keys. I can lock the door to my house and unlock the door to my house. That is what one key is used for, and it is used almost every day. I also have a key to the church, and I am able to lock and unlock the doors to the church whenever I want. Those are pretty important keys, don't you think? (*let them answer*)

After Jesus was resurrected from the grave, the people talked about the keys he had and how he used them. They weren't real keys like the ones I have shown you. Instead, they were imaginary keys. You remember how Jesus was the first person to come back from being dead to live again? (*let them answer*) When God raised Jesus from the dead, he also gave him the power over all the people who had ever died or who were going to die. Jesus was put in charge of the dead, just like I am in charge of things where I have keys to lock and unlock the doors. That was a great happening, the time when Jesus came back to life again, because it meant that now Jesus was put in charge of the dead, and he could raise them from the dead just like God the father had raised *him* from the dead.

And that is exactly what Jesus promised to do. Jesus said that since he is in charge of all of the people when they die, he will also raise them from the dead if they believe in him as the Son of the Living God. That is what the Bible means when it says that Jesus has the keys for death. It means that he is in charge of death and he can bring back to life those who have died.

The next time you see a key, or if you have your own key, think about the power that Jesus has. And remember, since he is living and no longer dead, he also has the power over death.

What About Heaven?

Revelation 5:11-14

Then I looked, and I heard the voice of many angels surrounding the throne and the living beings and the elders.... (v. 11)

Object: some cutouts from construction paper of clouds, angels, harps, and a throne

Good morning, boys and girls. Today we are going to do something different from usual. You have heard me talk to you about heaven many times, and so today I am going to ask you to tell me what your ideas of heaven are. When you think of heaven, what do you think about? (*let them answer*) You think of angels, but what else do you think about? (*continue to get as many answers as you possibly can from them; resist the temptation to get laughs from what they say and they will tell you many interesting things about their view of what heaven is like — if they feel that they are being made fun of at this point, they will keep their imaginations to themselves*) Those are very good answers. I thought that you might say some of the things you did so I had some things like angels and clouds and harps cut out of construction paper and when we are finished this morning, you can take them with you.

But heaven is a real place just like any of the other places that we have only heard about but never visited. I have read about Africa and India, but I have never visited them. The only thing about heaven is that you don't visit heaven any more than you visit the earth. Heaven is not a place in the sky, but I am not really sure where it is. I think that it is good for us to find out all we can about heaven though, since most of us — all of us — plan to spend time with God in this place that we call heaven.

Certainly the writer of Revelation, a man called John, thought a lot about heaven, and he had some real ideas about it. He often talked of the angels and their singing. He knew that there were other people there also. But most importantly, John knew that God was there, at work, making a place for you and me. It will be different from any place that we have known but it will also be the best place that we have ever lived. I hope that maybe you will take your angel or harp or whatever you think will be important for you to know about in heaven and then go home and find out with your parents everything that you can about this place called heaven. Remember, we all hope that someday we will live and share our lives together in heaven.

Would you like to take a cloud or angel cutout home? Good. I hope you will put them on your dresser so that you can think about our talk today.

Counting Sand

Revelation 5:11-14

Then I looked, and I heard the voice of many angels surrounding the throne and the living creatures and the elders; they numbered myriads of myriads and thousands of thousands.... (v. 11)

Object: a handful of sand and a piece of paper

Good morning, boys and girls. How many angels do you think there are in heaven? (*let them answer*) What do you think these angels do? (*let them answer*) We know, of course, that many of the angels are messengers of God to people on earth. We also know that the angels work for God in many other ways. But I wonder, this morning, if you or I know how many angels there are in heaven? (*let them answer*) We know that there are over 200,000,000 people in the United States. Do you think there are more people in the United States than there are angels, or do you think there are more angels than there are American citizens? (*let them answer*)

I brought along something that I thought might help us. I have a handful of sand that I want to spread out here on this piece of paper. Let's see how many grains of sand there in a handful. Who would like to help me count them while I tell the rest of the story for today? (*select a volunteer*)

A man named John had a vision of the angels in heaven singing their praises to Jesus, who had died for all of the people on the earth. It was like a great, great choir saying over and over again that this Jesus should receive all of the power, and all of the wealth, and all of the knowledge that there was in the world for the great thing he had done when he died for people's sins. Now how many were there? (*ask the volunteer counter*) We could ask our volunteer to tell us how many grains of sand he has counted by now, and see how that compares with the number of angels that there are in heaven. How many have you counted by now? (*let him give you a number*) How long do you think it would take you to count all of the grains of sand that I put on this paper? (*let him answer*) I think it would take you more than a day. But it would be safe to say that there are thousands and thousands of grains of sand here. The Bible writers could not count the number of angels either, so they just said that there were myriads of myriads, which is another way of saying, "More than any number that could be counted."

Maybe the next time you are on a beach, or the next time you see a bucket of sand, you will think about the angels and how many there are. When you are thinking about that, I want you also to think about the way they praised Jesus for saving us from our sins. If the angels are thanking Jesus for loving and caring about us, don't you think that it would be a good idea if we did the same, and told him how grateful we are for what he did for us? I think we should, and I am happy that we do.

He Cares For Our Hurts

Revelation 7:9-17

And God will wipe every tear from their eyes. (v. 17b)

Object: a box of tissues

Good morning, boys and girls. How many of you have ever felt so sad and blue that you wanted to sit down somewhere and cry big tears? Not many of us like to talk about those times, and I know a lot of boys who will tell you that they never cry. But I know differently. Boys cry just as girls cry when they are hurt, or when they feel like they have done something terrible and don't know what else to do. I remember a lot of times when I have been hurt and the tears come to my eyes faster than the awful feelings come to my tummy. Feeling bad and crying just go together. A tear can be a beautiful thing when it is a tear of sorrow. Most people don't cry when they feel hate or anger, but when they are hurt or are sorry they have tears.

I have something that goes along with tears. I imagine that one of these has been used on almost every boy and girl who has ever had a tear. Do you know what we call one of these things that I have in my hand? (*let them answer*) That's right; tissues. It feels good when your mother or father brushes away the tears with this very gentle tissue paper. It feels soft, and somehow it helps you to know that things are going to be all right. I remember that I used to think that my mother cared a lot when she would take a tissue out of her purse and wipe away my tears with it. And when I knew that she cared I knew that everything was going to be all right.

The Bible tells us that God does a lot of things that our mother and fathers do. As a matter of fact, the Bible tells us that another name for God is Father. Jesus called God his Father. One of the things that the Bible tells us that our Father in heaven is going to do is wipe away all of our tears when we join him in his new world. When we come to him it may be because we have been sick or injured, or just plain worn out, but the Bible tells us that when we come close to God, he is going to wipe away our tears. He is going to make us feel a lot better. Do you remember that no matter how bad you felt when you were crying, after your mother or father wiped away your tears you were laughing in minutes? I think that is what the Bible is talking about when it mentions that God our Father is going to wipe away our tears. It sure makes you feel good to know that he cares.

The next time that you see a tissue, I want you to think about how much God cares and how he makes us happy by taking care of our hurts.

A Brand New World

Revelation 21:1-5

And the one who was seated on the throne said, "See, I am making all things new." (v. 5)

Object: a used piece of furniture like a chair; some paint, sandpaper, some fresh wood, and hammer and saw

Good morning, boys and girls. Today I want you to learn something about the way God had planned his world. When we think about living and dying, it sometimes scares us because we are not sure what it will be like after we die. Are we going to be old like our grandparents, or are we going to start over like a tiny baby, or just how will we be? What will the world look like? Is it going to look just like this one but without pollution, or will it be all sunny days with white fluffy snow that doesn't melt? What do you think it will be like? (*let them answer*)

I don't know for sure what it will be like, but I do know one thing. It will be brand new! How many of you have ever painted a piece of furniture or watched your mom and dad paint a piece like this old chair? (*show them the chair and the paint*) That will make that chair look like brand new, won't it? It surely will, but you and I know that it is not brand new. Underneath the paint is the same old chair that it used to be. Now some people like that kind of furniture as well or better than new furniture. But paint doesn't make the chair new. If you want a new chair, you must go and buy one or you must take your hammer and saw and some fresh wood and make it. When you buy a new chair or make a chair out of wood like this, then you know that it is new. Do you see a difference?

God tells us that the next world will be a brand new one and everything in it will also be brand new. Whatever it is like, it will be brand new. I think that is great! When you and I come into God's world, it will be brand new, freshly made by God. The world won't have a newly painted sun, or some stars with some extra sparkle. No, sir, they are going to be brand new. That's what the Bible says, and I can hardly wait to see it when it happens.

Railroad Crossing

Revelation 21:6a

And he said to me, "It is done! I am the Alpha and the Omega, the beginning and the end." (v. 6a)

Object: a railroad crossing sign

Good morning, boys and girls. I have brought a sign with me today and I want to see if you can tell me where you've seen it. (*hold up sign*) That's right; at a railroad crossing. What do most of you do when you see this sign? You must look both ways, mustn't you, so in case you don't hear the train's whistle, you will certainly see the train coming.

As Christians we are asked to look both ways a lot of times. We are asked first of all to look back to the time when Jesus lived and even before Jesus to find out what God has taught us about living on his earth. It is important to know what God thinks about how we should live. Is it all right to be angry? How should we treat people who hate us, and who is our neighbor? Those are some of the questions we have and we must look one way to find the answers to those questions and many like them. We can read all about the things that Jesus taught in the Bible and find out what God meant when he answered our questions long ago.

But God doesn't want us to spend all of our time looking in one direction. God teaches us to look forward to when someday we will live with him forever. God says that there will be a special place for Christians and that someday in the future every one of us will enjoy living with him in heaven. God is all around us and we must look every way to find him.

So remember when you see this railroad sign that just as you must look both ways to know if a train is coming, so, too, you must look both ways to fully know and enjoy God.

A Place Of Light

Revelation 21:9-11, 22-27 (22:1-5)

And the city has no need of sun or moon to shine on it, for the glory of God is its light, and its lamp is the lamb. (v. 23)

Object: a night light

Good morning, boys and girls. Today is going to be a special day because we are going to discover something about the world that we are going to live in forever and how it is going to be different from the one that we live in today. Did you know that you were going to live forever? (*let them answer*) Well, you are going to live forever, and that is one of the things that the Christian faith is all about. Jesus promised us that because he died for our sins and we believe in him, that we would live forever with him and his Father in heaven.

What is heaven going to be like? That's what everyone wants to know. Some people wish that God would take a movie of heaven and show it to us, so that we could know how wonderful it is. But God has his own reasons for not taking a movie or showing us in this way. We are going to have to wait until the right time to find out.

There was a man named John who thought a lot about heaven. He prayed and dreamed about it a lot. He even wrote a book in the Bible that talked a lot about heaven and what it would be like. One of the things that he said is what I am going to tell you about right now. I brought along with me something that a lot of you use. (*take out the night light*) Do you know what this is? (*let them answer*) That's right; a night light. Do you know when you use it? (*let them answer*) You're right again. You use it at night, so that, if you must get up and walk around, you will not trip and fall. Night is very dark, and unless you are outside, and the moon is very bright, it is hard to see. A night light helps keep us from falling in the dark.

John discovered that heaven was never going to be dark. There was never anything to be afraid about, like falling in the dark, or not being able to see something and bumping into it. He talked about God's glory as being so bright that we would not even need a sun or a moon. He said the Father would supply more light than we would need during the day, and Jesus would be like a lamp for us at night. What John meant was that there is nothing to fear about the new world that we are going to live in forever. Everything will be light and beautiful and nothing bad will ever happen to us.

That is wonderful, and we are glad to know that in heaven Jesus will be with us forever, and that we will never have to worry, for even a moment, about anything. Jesus is like a night light that keeps us from falling, or even having to worry about falling. God bless you.

Jesus Is A And Z

Revelation 22:12-14, 16-17, 20

"I am the Alpha and the Omega, the first and the last, the beginning and the end." (v. 13)

Object: a package of film, a camera, and some snapshots

Good morning, boys and girls. When we read the Bible, pray our prayers, and sing our hymns, we are talking about the way we belong to Jesus and the way Jesus belongs to us. Sometimes people wonder if Jesus was just someone who lived a long time ago like other people and then died and went away. Is Jesus like other men or is he different? Today we have one of those answers. The Bible tells us that Jesus was at the beginning of the world and that we will be at the end of it. He said it a little differently when he called himself the A and the Z, the beginning and the end.

Let me show you in a different way. If I showed you my camera and told you that I wanted to take your picture, you would want to know if I have any film in the camera. Is that right? (*let them answer*) You need film to start with, don't you? (*let them answer*) The film is the beginning and I cannot do anything without film. Jesus is like the film. He was at the beginning of the world, just like my film is the beginning of the picture-taking. I am going to put my film in the camera so that when I take a picture of you, there will be an end. Do you know what the end of picture-taking is? (*let them answer*) That's right; a picture. After today's worship service is over, I will take all of your pictures with my film in the camera, outside of the church. Next week I will be able to show you what you look like today because your pictures will be printed on some special paper. This print, or picture, is also like Jesus because he said that he is not only at the beginning of the world, but also at the end of it, waiting for us. Jesus is the A and Z, the beginning and the end, the film and the picture.

It makes me feel good to know that Jesus did not just make the world, live in it for a little while, and then leave it. Jesus did make it, he lives in it, works in it, and will be here at the end when he will make a new world for all of us who love him.

Jesus is the beginning and the end, and the next time that you see someone take a picture and you know that there is film in the camera, I hope that you will think about what we said about Jesus today.

Alphabetical List Of Objects

291